Praise for the book

Riddles of Hinduism is a searing challenge to the entire intellectual order. The neglect of this text has itself become a metaphor for the ways in which the privileged have avoided a serious and honest engagement with Ambedkar. It is an important event that this text is finally being published with proper annotations and scholarly apparatus. The editors have done a wonderful act of recovery. Ambedkar was always meant to disconcert, and to shake our very foundations. This is a text that shows him at his forensic best. Whether you agree or disagree, this text should start an honest conversation. We cannot continue to hide behind the platitudes that Ambedkar so effectively pierces.
—**Pratap Bhanu Mehta**, president, Centre for Policy Research

There is not a shadow of doubt that B.R. Ambedkar's *Riddles in Hinduism* has been annotated with both love and care. The punctiliousness with which the notes have been written will certainly make the riddles less riddle-like to lay as well as informed readers. Decidedly, this edition, aided by Kancha Ilaiah's lucid and pointed introduction, will go a long way in dispelling some of the views apropos tradition that have become commonsensical by the act of constant repetition. Passionate yet scholarly, confrontational yet fortified by a strong sense of textual integrity, *Riddles in Hinduism*, composed almost sixty years from today, once again offers us the chance to engage in meaningful and sane dialogues.
—**Sibaji Bandyopadhyay**, author of *Three Essays on the Mahabharata: Exercises in Literary Hermeneutics*

Bhimrao Ramji Ambedkar was born in 1891 into an 'Untouchable' family of modest means. One of India's most radical thinkers, he transformed the social and political landscape in the struggle against British colonialism. He was a prolific writer who oversaw the drafting of the Indian Constitution and served as India's first Law Minister. In 1935, he publicly declared that though he was born a Hindu, he would not die as one. Ambedkar eventually embraced Buddhism, a few months before his death in 1956.

Kancha Ilaiah is Director, Centre for the Study of Social Exclusion and Inclusive Policy, Maulana Azad National Urdu University, Hyderabad. He is best known for his work, *Why I am Not a Hindu: A Sudra Critique of Hindutva Philosophy, Culture and Political Economy*. He has authored several books including *Buffalo Nationalism: A Critique of Spiritual Fascism* and *Post-Hindu India: A Discourse in Dalit-Bahujan, Socio-Spiritual and Scientific Revolution*.

S. Anand is the publisher of Navayana. He is the co-author of *Bhimayana*, a graphic biography of Ambedkar, and has annotated the critical edition of Ambedkar's classic *Annihilation of Caste*.

Shobhna Iyer studied ancient history at Jawaharlal Nehru University, New Delhi.

Unnamati Syama Sundar is doing his doctoral research at Jawaharlal Nehru University on the art and visuals used in the popular Telugu children's magazine, *Chandamama*. He is currently teaching history at SRR College, Vijayawada.

Riddles in Hinduism

An exposition to enlighten the masses

B.R. Ambedkar

The annotated critical selection

edited and annotated by
S. ANAND and SHOBHNA IYER

Introduced by **KANCHA ILAIAH** with the essay

**The Riddle of Ambedkar:
Why did he say he was born a Hindu?**

navayana

Riddles in Hinduism: An Exposition to Enlighten the Masses
The Annotated Critical Selection

10 8 6 4 3 5 7 9

ISBN 9788189059774

Navayana Publishing Pvt Ltd
155 2nd Floor
Shahpur Jat, New Delhi 110049
navayana.org

Typeset in Bembo and Optima at Navayana

Printed by Sanjiv Palliwal at Param Offset, New Delhi
Subscribe to updates at navayana.org/subscribe
Follow on facebook.com/Navayana

Contents

Preface

Riddles in Hinduism is one of his many works B.R. Ambedkar did not get to publish in his lifetime. As we began the process of selecting and annotating the *Riddles*, the book itself posed a major riddle. While the first and second editions of an iconic work like *Annihilation of Caste* (1936, 1944) that Ambedkar oversaw to the last detail could be traced, we had no choice but to base our edition of *Riddles* on the version that appears in Volume 4 of the ongoing multi-volume series called 'Dr Babasaheb Ambedkar: Writings and Speeches', known by the acronym BAWS, produced by the Maharashtra government's education department. All that the editors say of *Riddles in Hinduism* is this:

> The manuscripts of "Riddles of Hinduism" have been found in separate chapters bundled together in one file. These chapters contain corrections, erasures, alterations, etc. by the hands of Dr Ambedkar himself. Fortunately, the introduction by Dr Ambedkar is also available for this book. *We, however, regret that the final manuscript of this volume has not been found.* The Committee has accepted the title "Riddles in Hinduism", given by Dr Ambedkar in his Introduction to the Book.... The Editorial Committee has found a chapter on "Riddles of Rama and Krishna" which might have been intended for the volume "Riddles in Hinduism". The 24 riddles as proposed in his original plan were changed often in blue-prints. The seriatim of the contents and chapters and the arrangement of the file do not synchronize. The chapter on Rama and Krishna did not find a place in the listing of the contents of the book. However, we are including it in the volume on Riddles (BAWS Vol 4, 1987a, xiv–xv, emphasis added).

How the Ambedkar papers came into the possession of the state of Maharashtra and how the state was literally forced into publishing his works makes for an interesting and sad story. After he resigned from Nehru's cabinet in September 1951 following the impasse over the Hindu Code Bill (which Kancha Ilaiah discusses in his introduction), Ambedkar's spent his last years in Delhi at 26, Alipur Road, a bungalow he rented from the former Raja of Sirohi (a princely state in southern Rajasthan). He lived here with his wife Savita Ambedkar, a Saraswat Brahman medical doctor he'd married in 1948 in his fifty-sixth year (a marriage the *New York Times* described as more significant than the wedding of a royalty to a commoner).

Once he resigned, Ambedkar did not have any official secretarial staff to help him. At this point, he asked Nanak Chand Rattu, a Punjabi Ad-Dharmi Dalit who had expressed his keenness to assist Ambedkar since their first meeting in January 1940 and who now worked as a typist in a central government office, if he would help him with secretarial work and be his factotum. Rattu readily agreed and would show up at Ambedkar's house every evening after office hours and work till well past midnight. From October 1951 to December 1956, he typed out almost all of Ambedkar's letters and papers. Ambedkar died on 6 December 1956, intestate. Rattu published two worshipful memoirs about his time with Ambedkar—*Reminiscences and Remembrances of Dr B.R. Ambedkar* in 1995 and *Last Few Years of Dr Ambedkar* in 1997. The following account is based on these books.

According to Rattu, in 1966, ten years after Ambedkar's death, one Madan Lal Jain came to purchase the ten-room Alipur Road bungalow in 1966. Jain allowed Savita Ambedkar, who'd been living there, to retain two rooms. He gave one portion to his son-in-law, and rented one part of the building to an additional sessions judge. But soon, he sought to evict Mrs Ambedkar and the Additional Rent Controller served her a notice on 17 January 1967. On 20 January, Savita Ambedkar left for Alwar (Rajasthan), perhaps in the hope that nothing would happen in her absence. (Rattu, in his account, sounds paranoid and suspicious of Savita Ambedkar and her motives, even implying that she saw to it that an ailing Ambedkar did not get the right kind of medical treatment in the years leading to his death.)

With Mrs Ambedkar away, Jain and his son-in-law entered the premises with three bailiffs and twenty musclemen and forcibly opened the rooms, wresting the keys from Mrs Ambedkar's servant Mohan Singh. Jain and his men removed all the papers that had been neatly arranged in several racks in a big storeroom. These were recklessly dumped in an open yard. The room contained several of Ambedkar's "countless precious documents and important papers, nicely kept in several racks… and manuscripts of his several writings" (Rattu 1997, 202). Luck was such it rained that night. Several of Ambedkar's papers were irrevocably destroyed. That for over ten years Ambedkar's papers had remained unexamined and untouched in a storeroom in Delhi—even if Rattu says he dusted them on and off and fumigated them—is tragedy enough. They should have been part of the National Archives of India.

Upon her return from Alwar, Mrs Ambedkar sought the help of Home Minister Y.B. Chavan and the Lt Governor of Delhi A.N. Jha to access the premises and excavate her belongings. Soon, the building where Ambedkar lived was brought down, and the property changed hands. Though the sequence of events from hereon is not clear, the custodians of the Delhi High Court took possession of what remained of the Ambedkar papers. The BAWS editors narrate the story thereafter, without thinking it necessary to accord for the lost time:

> Later, these papers were transferred to the Administrator General of the Government of Maharashtra. Since then,

> the boxes containing the unpublished manuscripts of Dr Ambedkar and several other papers were in the custody of the Administrator General. It was learned that Shri J.B. Bansod, an Advocate from Nagpur, had filed a suit against the Government in the High Court Bench at Nagpur which was later transferred to the High Court of Judicature at Bombay. The petitioner had made *a simple request* seeking permission from the court to either allow him to publish the unpublished writings of Dr Ambedkar or to direct the Government to publish the same as they had assumed national significance. This litigation was pending before the Bombay High Court *for several years* (BAWS Vol 4, 1987a, xi–xii, emphases added).

In other words, the Maharashtra government was asked by a Dalit advocate, representing the aspirations of several Dalits (unfortunately but unsurprisingly not shared by non-Dalits) to explain why it was sitting on Ambedkar's papers (or what remained of them), for years, virtually doing nothing. Meanwhile, the already published writings of Ambedkar were kept in print by Dalit activists across India. Touchable India did not quite care for this Untouchable who constantly and relentlessly questioned Brahmanism and Hinduism till his last breath—and *Riddles in Hinduism* is testimony, as you will see.

The 1970s also saw great political ferment. The radical Dalit Panthers was formed in Bombay in 1972. Inspired by the Black Panther Party, it explored the convergence of Ambedkarism, Marxism and Buddhism. In 1978, the issue of renaming the Marathwada University in Aurangabad after Babasaheb Ambedkar—what could have been a benign gesture of symbolism—ran aground with the Shiv Sena and the Maratha community vehemently opposing the move. The Shiv Sena chief Bal Keshav Thackeray had responded with this infamous statement: "*Gharaat nahi peeth, magtaay vidyapeeth.*" "They've no bread to eat but demand a university." The fact is, in 1950, Ambedkar had started the first ever degree college—

Milind College, on behalf of People's Education Society—in Aurangabad, the administrative headquarters of Marathwada. A caste war broke out, lasting 67 days. About 1,200 villages were affected in three districts, nineteen Dalits were killed, Dalit women were molested and raped, and Dalit homes were burnt and pillaged. It was only in 1994 that the university was renamed Babasaheb Ambedkar Marathwada University (BAMU)—but it is still called Marathwada University in administrative speak and town parlance.

It was against this background that in 1976—twenty years after Ambedkar's death—the state government formed the Dr Babasaheb Ambedkar Source Material Publication Committee, appointing Vasant Moon as Officer on Special Duty. The first volume was published in 1979 and subsequently twenty-two volumes of speeches and writings have been printed, volumes that are almost impossible to find in regular bookstores.

The question before us now is which version of *Riddles in Hinduism* are we reading, especially since the BAWS editors "regret that the final manuscript of this volume has not been found"? Why did Ambedkar not publish this work in his own lifetime? When exactly did he work on this mammoth exegetical exercise that runs to ground everything people with caste hold dear?

Rattu records that Ambedkar began writing *Riddles in Hinduism* in the first week of January 1954 and completed it by the end of November 1955. He made "four press copies" that Rattu typed out "on a fine strong paper". When Rattu submitted that making four typed copies of the same manuscript seemed unnecessary, Ambedkar responded "with a smile":

> "Look," he said, "what is the title of the book—Riddles in Hinduism—which is itself a reply. I haven't got my own press and naturally it has to be given to some Hindu press for printing. It can be lost, burnt or destroyed and my several years

of hard labour will thus go waste. Doesn't matter what the cost involved. I must have a spare copy with me" (1997, 63).

Rattu says the book was complete in all respects, but its publication was held up as Ambedkar wanted to add two important photographs. The first was of Dr Rajendra Prasad, the first president of the republic, visiting Benares in 1952, worshipping Brahmans, washing their feet and drinking the water. The second photo related to Pandit Jawaharlal Nehru who on 15 August 1947 sat at the yagna performed by the Brahmans of Benares to celebrate the event of a Brahman becoming the first prime minister of free and independent India. Nehru is said to have worn the Raja Danda given to him by the Brahmans and drank the water of the Ganga brought by them. Rattu notes that while "Dr Rajendra Prasad's photo had become available, search was on for the photo of Nehru."

Ambedkar too makes note of these two incidents in his work *Thoughts on Linguistic States* (a critique of the report of the States Reorganization Commission) completed in December 1955:

> Did not Prime Minister Nehru on the 15th of August 1947 sit at the yajna performed by the Brahmins of Benares to celebrate the event of a Brahmin becoming the first Prime Minister of free and independent India and wear the Raja Danda given to him by these Brahmins and drink the water of the Ganges brought by them? How many women have been forced to go Sati in recent days and immolate themselves on the funeral pyre of their dead husbands. Did not the President [Rajendra Prasad] recently go to Benares and worship the Brahmins, wash their toes and drink the water? (BAWS Vol 1, 1979, 149).

Through the 1950s, Ambedkar was under tremendous financial stress and in a hurry to publish as many books as he could, given his failing health. Rattu lists (1997, 59) the following titles: (i) Buddha and His Dhamma, (ii) Buddha and Karl Marx, (iii) Revolution and Counter-revolution in Ancient India, (iv) Riddles in Hinduism, (v) Riddle of Rama and

December, 1952 FILMINDIA

The December 1952 issue of *Filmindia*, founded and edited since 1935 by Baburao Patel, featured this cartoon. Two prominent cartoonists used to draw for this magazine—Earan and B.K. Thackeray (Bal Keshav Thackeray). *Filmindia* used to publish highly controversial cartoons attacking religious fundamentalism, both Hindu and Islamic. Cartoonists therefore rarely signed their cartoons. Based on style one can infer that this is by Earan. Source: National Film Archive Library, Pune. Ascessed in February 2013 by Unnamati Syama Sundar.

Krishna, (vi) Riddle of Trimurti and (vii) Riddle of Woman. Of these, he gave priority to *The Buddha and His Dhamma*—an unfair but tactical choice he was forced to make. Even to publish this opus, he wrote out several letters seeking financial assistance including a few to M.R. Masani, Chairman of Tata Industries Ltd. In a reminder on 17 March 1956, Ambedkar says, "I'm dreadfully in a hurry and if Mr Tata refuses my request I'd like to go with my bowl to another door" (cited in Rattu 1997, 60). After assuring themselves that a book on the Buddha might not be "controversial", on 1 May 1956, the Sir Dorabji Tata Trust sanctioned Rs 3,000. Needing another Rs 20,000 to cover printing expenses, Ambedkar then abjectly wrote to Nehru on 15 September 1956, asking "if the Government of India could purchase 500 copies for distribution among the various libraries and among the many scholars whom it is inviting during the course of this year for the celebration of Buddha's 2,500 years' anniversary" (BAWS Vol 17, Part 1, 2003, 444–5). He was turned down, politely of course. (The proposed Ambedkar memorial at Indu Mills in Mumbai has a budget of Rs 425 core.)

While *The Buddha and His Dhamma* was published soon after Ambedkar's death, *Riddles in Hinduism* (and several other works) had to wait for three decades before being exhumed. When it was finally published in 1987 under BAWS Volume 4, copies of the book were burnt publicly at a Maratha Mahamandal meeting in Amravati in January 1988. The state government withdrew the book when the Shiv Sena rioted in Bombay for the removal of the chapter, "The Riddle of Rama and Krishna". When thousands of Dalits staged counter-protests across Maharashtra, the chapter was reinstated but with a caveat that the government did not "concur with views expressed in this chapter". The government edition carries this disclaimer till date.

Ambedkar's fears that the book could well be lost or destroyed by the Hindus is not unfounded. It has a historical basis. After all, scholars acknowledge that most Buddhist manuscripts from the subcontinent that have survived were found outside the subcontinent, owing to the efforts of Buddhist missionaries to find a safe place for them: the Brahmans sought to destroy whatever they could lay their hands on. If *The Buddha and His Dhamma* was Ambedkar's gospel, *Riddles in Hinduism* is the kind of critique that is similar to what the Buddha himself and other Sramanic traditions such as the Lokayata school undertook.

When the Buddha went about calling Brahmans to dialogue with him, they came forward. He defeated them in intellectual debates and even won some of them over to his Sangha. But Ambedkar did not enjoy that luxury. Unlike Siddhartha who was a Kshatriya prince, Bhimrao Ambedkar was an Untouchable, and only Dalits embraced his re-invented Navayana Buddhism, which was premised on the negation of Brahmanic Hinduism. This explains India's collective neglect of the nonviolent egalitarian revolution he charted, and the Prabuddha Bharat he sought to usher.

Riddles in Hinduism as published under BAWS Volume 4 features twenty-four riddles and eight appendices classified under three heads: Religious, Social and Political. Several of Ambedkar's notes are incomplete and sometimes even chapters end with the BAWS editors saying, "Incomplete. Further text missing."

The work runs to over 170,000 words and reissuing it in its entirety, with annotations, would have made for a bulky book of at least eight hundred pages. Therefore, ten riddles and one addendum have been selected from Ambedkar's fifteen religious, five social and four political quandaries. These better represent the social and political charades that Buddhism sought to uproot but textual Hinduism, as Ambedkar argues, made possible. By attacking the abstractions that ironically form the 'Sanatan' bedrock of Brahmanic theology—like varnashrama, Vedic scriptural authority, the appropriation of ahimsa, the shifting sacrality of Hindu gods, the laws of Manu, and the enduring Ḳali Yuga—these questions and their answers are stellar examples of Ambedkar's scholarship that go a step beyond cataloguing inequality to also asking the difficult, but ethical, question of justice. Primarily, they mount a moral critique on Hindu 'spirituality' or rather the absence of it. The riddles in this edition comprise the more identifiable 'tenets' of Hinduism that continue to be milked for their profitability today.

This editorial intervention was needed keeping in mind issues of space, relevance and accessibility while also undertaking the debatable, but ultimately contingent, task of introducing Ambedkar's sustained tirade on Hinduism to as wide and uninitiated an audience as possible. This is by no means a comprehensive or definitive selection; it is at best an indicative one, and what was possible given our limitations.

Ambedkar often presumes a minimal familiarity with textual debates and knowledge of Brahmanic theology and mythology in his readers. We therefore set ourselves two tasks: to go back to the primary sources Ambedkar refers to, and to find out what the latest available scholarship says on this. What was most fulfilling about this exercise was to realize that the questions Ambedkar raises—be it on the suspicious interpolation of the Purusha Sukta hymn into the *Rig Veda* or the gobbledygook around Varna and ashrama and the collapsing of the two at a historical juncture—have been echoed and validated in later scholarship. One of the most challenging yet enjoyable aspects of crafting the annotations was parsing through Ambedkar's notes where he refers to several texts on a single topic. Considering how long it took us to verify each source and make corrections where needed, it is awe-inspiring to consider that Ambedkar did this some sixty years ago, all by himself.

Given the irony of both the annotators being born Brahman, this exercise in writing a commentary on Ambedkar's text made us self-conscious about following what ultimately seems a Brahmanical *bhashya* tradition. But truth be told, reading Ambedkar's work only exposed our own profound ignorance of the texts and theology he so consummately discusses and demolishes. And how else is one to join Ambedkar's Sangha than by aiding and abetting him? Is redemption ever possible for a Brahman may well be another lost riddle.

S. Anand
30 March 2016
New Delhi

Introduction

The Riddle of Ambedkar:
Why did he say he was born a Hindu?

Kancha Ilaiah

On 13 October 1935, Bhimrao Ramji Ambedkar announced at the Depressed Classes Conference in Yeola, in the Bombay Presidency: "I had the misfortune of being born with the stigma of an Untouchable. However, it is not my fault; but I will not die a Hindu, for this is in my power" (in Zelliot 2013, 147). A few months later, in May 1936, he published *Annihilation of Caste*, a devastating critique of Hinduism focusing on its most distinguishing and dogmatic feature, caste. Towards the end of this address to the Hindus, whom he calls "the sick men of India", he says: "This would probably be my last address to a Hindu audience on a subject vitally concerning the Hindus" (2014, 311).

He then makes it abundantly clear that he is determined to quit Hinduism:

> I am sorry, I will not be with you. I have decided to change. This is not the place for giving reasons. But even when I am gone out of your fold, I will watch your movement with active sympathy, and you will have my assistance for what it may be worth (316).

On 14 October 1956, a few months before he died, Ambedkar formally embraced Buddhism with an estimated half a million followers in Nagpur, a city that happens to be the headquarters of the ultra-right Rashtriya Swayamsevak Sangh that today, with remarkable lack of shame, claims Ambedkar as its own.

According to the sources this new annotated edition has helped unearth, we may infer that Ambedkar wrote *Riddles in Hinduism* in 1954–55. Like the majority of his writings, *Riddles* was published posthumously.

After I wrote *Why I am Not a Hindu* in 1996, several people asked me, and continue to ask: 'If an Untouchable like Ambedkar admitted that by birth he was a Hindu and had to formally renounce it, how can a Shudra like you say you are not a Hindu by birth?' The question is understandable, especially since Shudras—today officially listed under Backward and Other Backward Classes—figure within the four-fold varna order, even if placed at the bottom of the heap. They may not enjoy the dwija (twice-born) status of those that claim to be Brahman, Kshatriya, or Vaishya, meant to serve these three classes, but they nevertheless have been regarded as Hindu and hence could be counted as Touchables. Ambedkar, too, regarded them as Hindus. But the riddle Ambedkar leaves us with is this: why and how did Ambedkar, as an Untouchable, come to deem himself a Hindu, although it seems the label was thrust upon him? Like one of the advance readers of this draft introduction asked: Why is a Gandhi cap called a Gandhi cap when Gandhi did not wear one?

Still, the issue needs to be sorted out. In the recently published series, *The Norton Anthology of World Religions*, Wendy Doniger, the committed American Indologist, had the honour of editing the volume titled *Hinduism*. The compilation, featuring several works oddly lumped as Hindu texts, includes Ambedkar's speech at the historic Mahad Satyagraha of 1927. Doniger introduces him as a "Dalit Hindu"—something that could curiously please her rightwing detractors in India and abroad. An excerpt from *Why I am Not a Hindu* is included as well, and she characterizes me as an "outsider within" Hinduism (Doniger 2015, 622). As a matter of fact, several people who claim a distinct identity from Brahmanical Hinduism, such as the Lingayats of southern India, or even the Adivasi Gonds of central India, are included as part of the procrustean edifice of Hinduism. In this, Doniger seems to be doing what several Orientalists assisted by nationalist Brahmans have done since the eighteenth century—that is, see everything that is not identifiably Muslim or Christian in the subcontinent as being Hindu by default. We must also remind ourselves that Hinduism was a neologism coined in the early nineteenth century. As the historian Upinder Singh reminds us in *A History of Ancient and Early Medieval India*, "The English word 'Hinduism' is a fairly recent one and was first used by Raja Rammohun Roy in 1816–17" (2009, 433).

First, we need to understand that Ambedkar made the statement—that he was unfortunate to be born an Untouchable 'Hindu' but shall not die as one—when he was unsure if or when the British would leave India. He made it at a time when the anticolonial struggle was taking a definite shape under the leadership of a slightly reform-minded Bania leader Mahatma Gandhi, who was later killed by a Brahman terrorist who espoused the supremacist ideology of the Hindu Mahasabha. Gandhi was perceived to be paying a reformist's role in 1947–48, and even seen as pro-Muslim, though the unstated reason that fuelled the right-wing's 'revolutionary' credo was that as a non-Brahman Vaishya raised on Jain notions of ahimsa, he was seen as meddling with Brahmanic Hinduism—something the Brahmans of western India as well as the Sankaracharyas, self-appointed pontiffs, deeply resented.

In 1935, Ambedkar was perhaps of the opinion that such a statement from him would make the Brahmans take a more serious reformist course, for he knew that Brahmans, though numerically insignificant at an estimated three to five percent of the population, were actually in real control of caste-infested Indian society, despite Gandhi being seen as the leader of the political movement at the time.

Ambedkar extensively researched Hinduism and recorded his distaste for this religion in several works. Subsequently, his role—both as the chief architect of the Constitution and as a modern-day Bodhisatta—has had a double edged impact on Dalitbahujan society. By Dalitbahujan, I mean the Dalit Untouchables (17 percent of the population), the Backward and Other Backward Classes formerly categorized as Shudra (55 percent), and the indigenous population of tribals (8 percent) together comprising seventy percent, and thus constituting a staggering oppressed majority.

At the outset, there is need for clarity on one crucial issue. The Hindu liberals argue that Hinduism as such is good, and that Hindutva is bad. They say there is a fundamental difference between Hinduism as a religion, as practiced by the elite castes, and Hindutva which is a 'modern' twentieth-century political response that coincided with the forming of organizations such as the Arya Samaj, Rashtriya Swayamsevak Sangh and the Hindu Mahasabha. We have even had communists, from S.A. Dange to A.B. Bardhan—in fact a whole spectrum of 'left-liberal-secular' intellectuals—extolling the greatness of Hinduism and decrying Hindutva as a perversion. This Hinduism–Hindutva binary does not hold much water. It is at best a good-cop–bad-cop strategy.

Ambedkar's thorough exposé of the Hindu texts and everything the Hindus hold dear shows that there is no scope to evolve a positive, nonviolent, egalitarian religion based on these texts. In *Annihilation of Caste* he says emphatically:

> You must not forget that if you wish to bring about a breach in the system, you have got to apply the dynamite to the Vedas and the shastras, which deny any part to reason; to the Vedas and shastras, which deny any part to morality. You must destroy the religion of the shrutis and the smritis. Nothing else will avail (2014, 303–4).

Bulking up Hindus

Today, the nation is being ruled by a strident Bharatiya Janata Party, which proclaims that the establishment of a Hindu Rashtra—a Hindu theocratic state—is its ultimate goal. As part of this agenda, it is also trying to coopt Ambedkar in major ways despite the bare fact that he repeatedly and vehemently critiqued this religion and wished for its annihilation. He refused to die with the label of an 'Untouchable Hindu'. After saying that he'd not like to die a Hindu, if only Ambedkar had immediately converted to Buddhism—or, even better, to a non-Indic religion—such cooption would have been impossible. Any keen student of Ambedkar would agree that Buddhism was indeed best suited to someone of his philosophical disposition. After all, as he recalls in his unpublished preface to *The Buddha and His Dhamma* (1956), he was gifted a biography of the Buddha by Arjunrao Keluskar upon completing his matriculation in 1907, and the book left an abiding impression on him. However, the reason why Buddhism lends itself to easy cooption is because of a provision in the Constitution that, ironically, Ambedkar himself oversaw.

Explanation II of Article 25(2)(b) of the Constitution categorizes Buddhists, Sikhs and Jains as "Hindu", even if "only" for the purpose of "providing social welfare and reform or the throwing open of Hindu religious institutions of a public character to all classes and sections of Hindus". For all purposes the law of the land treats Buddhism, Sikhism and Jainism as *sects* of Hinduism. Later, codified Hindu personal laws, like the Hindu Marriage Act, 1955, the Hindu Succession Act, 1956, etc, merely reinforced this position, and these statutes were applied to Buddhists, Sikhs and Jains. Pertinently, under Indian law even an atheist is automatically classified as Hindu.

Had Ambedkar therefore opted for say Islam or Christianity, it would have sent a different message to the Dalits as well as to the Hindus. There are many who ask, what is wrong if the BJP promotes—rather appropriates—Ambedkar in various ways. Some Dalits who say Ambedkar is their messiah have colluded with the Hindutva party—prominently Udit Raj (BJP member of parliament from Delhi and chairman of All India

Confederation of SC/ST Organizations) Ramdas Athawale (of the Republican Party of India (Athawale), and member of the Rajya Sabha from Maharashtra), Ram Vilas Paswan (Union minister of Food and Public Distribution in the Modi cabinet and long-term BJP ally) and Ram Shankar Katheria (the BJP's own RSS-trained Dalit leader and minister of state for Human Resource Development in the Modi cabinet). We may recall that Udit Raj was once Ram Raj, and when he tried to stage a mass conversion of Dalits to Buddhism in 2001 at Delhi's Ram Lila grounds, the then BJP-led government made every effort to sabotage the event. However, Dalit politicians joining or hobnobbing with the BJP is a political move and has little to do with Dalits—or rather Ambedkarites—becoming rightwing. Decades ago 'Harijans' worked for the Congress to even defeat Ambedkar in electoral battles.

By the time Ambedkar embraced Buddhism in 1956, the Buddha himself was being coopted into Hinduism. He was declared to be one of the ten avatars of the second most powerful of Hindu godheads—Vishnu. During the nationalist struggle that Ambedkar too was a part of, various interpretations of Hindu scriptures were undertaken. From the *Rig Veda* to the *Bhagavad Gita*, everything got translated and interpreted, with extensive commentaries and notes, so that they could be accepted as part of the nationalist ethos of India being manufactured. The Sacred Books of the East (SBE) series anchored by Max Müller, the German Orientalist who became an unabashed fan of the Vedas and Hinduism and wrote books such as *What India Can Teach Us*, became popular. To counter the 'foreigner'-heavy approach of the SBE series, 'nationalist' Indian historians started the reactionary Sacred Books of the Hindus (SBH) series at their Panini Office in Allahabad under the supervision of Major B.D. Basu who had retired from the Indian Military Service. Rightwing nationalists such as Bal Gangadhar Tilak got into the act and came to seriously believe that the Aryans were a fair-skinned race who migrated from the icy Arctic circle, destined to be the ruling class of India and the world. Several scholars and philosophers in the West—from Schopenhauer to Nietzsche—believed in Aryan supremacy at a time when the whites were trying to justify both racism and imperialism. Even Gandhi during his South African years espoused the innate superiority of high-caste Indians, given their 'Aryan blood', over the native blacks. This sentiment was to then fuel the racist ideologies of Hitler and Mussolini. The point is that Brahmanic Hinduism, even before it assumed the garb of Hindutva, had a fascist tendency.

While an interpretation of Buddhist texts was also undertaken around the same time as part of the Sacred Books of the Buddhists series, overseen by the British scholar-couple of T.W. Rhys Davids and C.A.F. Rhys Davids, these did not ignite the general imagination as much as Müller's project did. Only in his last but major work, *The Buddha and His Dhamma*, published posthumously, did Ambedkar offer an interpretation of Buddhist texts. Surprisingly, even Indian communist leaders who claimed to be atheists have not offered meaningful interpretations of Buddhist and other sramanic works. Following the Indological/Orientalist scholarly lineage, they too were more preoccupied with Hindu texts like the Vedas, Upanishads, *Ramayana*, *Mahabharata*, *Bhagavad Gita*, Puranas and so on.

However, Ambedkar spent considerable time reading and demolishing the Hindu texts that saw a revival during the colonial-nationalist period. He had perhaps hoped that his eviscerating critiques would trigger some introspection and lead to the reform of Hinduism. After he became the chairman of the drafting committee of the Constitution, his relationship with Gandhi and Jawaharlal Nehru changed considerably. He held no grudges against the leaders who, during elections of the Constituent Assembly from Bombay in 1946, had sabotaged his chances using Congress–Hindu majoritarianism. Once on board, he behaved more like a statesman rather than as a radical or a social reformer. He did not allow for the searing anger that we find in the pages of works like *Annihilation of Caste* or *Riddles in Hinduism* to affect his approach to the making of the Constitution.

If Ambedkar just wanted to keep away from reforming a religion that kept Untouchables like him outside the fold at the social, spiritual and political realms, he would not have thus laboured examining the Hindu shastraic literature, nor would he have waged a four-year struggle (1923–1927) around issues such as access to water in the Chavadar Tank in Mahad. In 1930, when Ambedkar participated in the Kalaram temple satyagraha (a struggle that carried on till 1935), a riot broke out and his lieutenants shielded him from a stone-pelting mob by covering him with an umbrella.

Rather early in his political career, on returning from his studies in New York and London, Ambedkar presented evidence before the Southborough Committee on Franchise in 1919. Ambedkar quoted the Aga Khan Committee report of 1909 submitted to the British Viceroy to argue that the Untouchables were indeed *not* Hindus. Based on this report, the J.H. Hutton-led Census of 1911 separated the Untouchables from the category of Hindus, and by 1916 the bureaucratic term 'Depressed Classes' came to be officially used by the British government (later renamed 'Scheduled Caste' after the Government of India Act of 1935). Why was the category of Untouchables as Depressed Classes created in the 1911 census? It is important that we come to terms with what Ambedkar says in his work *The Untouchables: Who Were They and Why They Became Untouchable* (1948). The major question before Ambedkar at that time was to prove why the Untouchables were a separate and distinct category from the Hindus and therefore deserved minority status. The criteria

Ambedkar discusses are worth listing *in extenso*:

> What is important is to know the basis adopted by the Census Commissioner for separating the different classes of Hindus into (1) those who were hundred per cent Hindus and (2) those who were not.
>
> The basis adopted by the Census Commissioner for separation is to be found in the circular issued by the Census Commissioner in which he laid down certain tests for the purpose of distinguishing these two classes. Among those who were not hundred per cent Hindus were included castes and tribes which:
>
> (1) Deny the supremacy of the Brahmans.
> (2) Do not receive the Mantra from a Brahman or other recognized Hindu Guru.
> (3) Deny the authority of the Vedas.
> (4) Do not worship the Hindu gods.
> (5) Are not served by good Brahmans as family priests.
> (6) Have no Brahman priests at all.
> (7) Are denied access to the interior of the Hindu temples.
> (8) Cause pollution (a) by touch, or (b) within a certain distance.
> (9) Bury their dead.
> (10) Eat beef and have no reverence to the cow.
>
> Out of these ten tests some divide the Hindus from the Animists and the Tribal. The rest divide the Hindus from the Untouchables. Those that divide the Untouchables from the Hindus are (2), (5), (6), (7), and (10). It is with them that we are chiefly concerned (BAWS 7, 1990, 312–13).

There is much to be read between the lines here. Ambedkar says points 2, 5, 6, 7 and 10 help establish the division between Hindus and Untouchables. He uses a mathematical metaphor to say that even if one of these criteria is not met, a person cannot be "hundred per cent" Hindu. In other words, one can be partly Hindu, but never fully Hindu unless you are a Brahman. These criteria, of course, were devised for the 1911 Census using both shastraic prescriptions and the ways in which caste was practised in day-to-day life. These leave us with the conclusion that most people who are counted as Hindu are never fully Hindu.

Bureaucratic definitions apart, Ambedkar strongly believed that the Untouchables were not Hindu, and in all his formal writings and speeches he uses the words Hindus and Touchables synonymously, and refers to Untouchables as such. While he says it was his misfortune to be *born* a Hindu, he never says 'I'm a Hindu'. In fact, the editors of the BAWS volumes in their introduction to *Riddles in Hinduism* (Volume 4) point out that among the various papers of Ambedkar, they found a book plan with detailed chapterization. The title of the book was "Can I be a Hindu?" (BAWS Vol 4, 1987a, xvi). It has not been established whether Ambedkar did eventually write this book.

How is one a Hindu?

In the first of his *Riddles*, "The Difficulty of Knowing Why One is a Hindu", Ambedkar looks at the importance of religion in one's life. But he comes to the conclusion that the idea of being a Hindu does not share the definiteness that belonging to Islam, Christianity or Zoroastrianism gives a person. At best, there is a vague connotation of religion with polytheism as its core value. There can be many gods and but there is no set of core principles that constitute a system of beliefs. There is nothing that anchors or *binds* people. After all, the word religion comes from the Latin root *religare*, which means to bind and to be bound by an obligation.

If we consider those who converted to Islam in the Indian subcontinent, they too allowed for certain aspects of the Hindu caste ideology to infiltrate their belief system and such values govern their lives to an extent till date. The egalitarian values of Indian Muslims would have collapsed if they had not realized that their notion of a universal god is different from the regional

Hindu notion of god (that is bound to the subcontinent) and Hindu polytheism and idol worship. Muslims in India adopted the caste system and created a sometimes unbridgeable caste divide between the supposedly superior category of Ashrafi Muslims (Syed/ Sheikh/ Mughal/ Pathan) and the so-called converts who were classified as Ajlaf and even Kamina or Itar (meaning 'base'). This has led to the contemporary pasmanda movement, 'pasmanda' being a Persian term that means 'those who have fallen behind', referring to Muslims of Shudra and Ati-Shudra origins.

The Christians, particularly the Catholics, also fell prey to the caste trap under the garb of acculturation. Their educational institutions turned out to be centres where the Brahmanical classes were trained in English. High-caste Hindus then converted these Catholic schools into modern gurukulas, keeping the Shudras and Ati-shudras out. In turn, Brahmanic intellectuals trained in English in Christian educational institutions treated Ambedkar as an intellectual outcaste for decades. The Orientalist Christian scholars also treated the Hindu works that Ambedkar critiqued as books sacred to all Indians—including Dalits, Tribals and Other Backward Classes. Jesuits saw wisdom in the Vedas and Vedanta, whereas Ambedkar, coming from a sramanic tradition, repudiates the Veda and all the texts that are post-facto subjected to the adjectival tyranny of 'Hindu'. Hinduism, thus, became an elephant—rather a holy cow—with spiritually blind men and women groping around it. Ambedkar, following in the tradition of the Buddha and the Lokayata philosophers, repeatedly dissected this sacred cow.

Ambedkar's *Riddles* does not deal with how textual Hinduism treated the historical Untouchables or Shudras. Instead, he is dispassionately focused on the absolute lack of morality and the absence of even a semblance of what may be regarded as 'sacred'. Contemporary scholarship, including scholarship by Dalits, regards all Shudras, both the Backward Classes and the lower placed Other Backward Classes, as a part of the Hindu cultural or textual heritage. From Ambedkar's examination of the riddles in Hinduism, it is clear that the labouring Shudras—as cattle-rearers, tillers of the soil, pot-makers, fisher-folk, weavers, carpenters, barbers, etc—are not discussed in the Hindu texts at all. Untouchables, too, seldom get mentioned, except in terms of injunctions in the post-Vedic texts on how to avoid them such as in the *Manusmriti*, the *Yajnavalkyasmriti* and the Dharmashastras. Not that these social divisions did not exist at the time when these texts were composed. All the broad divisions, based on the chaturvarna system, were in place, and the divisions were based on occupation and livelihood. Ambedkar's entire effort in *Riddles* appears to be able to tell the world that the Hindu spiritual texts hardly contain anything spiritual in them, and he did this at a time the world was besotted with what Indian texts could teach it.

If Ambedkar worked on these riddles about the same time as he composed his opus *The Buddha and His Dhamma*, at the heart of his scholastic disputations there appears to be a search for something spiritual. He comes to the conclusion that the Hinduism being practised around him—and as obtained in ancient texts—had indeed none of the universal values associated with religion. Yet everyone around him—not just conservatives like Tilak and reformists like the Arya Samajists, but even those considered more open-minded like Gandhi and Nehru—were praising textual Hinduism as great and worthy of being admired, followed and preserved. Yet there were serious internal disputes, so much that the Hinduism espoused by the Hindu Mahasabha and the Rashtriya Swayamsevak Sangh brazenly executed Gandhi for what they regarded as his flawed understanding of Hinduism. Why is it that most Hindu gods and goddesses bear arms and kill at the slightest provocation to establish dharma, like an army does in an occupied territory? Why does Hindu dharma espouse such intense intellectual and physical violence? For answers, Ambedkar wanted to examine the moral strength of textual Hinduism: be it Vedic incantations that are full of magic or the latter-day mythological fables, or gods who display an absolute and habitual disregard for morals.

What was Ambedkar's methodology? In Columbia University (1913–16), Ambedkar majored in Economics, with Sociology, History, Philosophy, and Anthropology as other subjects of study, was called to the bar at Gray's Inn in 1916, and further studied Economics at the London School of Economics and Political Science. (Few people remember that his 1923 doctoral thesis on the Indian rupee at the LSE ran into trouble because of its subversive, anti-British implications.) His engagement with Hindu texts is therefore multidimensional. We must also remember that Ambedkar juggled several roles. As someone fiercely committed to Dalit rights and the welfare of the larger mass of caste-infected Indians, he was involved with the drafting of the Constitution and participated in the Constituent Assembly debates. Often times, his knowledge of the Hindu shastras helped him counter any reactionary Brahman pandit in the Constituent Assembly when the challenge arose.

What is remarkable about Ambedkar is that he does not allow his scholarship to be influenced by his politics or communitarian victimhood, though his furious critique comes from an experiential position. Such scholarship, sometimes, has its limitations. This approach refuses to compare what is obtained from the texts with the practice of the religion on the ground. This, at one level, is the problem of operating within the Orientalist methodological paradigm. He was never too concerned, unlike Phule or Periyar, with the day-to-day lives of the Brahmans and Banias. Phule characterized them as Shetjis and Bhatjis, whose essential characteristics were that of oppression and exploitation, and producing a culture of hatred for labour. Ambedkar was more intellectual and philosophical in his approach, and hence described Indian society as "a gradation of castes forming an ascending scale of reverence and a descending scale of contempt—a system which gives no scope for the growth of the sentiments of equality and fraternity so essential for a democratic form of government" (in Bhagwan Das 2010, 25). Also, as Ambedkar says in *Annihilation of Caste*, "the caste system is not merely a division of labour. *It is also a division of labourers*" (2014, 233, emphasis original). But in *Riddles in Hinduism*, Ambedkar does not deal with this contempt for labour.

The Brahmans and Banias have never been involved in the production of food and any form of activity that organically sustains the lives of fellow human beings and the larger ecosystem we are a part of. And yet, thanks to this system, they extract enormous surplus and accumulate social, cultural and political capital, and justify all this in the name of religion. No religion offers an elaborate justification for such injustice as Hinduism does. It is this indefensible theoretical edifice that Ambedkar launches himself against in *Riddles in Hinduism*.

The sanctity of the caste system became the basis for enormous inequalities not only in India but the world over ever since casteist Hindus began to settle overseas, whether in the UK, USA, Canada, Australia, South Africa, the Caribbean, or Southeast Asia. Wherever they went, they took caste with them. If the Brahman-led science establishment in India does manage to land on Mars using foreign technology for this purpose, we can be sure they shall introduce caste there—after all, a replica of India's Mars Orbiter Mission was personally taken by the Indian Space Research Organisation's chairman to propitiate Lord Venkateshwara at the Tirupati temple before the launch of the actual spacecraft from Sriharikota in 2013.

While ordinary foreigners come to think of Hinduism as a benign religion of ahimsa/nonviolence and vegetarianism, they know or care little about the violence and untouchability that the so-called sacred books of the Hindus propound. Even the Orientalist and Indological scholars—from William Jones to Sheldon Pollock—were and are more fascinated by Hinduism and its many manifestations than horrified by it. But Ambedkar, even while forced by circumstances to depend on the work of these Orientalist scholars, comes to conclusions that are the very opposite.

The Reformer and the Radical

Even a look at the titles of the chapters included in this annotated selection will reveal that Ambedkar had a deep desire to reform Brahmanic Hinduism. One of his key concerns was to expose the brazen contradictions that exist within the texts of Hinduism. In "Riddle No. 18: Manu's Madness or the Brahmanic Explanation of the Origin of the Mixed Castes", he offers painfully elaborate tables about the different varna categories into which various *smritis* fit the progeny of varna-samkara, that is miscegenation or the intermixture of jatis resulting in a further proliferation of jatis. He concludes:

> Some of the names of the mixed castes mentioned by Manu and the other Smritikaras appear to be quite fictitious. For some of the communities mentioned as being of bastard origin have never been heard of before Manu. Nor does anyone know what has happened to them since. They are today non-existent without leaving any trace behind. Caste is an insoluble substance and once a caste is formed it maintains its separate existence, unless for any special reason it dies out. This can happen but to a few (147).

Ambedkar may seem unsparing and unrelenting in the *Riddles*, but his reformist impulse is more evident in public interventions such as the Hindu Code Bill (1951–55), a large-scale exercise in the repair of Hinduism. Opposition to the Bill came from almost all Hindus. The scholar Sharmila Rege in her analysis of Ambedkar's writings on Brahmanical patriarchy, explains the scenario:

> Intense opposition came from all quarters. For one, the President threatened to stall the Bill's passage into law. Hindu *sadhus* laid siege to parliament. Business houses and landowners warned a withdrawal of support in imminent elections ... the Hindu Code Bill posed the imminent threat of women gaining access and control over resources and property, the possibility of removal of the restrictions of caste in marriage and adoption, and the dawn of the right to divorce. All this seemed to intimidate the structural links between caste, kinship and property that form the very core of Brahmanical patriarchy (2013, 200).

Despite having a huge majority in both houses of parliament, Nehru succumbed to the rightwing and scuttled the Bill. Nehru, for all his liberalism and progressiveness that the self-styled left-liberal-secular intelligentsia in India admires and loves him for, succumbed to the pressure of Brahmanic Hindus both in his own government and parliament. Even the communist parties and the broader Left were under the spell of the ideology of Brahmanic Hinduism. Someone like Dange argued that there was evidence of primitive communism in the Vedas. Others like P.C. Joshi, B.T. Ranadive and E.M.S. Namboodiripad opined that an issue like untouchability was "mundane" compared to the "freedom movement". Nor did Brahmanic patriarchy bother them like it did Ambedkar. Nehru, though an avowed rationalist, compromised with the Brahmanical forces in order to save his government. He sacrificed his impassioned colleague and law minister of four years, choosing instead to please the conservatives, the very same lot that celebrated Gandhi's assassination at the hands of a Hindu Right fanatic. Ambedkar resigned over these developments, setting an example, showing that he was a statesman and not a selfish power-hungry politician. Writes Rege, "The Hindu Code Bill is seen as a manifesto of women's liberation, and Ambedkar's resignation as Law Minister over the sabotaging of the Hindu Code Bill is viewed as an act unparalleled in history" (2013, 48).

All this goes to show how Ambedkar, despite the hurdles, was rather keen to reform Hinduism, for he believed that if a religion that was by default the majority's has such a weak moral and communitarian outlook, the future of India was rather bleak. He believed that the liberation of the Untouchables was contingent upon the liberation and humanisation of the Hindus, and hence made earnest attempts to rid Hinduism of its contradictions.

From the 1935 declaration that it was his misfortune to be born a Hindu, to his final battle to reform Hinduism culminating in 1955, Ambedkar tried everything in his power to make the Hindus see reason for over twenty years. While at it, he drew upon his study and knowledge of Buddhist texts, which offered a counter to the 'sacred' Hindu texts totally lacking in morality and ethics. The Buddhism that Ambedkar drew moral strength from is very much Indian in the geographical sense, and this fits in with the demands of nationalism that are often made of people who stand at the nation's margins and are critical of the dominant paradigm. There's enough evidence we gather from his other works, and his interventions in the Constituent Assembly debates, that Ambedkar had made a proper study of all Abrahamic religions and their approaches to morality and ethics. For instance, the introduction to *Riddles* features a lengthy quote from the Book of Daniel in the Old Testament, where he compares Brahmans and Jews and shows how the Brahmans, unlike Jews, never were steadfast to their gods. He writes:

> Indeed the Brahmans have made religion a matter of trade and commerce. Compare with this faithlessness of the

> Brahmans the fidelity of the Jews to their Gods even when their conqueror Nebuchadnezzar forced the Jews to abandon their religion and adopt his religion (51–2).

However, throughout *Riddles in Hinduism*, Ambedkar quite consciously does not deploy a comparative approach between these various textual traditions to score easy points. Nor does he compare the Hindu sacred texts with the secular philosophical works of the Greeks, for instance. He examines these texts from a humanist and personal ethical–moral point of view, and counters their irrationalism with cold logic and reasoning. Take, for example, the divine himsa (violence) practised by spiritually authenticated Hindu heroes turned into gods like Rama, Krishna, Indra, Vishnu, Narasimha and others in the name of *dharma rakshana*—protection of the Hindu dharmic order—against the highly evolved message of compassion and universal brotherhood that Gautama Buddha espouses. While the Buddha never believed in killing anybody for whatever reason, all that the Hindu gods do is wreak vengeance in a mindless fashion till they reach their final goal, which could be just a piece of property as seen in the *Mahabharata*. M.S. Golwalkar, the RSS leader, had once said: "Obviously we did not expand into Central Asia and South-East Asia by sermons alone. It is significant that every Hindu god is armed" (cited in K.R. Malkani 1980, 42).

Buddhism, given its propensity to peace and the larger wellbeing of not just humans but the world we live in, became a beloved universal religion because of its advocacy of the middle path. Unlike the other sramanic religion, Jainism, it does not advocate extreme nonviolence as a reaction to Hinduism's path of extreme violence. Buddhist kings in the past have waged wars and no Buddhist nation has disbanded its armed forces. (We also have the nearly theocratic Buddhist state in Sri Lanka that has unleashed genocidal violence on the minority Tamil people who happen to be Hindu. Discussing this, or the state-backed violence against Rohingyas in Buddhist-dominated Myanmar, however, is beyond the scope and purpose of this essay.)

The books that the Hindus regard as sacred have always justified the regular use of massive violence against those it regards as Untouchables, tribals and Shudras—demonized as rakshasas. Invoking violence against the productive castes of the subcontinent is part of the institutional practice of varna vyavastha—the caste order. The Buddha always spoke against the use of violence against any social force; he delinked the worth of a person from the birth of a person. The Hindu Brahmanic forces, both in ancient and contemporary India, believe in using violence in the name of god, often times against their own people. It is not as if the Crusades did not happen, and it is not that Islam and Christianity do not have histories of violence; but Abrahamic religions surely do not ask people of faith to wage a war against their own people. The bloodlust of Brahmanism killed Gandhi too, whereas Ambedkar sought only to intellectually vanquish Gandhi and never sought the physical extermination of his most bitter rival. In fact, when Gandhi blackmailed Ambedkar with an unreasonable fast-unto-death in 1932 over the issue of separate electorates for Untouchables, it was Ambedkar who saved Gandhi's life, staking the rights of his people.

Texts and Access

Ambedkar's work assumes renewed significance today since we are witnessing a dangerous revival of text-based Hinduism. The present BJP-led National Democratic Alliance government, like its predecessor in 1999–2004, is re-imposing the hegemony of Sanskrit in not just temples but as an academic discipline. In Anglo–American universities, proto-Hindutva NRI bodies are promoting Sanskrit chairs. It appears that Hindu gods understand only a near-dead language. The same Brahmans who controlled Sanskrit also acquired control over the English language and established their hegemony in courtrooms, government offices and in intellectual and cultural spheres including the great Indian diaspora. In some ways, the text-based ritual-oriented Sanskritic Hinduism and the market-oriented English-language friendly Hinduism have both become cunning cultural tools. This has become clearer now than it was during Ambedkar's time.

The Brahmanic forces could also make friendly alliances with the Christians—more so with the Catholics and Jesuits. That is because the Christian social forces gave them the weapon of English to retain their hegemony in the modern world. If the Christians had not educated the Indian Brahmanic forces in colleges like St Stephen's in Delhi, St Xavier's in Bombay, St Joseph's in Bangalore, and the chain of Loyola colleges in the south and Presidency College in Kolkata, there would not have been a good English-educated Brahmanical force in India. This has resulted in a situation where Brahmans, who continue to monopolize Sanskrit—a language that Ambedkar sought to learn but was denied in India—also use market-friendly English for profit. This Janus-faced, *janeu*-wearing, fork-tongued nationalism speaks both English and Sanskrit tongues at once.

Why should the absence of Dalitbahujans as priests in Sanskrit-oriented temples be an issue? When we say that the Dalits and OBCs are not Hindu anyway, why should their claim to enter the sanctum of temples and chant mantras in a dead language even be entertained? The logic is simple. As long as these hugely profitable temples exist—some like the rich Tirupati temple are also the biggest tax evaders in the country—managing their affairs and having the right to priesthood must be open to all according to the right to equality enshrined in Article 14 of the Constitution. It is as much a civil right as accessing the water in a temple tank, which is what the Mahad Satyagraha was all about.

However, in December 2015, a two-judge bench of the Supreme Court of India invoked Article 16(5) to hold that "exclusion of some and inclusion of a particular segment or denomination for appointment as archakas [priests] would not violate Article 14 [right to equality]". This gives unusual rights to the Brahmans to exclusively be the priests and controllers of Hindu religion in the name of Agama Shastras. A non-Brahman trained and proficient in priest craft will be ineligible because of the caste barrier. This proves that Brahmanic Hinduism's claim to perpetuating inequality—in other words, its inherent lack of spiritual democracy—is now backed by the highest court of the land. To accept this is no less than accepting the killing of some Dalits every day as a necessary Hindu ritual—the National Crime Records Bureau says, as of 2012, every week thirteen Dalits are killed and every day at least four Dalit women are raped. Or, to accept that a section of Untouchables has to do sewer work clad in a loincloth while at the other extreme the Brahman maintains ritual purity. Those who believe in caste and untouchability can never wish for the welfare of all human beings. In fact, to be Brahman means you can never be the well-wisher of other communities.

It is in this context that Ambedkar's study of texts, and texts that someone in his station of life ought to not be even hearing, assumes immense significance. After all, in the *Ramayana* the 'Shudra' Sambuka is murdered by Rama for doing penance and studying the Vedas, for that causes anarchy (Ambedkar discusses this here in 230–32). The *Gautama Dharmasutra* lists severe punishments for a Shudra who comes even within hearing distance of a Veda. In George Bühler's translation:

> 4. Now if a Shudra listens intentionally to (a recitation of) the Veda, his ears shall be filled with (molten) tin or lac. 5. If he recites (Vedic texts), his tongue shall be cut out. 6. If he remembers them, his body shall be split in twain. 7. If he assumes a position equal (to that of twice-born men) in sitting, in lying down, in conversation or on the road, he shall

undergo (corporal) punishment (1879, 239).

Today, the Supreme Court more or less upholds this logic.

Absence of Production

Amedkar's critique of the sacred books of the Hindus also shows us that from the *Rig Veda* to the Puranas, there's hardly any discussion of human relations and actual processes of production in these texts. There's no concern with agricultural practices, or domestication and rearing of animals and their integration into settled human life. Scholars have often described Aryans as cattle raiders who staged enormous carnages in the name of Vedic sacrifices. At the yagna pit, thousands of cows, buffaloes and on occasion horses and even humans were sacrificed. Though in the stories about Krishna and his brother Balarama, cattle-rearers by caste, we do get some descriptions of pastoral life, the discourse around agriculture has never found significant space in Hindu texts. Equally, Shiva, a god with patently tribal characteristics, does not figure in an important way in the main corpus of Hindu texts, except at a later stage as an act of cooption. Ambedkar speaks of how the Brahmans have changed their gods as and when it suited them, and wonders how they can be so unfaithful to their own gods.

The Brahmans of today have not given up their anathema for production and continue to hold dear the purity–pollution theory. Even today, when forced by the odd case of penury, they would rather beg than take up agrarian work or any kind of physical labour they deem lowly. A majority of them have not even given up their so-called sacred thread (*janeu*), nor have they given up intra-caste marriage. They hold on as well to priesthood that demands rote-learning incantations in Sanskrit, a language even the Brahmans seldom understand. Ambedkar argues in "Riddle No. 17: The Four Ashramas: The Why and How about them" that none of the Brahmans really follows the four ashramas prescribed in the Shastras (especially Vanaprastha, retiring to the forest in old age). However, their admiration for textbook varnashrama, the four-fold caste order, continues. Hypocrisy has become a daily ritual now.

The text-centrism of Ambedkar does pose some problems, though. While examining the socio-cultural of life of people as reflected in these texts, he forgets that the lives of Dalitbahujans had almost nothing to do with the rituals and lives described in them. The socio-cultural differences that exist even today among dwija Hindus (Brahman, Kshatriya and Vaishyas) and that of Dalitbahujans and Adivasis are an extension of their ancient and medieval lifestyles. Ambedkar does raise the key issue of food culture. Why did the Brahmans who happily sacrificed cows and feasted every day on beef, with utter disregard to what this does to the economy, suddenly turn vegetarian? If everyday consumption of beef was one extreme, the total giving up of all meat is another. Both are unnatural. And we live in an age when a Shudra-origin chief minister cited Newton's third law of motion, that for every action there is an equal and opposite reaction, to justify one of the worst anti-Muslim pogroms in post-independence India, and got to become prime minister. He is vegetarian.

Ambedkar's critique of Hinduism also brings out one historical fact that matters more than any other—that the Hindu textual heritage shows a complete estrangement from the productive culture of the working castes of India. From the *Rig Veda* to *Bhagavad Gita*, all the texts deal with war, Brahman–Kshatriya and man–woman relations, their political, personal and social morality. Whether it is Al-Biruni's study of these texts in the early eleventh century or Ambedkar's twentieth-century study, or the studies of contemporary scholars like Wendy Doniger, none of them can possibly discuss Brahman or Kshatriya involvement in actual processes of agrarian production, whether it be the domestication and rearing of cattle for tilling, or its use for dairy and meat. All other spiritual texts of the world engage with the production processes the people were involved with in the ancient or medieval period. One example should suffice: the Book of Genesis speaks of Abel as a keeper of sheep, and Cain as a tiller of the ground.

The Hindu texts however remain not only silent on such life-sustaining occupations; they look down on such labour as Shudra–Chandala–Rakshasa tasks. This kind of spirituality that disregards labour is actually anti-life. Nowhere in the world did religion take such a devious course. This is not just an academic question confined to ancient texts but a question that has serious ramifications for our times since contempt for the labouring castes persists among the non-sweating elite castes.

While critiquing the Hindu texts, Ambedkar somehow gave the impression that they spoke for his community too. They did not. Even the European Orientalist scholars committed this basic methodological mistake in understanding Indian society through a textual reading of ancient and medieval life. It is this flaw in Ambedkar that makes him believe that he is born a Hindu and has to cease to be one at some point. It is this chink that the Sangh parivar wants to exploit—and do a *ghar-wapsi* for him—despite the fact that anyone reading Ambedkar will know that he has no regard whatsoever for Hinduism in any form.

The entire corpus of Ambedkar's writings and speeches bears testimony that he bristled with anger against Hinduism. *Riddles in Hinduism* makes it abundantly clear that Ambedkar can never be drawn into the Hindu fold.

Ambedkar laboured a lot to inject morality into Brahmanic Hinduism. In his copious works on various Hindu texts before he embraced Buddhism, he comes across as a true moral friend of the Brahmans, though they never saw him as such. He tried telling them that they had undergone a social revolution by transforming themselves from promiscuous sexists—who believed in child marriage and incest and enforced widowhood and sati—to slightly more moral beings thanks to several historical processes, including the advent of Buddhism and the colonial moment. As Ambedkar painstakingly documents, their moral life was—and is—rather bizarre, and the ancient books of the Hindus prove that they revelled in unnatural extremes.

Kali Yuga, the Best Time

Such is the abiding love Brahmanic Hindus have for the hollow texts of the past—Ambedkar coldly calls the Vedas a "worthless set of books"—that they regard any effort to infuse morality into their religion as a *fall* into the Kali Yuga. The present may well be the best of times to live in India, for all the citizens now have their rights secured in an enlightened Constitution and are not held hostage to some book that carries hymns of hate. In fact, even for the Brahmans, Kshatriyas and Vaishyas—and for women across castes—it is the present that is the best time. But led by the Brahmans, a majority of the Hindus believe that we live in Kali Yuga and this is an era of moral turpitude. Why? Because there is disregard for varnadharma—the Shudras and Untouchables have wrested some power—chaos reigns, and this will lead to complete destruction. Kali Yuga, then, according to the present Brahmanic understanding, is a Shudra–Chandala yuga. For them, it is a Reservation Yuga, where Dalitbahujans can aspire to anything they want—including staking claims to priesthood.

Hinduism as it exists and operates today, particularly after the implementation of the Mandal Commission report in 1990 and the demolition of the Babri Masjid in 1992, is not too different from what was described in the Hindu texts. Modern Hindu intellectuals, mostly from Brahman and Vaishya communities, think that if the Dalitbahujans are exposed to Islamic and Christian worldviews they would awaken to ideas of spiritual equality, and that would force the Brahmans into productive activity they so loathe. This is the reason why we see such a strong opposition to conversion even from people like Gandhi. In fact, the Partition of 1947 was a big relief for the Brahman–Bania forces because it reduced the scope for Muslims and the Dalitbahujans coming together and numerically submerging the Hindu system. The real battle in India is not between the Hindus and Muslims as the RSS and other Sangh parivar outfits would have us believe. It is actually between the Dalitbahujans and the Brahmanical forces. Once this battle settles, within the framework of democracy and the Indian Constitution, the full religious rights of even Muslims and Christians could be realized. What the RSS yearns for, an Akhand Bharat, could actually work in favour of the Dalitbahujan people of South Asia who have reason to embrace spiritual democracy. A pan-subcontinental Islam dominating a mega Indian nation would be a proposition Hindus would have had to deal with, for that would have been the situation had the British not left India or if the partition(s) had not happened.

History, in fact, validates such speculation. The founding of the Arya Samaj in 1875 in Lahore and its subsequent rise owed much to the demographic shifts that characterized the history of the Punjab due to its proximity to Central Asia and the predominance of Sikh and Muslim rulers in the region. In the nineteenth century, British rule was added to this list, and the conversions of the oppressed castes in large numbers to Islam and Christianity exacerbated the situation. The scholar Kenneth Jones discusses this at length (2006, 139–45). In the 1881 census of Punjab, the Hindus constituted 43.8 per cent of the population, the Sikhs 8.2 per cent and Christians 0.1 per cent. The Muslims, at 47.6 per cent, were well short of an absolute majority. But by 1941, the Muslims were in absolute majority in the Punjab accounting for 53.2 per cent of the total population.

The Hindus made 29.1 per cent of the total, the Sikhs 14.9 per cent, Christians 1.9 per cent, and others 1.3 per cent. The erosion in the percentage share of the Hindus was caused by the conversion of many Hindus—especially the 'lower castes', such as Chuhras, Chamars, Jhiwars and Malis—to Islam, Sikhism and Christianity (Krishan 2004, 77–89).

This fear of Islamization haunts Hindu institutions even today. They have not realized that their ancient texts and modern practices could not save the regions that are modern-day Afghanistan, Pakistan and Bangladesh from shifting their religious allegiance from Brahmanic Hinduism and Buddhism to Islam. The Hindu Brahmanical forces could succeed in all their wars against the native–producer masses but once the 'one-book–one-god' appeal of Islam came into the land, Hinduism lost what little spiritual power it had. Their mantras could not stall the exodus in several parts of the Indian subcontinent. Ambedkar nowhere talks about this historical shift towards Islam, especially the Sufi strain towards which a lot of Dalitbahujans in the cow-belt gravitated. This was the most major development in the religious sphere after Buddhism with even Southeast Asia witnessing a shift towards Islam from an earlier Sanskritic–Hindu base.

Ambedkar's examination of Hindu texts shows that he did not find a single redeeming feature in them. He finally embraced Buddhism. Given this reality, characterizing Untouchables, and especially someone like Ambedkar who always saw himself as outside the fold as a "Dalit Hindu", as Wendy Doniger does, is not only incorrect but is also politically fraught. In any religion, a certain level of inequalities may be permissible. For instance, class inequality and patriarchy are prevalent in societies governed by all religious cultures. But no other religion treats its own members as Untouchables or grades the entire population into fundamentally unequal people. For this reason, I'd be echoing Ambedkar in saying Hinduism does not deserve to survive at all.

References

Ambedkar, B.R. 1990. *The Untouchables: Who Were They and Why They Became Untouchable.* In BAWS Vol 7. Bombay: Education Department, Government of Maharashtra. (Orig. publ. 1948.)

———. 2014. *Annihilation of Caste: The Annotated Critical Edition.* New Delhi: Navayana. (Orig. publ. 1936.)

Bühler, George. 1879. *The Sacred Laws of the Aryas as taught in the schools of Apastamba, Gautama, Vashishta and Baudhayana, Part I: Apastamba and Gautama.* Sacred Books of the East Vol 14. Oxford: Clarendon Press.

Das, Bhagwan. 2010. *Thus Spoke Ambedkar, Vol1: A Stake in the Nation.* New Delhi: Navayana.

Jones, Kenneth W. 2006. *Arya Dharm: Hindu Consciousness in 19th Century Punjab.* Delhi: Manohar. (Orig. publ. 1976.)

Krishan, Gopal. 2004. "Demography of the Punjab (1849–1947)." *Journal of Punjab Studies* 11(1): 77–89.

Malkani, K.R. 1980. *The RSS Story.* New Delhi: Impex India.

Rege, Sharmila. 2013. *Against the Madness of Manu: B.R. Ambedkar's Writings on Brahmanical Patriarchy.* New Delhi: Navayana.

Singh, Upinder. 2009. *A History of Ancient and Early Medieval India: From the Stone Age to the 12th Century.* New Delhi: Pearson Longman.

Zelliot, Eleanor. 2013. *Ambedkar's World: The Making of Babasaheb and the Dalit Movement.* New Delhi: Navayana.

Riddles in Hinduism

An exposition to enlighten the masses

B.R. Ambedkar

Introduction[1]

This book is an exposition of the beliefs propounded by what might be called Brahmanic theology. It is intended for the common mass of Hindus who need to be awakened to know in what quagmire the Brahmans have placed them and to lead them on to the road of rational thinking.

The Brahmans have propagated this view that the Hindu civilization is Sanatana,[2] that is, unchanging. This view has been

---

1 The BAWS editors write: "This is a seven-page manuscript, with corrections in Dr Ambedkar's handwriting. Last few pages are additions in the handwriting by Dr Ambedkar to the typed script."

2 Orthodox Hindu leaders of the late nineteenth century, responding to reformist movements such as the Arya Samaj, defended Hindu orthodoxy as Sanatana Dharma, translated variously as "eternal religion" or "eternal law", "unshakeable, venerable order" and "ancient and continuing guideline" (Zavos 2001, 109). Sanatana dharmis opposed the the reformists' attempts to remove untouchability, sati and image worship. In 1936, Ambedkar said of Gandhi: "The Mahatma was a full-blooded and a blue-blooded Sanatani Hindu. He believed in the Vedas, the Upanishads, the Puranas, and all that goes by the name of Hindu scriptures; and therefore, in avatars and rebirth. He believed in caste and defended it with the vigour of the orthodox" (AoC 2014, 348). Gandhi—who was looked down upon by Sanatanis for what they perceived as his reformist position on untouchability and for his tolerance of Muslims—often claimed he was more Sanatani than the Sanatanists. This double-speak on Gandhi's part fractured the notion of the Sanatani from within. In a 1925 speech in Calcutta, Gandhi said: "Let the Sanatani Hindus understand from me who claims to be a Sanatani Hindu. I do not ask you to interdine with anybody; I do not ask you to exchange your daughters with the Untouchables or with anybody, but I do ask you to remove this curse [of untouchability] so that you may not put him beyond the pale of service" (*Amrita Bazar Patrika*, 2 May 1925). See Ambedkar, AoC 2014, 348n13.

reinforced by a good many of the European scholars who have said that the Hindu civilization is static.[3] In this book I have attempted to show that this view is not in accord with facts and that Hindu society has changed from time to time and that often times the change is of the most radical kind. In this connection, compare the Riddles from Himsa to Ahimsa and from Ahimsa back to Himsa.[4] I want to make the mass of people realize that Hindu religion is not Sanatana.[5]

The second purpose of this book is to draw attention of the Hindu masses to the devices of the Brahmans and to make them think for themselves how they have been deceived and misguided by the Brahmans.

It will be noticed how the Brahmans have changed and chopped.[6] There was a time when they worshipped the Vedic gods. Then came a time when they abandoned their Vedic

---

3 Ambedkar seems to be referring primarily to the work of J.S. Mill and Max Müller. Mill's *History of British India* was published between 1818 and 1823 and became the standard text of subcontinental history in the nineteenth century, dividing thousands of years of history into Hindu, Muslim and British 'periods'. For Mill, the Hindu civilization was "backward, irrational and unchanging", and the Muslim one only marginally better. Müller too considered the Indian past as unchanging; "passive, meditative and reflective". According to Romila Thapar, Mill saw the despotic state as default, and the British administration as the first attempt at establishing law and order. "These views were in part a reflection of the debate on current colonial policy, a debate that introduced corresponding interpretations of the Indian past" (Thapar 2009, 5).

4 Ambedkar seems to be referring to Riddles 13 and 14, featured in this annotated edition. However, according to the BAWS editors, Riddle No. 13 was originally listed in the Table of Contents as "How the Brahmans who were once cow-killers became the worshippers of the Cow?" See p.85.

5 Another ideological feature of the Sanatanis, including Gandhi, is the unabashed constant espousal of the 'ideal' varnashrama, where varna and ashrama are collapsed. The ceaseless harping on the complex of the varnashrama by the Sanatanis has resulted in a haze of historical amnesia, given that the ideas of the varna and the ashrama evolved along two different trajectories. Contrary to the 'Eternal Dharma' viewpoint, the tying of the knot between the two took place at a specific historical conjuncture, as explored by Ambedkar in Riddle No. 17; see notes 10, 16 and 17 to that riddle.

6 Ambedkar likely means "changed and chopped" both the texts and gods.

gods and started worshipping non-Vedic gods. One may well ask them—where is Indra, where is Varuna, where is Brahma, where is Mitra—the gods mentioned in the Vedas? They have all disappeared. And why, because the worship of Indra, Varuna and Brahma have ceased to be profitable. Not only did the Brahmans abandon their Vedic gods but there are cases where they have become the worshippers of Muslim Pirs. In this connection one glaring case may be referred to. In Kalyan near Bombay there is a famous Darga of a Pir called Bawa Malangasha on the top of a hill.[7] It is a very famous Darga. Every year an Urs (pilgrimage) is held and offerings are made. The person who officiates at the Darga as a priest is a Brahman, sitting near it, wearing the clothes of Muslims and receiving monies offered at the Darga. This he did for the sake of money. Religion or no religion, what the Brahman wants is *dakshina*. Indeed the Brahmans have made religion a matter of trade and commerce. Compare with this faithlessness of the Brahmans the fidelity of the Jews to their

---

7 This is the Hazrat Baba Haji Malang near Kalyan, present-day Maharashtra, where Baba Abdur Rehman Malang was buried. Malang was a Sufi saint, who is said to have come to India from Yemen in the twelfth or thirteenth century CE. Haji Malang is noted for being one of the few dargahs where a Hindu *vahivatdar* (manager) and a Muslim *mutavalli* (with distant lineage claims to the saint) both officiate at rituals and at the yearly festival. Many of the rites performed are distinctly Hindu, though the tomb itself is clearly Muslim in form and inscription (Hansen 2001, 107). According to news reports now (*The Tribune*, 15 May 2005), there's a rift between Hindutva groups and the Waqf board over the rightful ownership and administration of the shrine. From 1988 on, the Shiv Sena claimed the Malagadh Hill was an ancient Hindu shrine of the Nath yogi Machindranath, and that Haji Malang was a Muslim conqueror who destroyed the site (Hansen 2001, 107). Alternatively, another legend goes that Baba Haji Malang rescued the town from the darkness of "infidelity and oppression" (*kufr wa zulmat*) (Green 2011, 72). Consider here the case of Shirdi Sai Baba, a spiritual master from the nineteenth century. Though not a lot is known of his personal life, he appeared as a young man in the town of Shirdi, present-day Maharashtra, dressed as a Muslim fakir. But he was not a conventional follower of Islam, and over time Hindus—like with the sixteenth-century radical poet from Benares, Kabir—have come to assert that he was of Brahman origin and was orphaned and taken as a disciple by a Muslim ascetic (White 1972, 868). Sai Baba's religious practices blended Hindu and Muslim elements and he has come to be worshipped by people of all faiths.

gods, even when their conqueror Nebuchadnezzar forced the Jews to abandon their religion and adopt his (religion).[8]

> Nebuchadnezzar, the king, made an image of gold, whose height was three score cubits, and the breadth thereof six cubits; he set it up in the plain of Dura, in the province of Babylon.
>
> Nebuchadnezzar, the king, ordered the princes, the governors, the captains, the judges, the treasurers, the counsellors, the sheriffs, and all the rulers of the provinces to come to the dedication of the image which Nebuchadnezzar, the king had set up.
>
> Then the princes, the governors, the captains, the judges, the treasurers, the counsellors, the sheriffs, and all the rulers of the provinces, were gathered together unto the dedication of the image that Nebuchadnezzar the king had set up; and they stood before the image that Nebuchadnezzar had set up.
>
> Then a herald cried aloud, "To you, it is commanded, O people, nations, and languages, That at what time ye hear the sound of the cornet, flute, harp, sack-but, psaltery, dulcimer and all kinds of musick, ye fall down and worship the golden image that Nebuchadnezzar the king hath set up: And he who so falleth not down and worshippeth shall the same hour be cast into the midst of burning fiery furnace."
>
> Therefore at that time, when all the people heared the sound of the cornet, flute, harp, sack-but, psaltery, dulcimer, and all kinds of musick, all the people, the nations, and the languages fell down and worshipped the golden image that Nebuchadnezzar the king had set up.

---

8 [What follows is from Damet Ch. 3 (Old Testament).] The lengthy quote is from the Book of Daniel in the Old Testament. Nebuchadnezzar was the king of Babylon between c. 605 and 562 BCE. The construction of the Hanging Gardens of Babylon is usually ascribed to him. He is mentioned in several books of the Bible, the Book of Daniel being the most prominent. In the beginning of the Book, God allows Jerusalem to fall into Nebuchadnezzar's hands, and Daniel and his three companions are sent to Babylon, where they refused food and wine and prayed when it was illegal to do so. The Book of Daniel is meant to emphasize the Lord's protection of His followers while they were in captivity.

Wherefore at that time certain Chaldeans came near, and accused the Jews.

They spake and said to the king Nebuchadnezzar,

"O King, live for ever.

Thou, O king, hast made a decree, that every man that shall hear the sound of the cornet, flute, harp, sack-but, psaltery, dulcimer, and all kinds of musick shall fall down and worship the golden image;

And who so falleth not down and worshippeth that he should be cast into the midst of a burning fiery furnace;

There are certain Jews whom thou hast set over the affairs of the province of Babylon; Shadrach, Meshach, and Abed-nego; these men, O king, have not regarded thee; they serve not thy gods, nor worship the golden image which thou hast set up."

Then Nebuchadnezzar in his rage and fury commanded to bring Shadrach, Meshach, and Abed-nego. Then they brought these men before king.

Nebuchadnezzar spake and said unto them, "Is it true, O Shadrach, Mesach and Abed-nego, do not ye serve my gods, nor worship the golden image which I have set up?

Now if ye be ready that at what time ye hear the sound of the cornet, flute, hard, sack-but, psaltery, and dulcimer, and all kinds of musick, ye fall down and worship the image which I have made; well! but if ye worship not, ye shall be cast the same hour into the midst of a burning fiery furnace; and who is that God that shall deliver you out of my hands?"

Shadrach, Meshach, and Abed-nego, answered and said to the king, "O Nebuchadnezzar, we are not careful to answer thee in this matter.

If it be so, our God whom we serve is able to deliver us from the burning fiery furnace and he will deliver us out of thine hand. O King.

But if not, be it known unto thee, O King, that we will not serve thy Gods, nor worship the golden image which thou has set up."

> Then was Nebuchadnezzar full of fury, and the form of his visage was changed against Shadrach, Meshach, and Abed-nego; therefore he spake, and commanded that they should heat the furnace one seven times more than it was wont to be heated.
>
> And he commanded the most mighty men that were in his army to bind Shadrach, Meshach, and Abed-nego, and to cast them into the burning fiery furnace.
>
> Then these men were bound in their coats, their hosen and their hats, and their other garments, and were cast into the midst of the burning fiery furnace.
>
> Therefore because the king's commandment was urgent, and the furnace exceeding hot, the flame of the fire slew those men that took up Shadrach, Meshach, and Abed-nego.
>
> And these three men, Shadrach, Meshach, and Abed-nego, fell down bound into the midst of the burning fiery furnace.[9]

Can the Brahmans of India show such steadfast faith and attachment for their gods and to their religious faith?

Buckle[10] in his *History of Civilization* says:

> It is evident that until doubt began, progress was impossible. For as we have clearly seen, the advance of civilization solely depends on the acquisitions made by the human intellect and on the extent to which those acquisitions are diffused. But men who are perfectly satisfied with their own knowledge will never attempt to increase it. Men who are perfectly convinced of the accuracy of their opinions will never take

9 Daniel 3: 1–23.

10 Henry Thomas Buckle (1821–1862) was an English historian, who was educated privately and never attended university. His only work was an unfinished opus *History of Civilization in England*, which was meant to comprise fourteen volumes, but of which he only finished the first two before his death in Damascus in 1862. Buckle formulated several 'laws' of history that were in fact rationalizations of his own liberal views. Nonetheless, the two volumes had immense impact on English liberal thought in the second half of the nineteenth century, with its emphasis on the population rather than individual kings and heroes, and in looking at social life beyond politics.

> the pains of examining the basis on which they are built. They look with wonder, and often with horror, on views contrary to those which they inherited from their fathers; and while they are in this state of mind, it is impossible that they should receive any new truth which interferes with their foregone conclusions.

On this account it is, that although the acquisition of fresh knowledge is the necessary precursor of every step in social progress, such acquisition must itself be preceded by a love of inquiry, and therefore by a spirit of doubt; because without doubt there will be no inquiry and without inquiry there will be no knowledge. For knowledge is not an inert and passive principle which comes to us whether we will or not; but it must be sought before it can be won; it is the product of great labour and therefore of great sacrifice. And it is absurd to suppose that men will incur the labour, and make the sacrifice for subjects respecting which they are already perfectly content. They who do not feel the darkness will never look for the light. If on any point we have attained certainty, we make no further inquiry on that point; because inquiry would be useless, or perhaps dangerous. Doubt must intervene, before the investigation can begin. Here, then we have the act of doubting as the originator or, at all events, the necessary antecedent of all progress.[11]

---

11 Ambedkar is quoting from Chapter 7 of Buckle's General Introduction to the volume, "Outline of the History of the English Intellect from the Middle of the Sixteenth to the End of the Eighteenth Century." Following the 'age of reason', the nineteenth century in Western Europe is considered the first great 'age of doubt', when leading intellectuals battled the Church as scientific discoveries disqualified all they knew to be true from the Bible (Lane 2012, 2). Lucien Febvre has argued that atheism could only become a "thinkable" concept in the seventeenth and eighteenth centuries, when a new philosophical vocabulary developed and there were new expectations regarding the certainty of scientific, philosophical and theological propositions (in Frede 2011, 11). By making God, through their critical analysis of religious texts, unknowable and unprovable, many in nineteenth-century Britain found a release from faith and dogma (Lane 2012, 2). Doubt turned from a religious sin into an ethical necessity inseparable from belief, a much-needed antidote to unbridled religiosity, something that Blunt emphasizes here.

Now the Brahmans have left no room for doubt, for they have propounded a most mischievous dogma which the Brahmans have spread among the masses, the infallibility of the Vedas. If the Hindu intellect has ceased to grow and if the Hindu civilization and culture has become a stagnant and stinking pool, this dogma must be destroyed root and branch if India is to progress. The Vedas are a worthless set of books.[12] There is no reason either to call them sacred or infallible. The Brahmans have invested it with sanctity and infallibility only because by a later interpolation of what is called the Purusha Sukta, the Vedas have made them the lords of the Earth.[13] Nobody has had the courage to ask why these worthless books, which contain nothing but invocations to

---

12 Unlike Abrahamic religions, what passes for Brahmanism, Sanatanism or Hinduism and its variants do not ascribe to a single book. British scholars of Indology in the early colonial period emphasized the relationship between Sanskrit and certain European languages, leading to the primacy of Sanskrit texts as emblematic of Indian culture. The reliance on Brahman pandits led to the study of the Shastras, Vedas and the *Bhagavad Gita*, earlier restricted to Brahmans. Therefore, the Vedas as texts came to exist only after the 'Orientalist' scholars made them available. Ambedkar was not alone in considering the Vedas a "worthless set of books". A much earlier text, *Agganna Sutta*, the 27th sutta of the Buddhist 'Book of Genesis', *Digha Nikaya*, holds a similar view. After ridiculing the pernicious four-varna imagery outlined in the Purusha Sukta hymn (*Rig Veda* 10.90.12), the Buddha pronounces that it was those lazy Brahmans incapable of enduring meditations in the forest who settled on the outskirts of villages and towns and started to make books ('books' meaning the three Vedas); the term 'Ajjhayaka' ('professors', if you like) applies to those Brahmans who meditate not but are 'repeaters' (of the Vedas). See T.W. Rhys Davids and C.A.F. Rhys Davids 2007, 78–9, 90.

13 The Purusha Sukta or "Hymn of the Man" is hymn 10.90 of the *Rig Veda*. The Purusha Sukta contains the best known Vedic description of creation (Klostermaier 2007, 87). It derives everything from a ritual sacrifice of a thousand-headed *purusha*, primeval man. It is from this great sacrifice that the entire universe and four castes are said to emerge; Brahman from the mouth, Kshatriya from the arms, Vaishya from the thighs and Shudra from the feet. As Jamison and Brereton say in the introduction to their opus translation of the *Rig Veda*: "this hymn is generally considered to have been a quite late addition to the text, perhaps to provide a charter myth for the varna system after it had taken more definite shape" (2014, 58). This is the only portion of the *Rig Veda* that mentions varna, but even this seems to be a social ideal rather than a social reality (Jamison and Brereton 2014, 57). See also Riddle No. 16 on the four varnas, where the hymn is quoted in full.

tribal Gods to destroy the enemies, loot their property and give it to their followers (have been made sacred and infallible).[14] But the time has come when the Hindu mind must be freed from the *hold* which the silly ideas propagated by the Brahmans, have on them. Without this the liberation [of] India has no future. I have undertaken this task knowing full well what *risk*[15] it involves. I am not afraid of the consequences. I shall be happy if I succeed in stirring the masses.

---

14 The words in parenthesis were inserted by the BAWS editors.

15 The words 'hold' and 'risk' were introduced by the BAWS editors. Unless otherwise stated, all emphases are as used in the BAWS edition.

Riddle No. 1

The Difficulty of Knowing Why One is a Hindu[1]

India is a congeries of communities. There are in it Parsis, Christians, Mohammedans and Hindus. The basis of these communities is not racial. It is of course religious. This is a superficial view. What is interesting to know is why is a Parsi a Parsi and why is a Christian a Christian, why is a Muslim a Muslim and why is a Hindu a Hindu? With regard to the Parsi, the Christian and the Muslim, it is smooth sailing. Ask a Parsi why he calls himself a Parsi, he will have no difficulty in answering the question. He will say he is a Parsi because he is a follower of Zoroaster. Ask the same question to a Christian. He too will have no difficulty in answering the question. He is a Christian because he believes in Jesus Christ. Put the same question to a Muslim. He too will have no hesitation in answering it. He will say he is a believer in Islam and that is why he is a Muslim.

Now ask the same question to a Hindu and there is no doubt that he will be completely bewildered and would not know what to say.[2]

---

1 For most of the riddles in the BAWS edition, the editors begin with a note about where and in what state the riddle was found. Riddles 1, 3, 4, 5 and 6 do not however carry an explanatory note from the BAWS editors.

2 Derived from Sindhu, the native name for the Indus river, the term 'Hind' was first used in Persian and came to be established after the eleventh-century polymath Al-Biruni (973–1048), commissioned by the king Mahmud of Ghazni (in present-day Afghanistan), travelled to the Indian subcontinent in 1017 and wrote the

If he says that he is a Hindu because he worships the same god as the Hindu community does, his answer cannot be true. All Hindus do not worship one god. Some Hindus are monotheists, some are polytheists and some are pantheists. Even those Hindus who are monotheists are not worshippers of the same gods. Some worship the god Vishnu, some Shiva, some Rama, some

---

famous encyclopedic account of India called *Tarikh-al-Hind*. The word 'Hindu', derived thus, did not indicate a religious group but was used as a geographical demarcator for the inhabitants of the land near and east of the Indus. Later, the word may have been adopted by those inhabitants to distinguish themselves from the Muslims who came to initially rule the northern parts of India. The ancient texts that the so-called Hindus today claim their roots from—the Vedas, *Ramayana, Mahabharata, Bhagavad Gita*, Upanishads—do not ever use the terms Hindu or Hinduism. Kalidasa (circa fifth century CE) or the absolute-monist Sankara (ninth century) or the qualified non-dualist Ramanuja (twelfth century), simply no one—fictional characters, poets or philosophers—could have understood anything by the term Hindu. Yet, while expounding upon them it is customary today to prefix the word Hindu to their works. Recent research argues that the term came into vogue with Orientalist and colonial scholarship. For an overview of the debates around 'Hindu' and 'Hinduism' and a nuanced counter-argument see D.N. Lorenzen (2006, 7–10). In her essay "Syndicated Hinduism" (1989, 54), Romila Thapar says, "The term Hinduism as we understand it today to describe a particular religion is modern." Ambedkar, for his times, was far-sighted in seriously interrogating a term around which Indian nationalism and anticolonialism came to be constructed. Thanks to colonial taxonomy, the notion of the 'Hindu' became fixed: suddenly it came to stand for all those Indians who were not Muslim or British by birth. The word 'Hindooism'/'Hinduism' was gifted to the English language by Rammohun Roy. Upinder Singh says, "The English word 'Hinduism' is a fairly recent one and was first used by Raja Rammohun Roy in 1816–17" (2009, 433). The new coinage began to infiltrate modern reflections on tradition (see also Lorenzen 2006, 3). The cross-disciplinary scholar Sibaji Bandyopadhyay alerts us to the fact that Bankimchandra Chattopadhyay (1838–94), despite being a prominent father figure as far as the spawning of indigenously modern discourses is concerned, had great reservations about deploying the term 'religion' for Hinduism, which he saw as *dharma*; but in spite of his fulminations against the "the monstrous nature of misuse of a name", i.e., against the erroneous substitution of *dharma* (understood as 'custom') by *religion* and his unease over the circulation of the commodity called 'Hinduism' in the free-market of ideas Chattopadhyay too ended up using it (2015, 75–9 for Bankimchandra Chattopadhyay, 95 for Rammohun Roy). Negative in orientation in terms of two given sets of population, the *identity* of the 'Hindu' went on to become flexible—functioning as a free-floating signifier signifying nothing positive, the 'Hindu' could increasingly arrogate or appropriate to itself any group/sect that remained unaccounted for, excluding the already accounted-for Muslims and the British. It is likely that while trying to crack the riddle "Who is a Hindu?", Ambedkar is gesturing towards this answer: precisely, no one.

Krishna. Some do not worship the male gods. They worship a goddess. Even then they do not worship the same goddesses. They worship different goddesses. Some worship Kali, some worship Parvati, some worship Lakshmi.

Coming to the polytheists, they worship all the gods. They will worship Vishnu and Shiva, also Rama and Krishna. They will worship Kali, Parvati and Lakshmi. A Hindu will fast on the Shivaratri day because it is sacred to Shiva. He will fast on Ekadashi day because it is sacred to Vishnu. He will plant a *bel* tree because it is sacred to Shiva and he will plant a *tulsi* because it is dear to Vishnu.

Polytheists among the Hindus do not confine their homage to the Hindu gods. No Hindu hesitates to worship a Muslim Pir or a Christian goddess. Thousands of Hindus go to a Muslim Pir and make offerings.[3] Actually there are in some places Brahmans who own the office of a hereditary priesthood of a Muslim Pir and wear a Muslim Pir's dress. Thousands of Hindus go to make offerings to the Christian goddess Mat Mauli near Bombay.[4]

The worship of the Christian or Muslim gods is only on occasions. But there are more permanent transfers of religious allegiance. There are many so-called Hindus whose religion has a strong Mohammedan content. Notable amongst these are the followers of the strange Panch Piriya cult,[5] who worship

---

3 See 51n7.

4 The spelling used in the BAWS edition, *Mant* Mauli, seems like an error. Ambedkar could be referring to the Mount Mary Church in Bandra, Mumbai, officially the Basilica of Our Lady of the Mount. Besides Christians, Hindus, Parsis and Muslims throng it. According to Klostermaier, the local name "Mat Mauli" may be seen as a "Hinduization" of "Mount Mary" (Klostermaier 1972). According to the *Maharashtra State Gazetteer* of 1986 Mat Mauli could be "corruption" of "Mata" or "Mother" Mauli.

5 Panch Piriya is a term applied to the worship of the 'Panchon Pir' or five saints, of whom the most prominent figure seems to have been Ghazi Miya or Salar Mas'ud, the nephew of Mahmud of Ghazni. Muslim 'deities' have been incorporated into the pantheons of many rural Hindu and subordinated castes. In Punjab, where the

five Mohammedan saints, of uncertain name and identity, and sacrifice cocks to them, employing for the purpose as their priest a Mohammedan Dafali fakir.[6] Throughout India many Hindus make pilgrimages to Mohammedan shrines, such as that of Sakhi Sarwar in the Punjab.[7]

Speaking of the Malkanas, Mr. Blunt[8] says that they are converted Hindus of various castes belonging to Agra and the adjoining districts, chiefly Muttra,[9] Ettah and Mainpuri. They are of Rajput, Jat and Bania descent. They are reluctant to describe themselves as Musalmans, and generally give their original caste name and scarcely recognize the name Malkana.[10]

'cult' seems to have originated, the list of the Panchon Pir consists of prominent Sufi saints from the thirteenth and fourteenth centuries. Over time, there was a dilution of Islamic elements and the inclusion of local Hindu deities and deified dead (Hiltebeitel 1988, 255–6).

6 Hiltebeitel notes that despite the influence of the Arya Samaj and corresponding Muslim fundamentalist movements, Hindu attendance at the tombs of Muslim martyrs and saints remained a visible phenomenon. "In addition to the pilgrimage and tomb-centered worship which continues to this day, the five saints are worshipped in the homes as family deities. Daily, weekly, and annual worship is performed in the usual manner for household deities, often assisted by a Muslim Dafali, the hereditary priest of Ghazi Miya" (1988, 255–6).

7 Max Arthur Macauliffe, a colonial officer in Punjab between 1864 and 1893, wrote of the Sakhi Sarwar fair in 1875: "Hindus as well as Musalmans make offerings at the grave, and invoke the divine intercession of God's Musalman favourite" (Macauliffe 1875, quoted in Mir 2010, 108).

8 Edward Arthur Henry Blunt (1877–1941) was a British civil servant appointed to the United Provinces. In 1931, he wrote *The Caste System of Northern India with Special Reference to the United Provinces of Agra and Oudh*, which Ambedkar is referring to.

9 Present-day Mathura.

10 By passing the Indian Councils Act of 1909 the British granted Muslims a separate electorate and proportional political representation, after which the Arya Samaj looked to increase the ranks of the Hindu community. One of the ways this was done was through *shuddhi* or purification rituals, in which they converted/purified Chamars, Doms and other 'Untouchable' castes. One of the most important *shuddhi* campaigns, according to Christophe Jaffrelot, was of the Muslims Rajputs from the Malkana caste, which may explain their reluctance to identify as Muslim, despite the social fluidity (Jaffrelot 2010, 150–1).

Their names are Hindu; they mostly worship in Hindu temples; they use the salutation "Ram-Ram"; they intermarry amongst themselves only. On the other hand, they sometimes frequent a mosque, practise circumcision and bury their dead; they will eat with Mohammedans if they are particular friends.[11]

In Gujarat there are several similar communities such as the Matia Kunbis,[12] who call in Brahmans for their chief ceremonies, but are followers of the Pirana saint Imam Shah and his successors, and bury their dead as do the Mohammedans; the Sheikhadas at their weddings employ both Hindu and Mohammedan priests, and the Momnas,[13] who practise circumcision, bury their dead and read the Gujarati Koran, but in other respects follow Hindu custom and ceremony.

If he says that "I am a Hindu because I hold to the beliefs of the Hindus," his answer cannot be right for here one is confronted with the fact that Hinduism has no definite creed. The beliefs of persons who are by all admitted to be Hindus often

11 Paraphrased from Blunt 1931, 206–7.

12 D.D. Kosambi (1956/2008, 389) cites the colonial ethnographer R.E. Enthoven to say that the Matia Kunbis were low castes who were "half Hindu half Muslim by religion". The Kunbis (also Kunabis, Kanbi), broadly, are non-elite tillers in western India, included among the OBC (Other Backward Classes) in present-day Maharashtra. While the jati has Shudra origins, claims have been made to Kshatriya status and the hyphenated Maratha-Kunbi identity since the colonial period. The seventeenth-century Marathi saint-poet Tukaram identified himself as a Kunbi. Rosalind O'Hanlon tracks the aspiration for upward social mobility among the Kunbis since the 1860s (1985).

13 Ambedkar is relying on Census reports for such information. The 1911 Census has this to say: "In Gujarat there are several similar communities—such as the Matia Kunbis, who call in Brahmans for their chief ceremonies, but are followers of the Pirana saint Imam Shah and his successors, and bury their dead as do the Mohammedans; the Sheikhadas who at their weddings employ both a Hindu and a Mohammedan priest; the Momnas who practise circumcision...." (*Census of India*, 1911, Vol 1, 118). The Momnas apparently are a modern branch of the Aga Khan Ismailis who "belonged originally" to the Hindu caste of Leva Kunbis. See Lokhandwalla 1955, 117–18. On the role of the Census and other colonialist methods that sought to freeze fluid, evolving communities into fixed lists, see Dirks 2001.

differ more widely from each other than do those of Christians and Mohammedans. Limiting the issue to cardinal beliefs,[14] the Hindus differ among themselves as to which beliefs are of cardinal importance. Some say that all the Hindu scriptures must be accepted, but some would exclude the Tantras,[15] while others would regard only the Vedas as of primary importance; some again think that the sole essential is belief in the doctrine of karma and metempsychosis.

A complex congeries of creeds and doctrines is Hinduism. It shelters within its portals monotheists, polytheists and pantheists; worshippers of the great gods Shiva and Vishnu or of their female counterparts, as well as worshippers of the divine mothers or the spirits of trees, rocks and streams and the tutelary village deities; persons who propitiate their deity by all manner of bloody sacrifices, and persons who will not only kill no living creature but who must not even use the word "cut"; those whose ritual consists mainly of prayers and hymns, and those who indulge in unspeakable orgies in the name of religion; and a host of more or less heterodox sectaries, many of whom deny the supremacy of the Brahmans, or at least have non-Brahmanical religious leaders.

If he says that he is a Hindu because he observes the same customs as other Hindus do, his answer cannot be true. For all Hindus do not observe the same customs.

In the north, near relatives are forbidden to marry; but in the south cousin marriage is prescribed, and even closer alliances are

14 A cardinal belief is the basic principle on which a religion is hinged. For instance, though there are several Christian denominations, there are some core beliefs accepted as common (such as the trinity, the divinity of Christ and his bodily resurrection) that are foundational to all. A person who rejects any of these beliefs cannot be called a Christian. In Islam, there are seven articles of faith (such as belief in Allah and Judgment Day) that every Muslim believes in.

15 See Riddle No. 14, where Ambedkar discusses Tantrism and the Tantra texts.

sometimes permitted. As a rule, female chastity is highly valued, but some communities set little store by it, at any rate prior to marriage, and others make it a rule to dedicate one daughter to a life of religious prostitution.[16] In some parts the women move about freely; in others they are kept secluded. In some parts they wear skirts; in others trousers.

Again if he said that he is a Hindu because he believes in the caste system, his answer cannot be accepted as satisfactory. It is quite true that no Hindu is interested in what his neighbour believes, but he is very much interested in knowing whether he can eat with him or take water from his hands. In other words it means that the caste system is an essential feature of Hinduism and a man who does not belong to a recognized Hindu caste cannot be a Hindu. While all this is true it must not be forgotten that observance of caste is not enough. Many Musalmans and many Christians observe caste, if not in the matter of inter-dining certainly in the matter of inter-marriage. But they cannot be called Hindus on that account. Both elements must be present. He must be a Hindu and he must also observe caste. This brings us back to the old question: who is a Hindu? It leaves us where we are.

---

16 The religious practice referred to is the votive offering of pre-pubescent girls, known as Devadasis, to deities in Hindu temples, requiring them to become sexually available for community members. It is traditionally believed that the girls are 'serving' the society and have been ordained to do so. For her services to the temple, the Devadasi enjoyed grants made either to her personally or to the temple (Nair 1994, 3159). Communities like the Basavi, Matangi and Jogini connote similar practices in other regions. Devadasis are usually from Dalit and other oppressed castes, and the custom continues to this day, according to the National Human Rights Commission. See Kannabiran (1995) for a discussion on women, religion and the state in colonial and post-colonial India. Ambedkar, in a speech in 1936 to Vaghyas, Devadasi, Joginis and Aradhis in Kamatipura, spoke of the need to give up the profession as one they were forced into because of their oppressed caste position: "You will ask me how to make your living. I am not going to tell you that. There are hundreds of ways of doing it. But I insist that you give up this degraded life. You marry and settle down to normal domestic life as women of other classes do and do not live under conditions which inevitably drag you into prostitution." For more, see Rege 2013, 145–9.

Is it not a question for every Hindu to consider why, in the matter of his own religion, his position is so embarrassing and so puzzling? Why is he not able to answer so simple a question which every Parsi, every Christian and every Muslim can answer? Is it not time that he should ask himself what are the causes that has brought about this religious chaos?

Riddle No. 6

The Contents of the Vedas: Have they any Moral or Spiritual Value?

I

If the Vedas are to be accepted as binding and infallible, then what they teach must have ethical and spiritual value. Nobody can regard a rag to be binding and infallible because a philosopher like Jaimini came forward to lend his authority to such a proposal.[1] Have the Vedas any ethical or spiritual value? Every Hindu who regards the Vedas as infallible is bound to consider this question.

Modern writers have expressed views which deny any spiritual value to the Vedas. As an illustration one may refer to the views of Prof. Muir.[2] According to Prof. Muir:

> The whole character of these compositions and the circumstances under which, from internal evidence, they

---

1 Jaimini is an ancient sage associated with the Mimamsa school of exegesis, concerned with the understanding of Vedic ritual injunctions. Around the fifth century BCE, the authority of the Vedas was being undermined by heterodox thinkers, such as the Buddha. The Mimamsa school developed as an exegetical exercise to resolve contradictions and inconsistencies in the scriptures, and Jaimini's *Purva Mimamsa Sutras,* dated sometime between the second century BCE and second century CE, form the textual basis of this school, emphasizing the eternal authority of the Veda. See also note 11 to this riddle.

2 John Muir (1810–1882) was a Scottish Indologist whose work *Original Sanskrit Texts on the Origin and History of the People of India, their Religion and Institutions,* written between 1852 and 1870 in five volumes, was a study of some of the important Sanskrit sources of ancient Indian history.

> appear to have arisen, are in harmony with the supposition that they were nothing more than the natural expression of the personal hopes and feelings of those ancient bards of whom they were first recited. In these songs the Aryan sages celebrated the praises of their ancestral gods (while at the same time they sought to conciliate their goodwill by a variety of oblations supposed to be acceptable to them), and besought of them all the blessings which men in general desire—health, wealth, long life, cattle, offspring, victory over their enemies, forgiveness of sin, and in some cases also celestial felicity.[3]

It would no doubt be objected that all foreign scholars are prejudiced and that their views cannot therefore be accepted. Fortunately we are not altogether dependent upon the views of foreigners. There are leaders of indigenous schools of thought which have taken the same view. The most notorious example is that of the Charvakas.[4]

The opposition of Charvaka[5] can be seen from the following

---

3 Muir 1870, Vol 3, 210–11.

4 Charvaka or Lokayata was a materialist this-worldly school of thought that evolved around the seventh century BCE, whose doctrines only remain as extracts in Vedic, Buddhist, Jain and Brahmanic texts that refute them. The Charvaka rejected the existence of the afterworld, karma, moksha, the authority of the Vedas, etc. The Charvaka doctrines are discussed in Madhavacharya's *Sarva-Darsana-Samgraha*, a fourteenth-century compendium that offers a review of the sixteen different systems of Brahmanic philosophy. Even as Madhavacharya—who following in the line of the ninth-century brahmanist Sankara espouses Advaita Vedanta—refutes the arguments of Buddhism and Lokayata, he extensively quotes from the Charvaka school, and Ambedkar cites from the translated edition of this work. However, as the scholar Ramkrishna Bhattacharya (2011a) says, we must be cautious of how we read Madhavacharya's digest. Bhattacharya refutes the charge that the Lokayata were hedonists permitting immorality by denying any ethical consequences. "The one verse found at the end of the *Sarva-darsana-samgraha*, chapter 1, which urges people to drink clarified butter even by incurring debt (*mam krtva ghrtam pibet*) is a gross distortion of the original reading of the half-line, 'nothing is beyond the ken of death' (*nasti mrtyor agocarah*)." Bhattacharya also says Lokayata *does not* mean materialism but signifies *Vitandashastra,* the art of disputation. "Another oft-used term, *nastika,* means the denier of the other-world but also the defiler of the Veda." See also Bhattacharya 2011b and Debiprasad Chattopadhyay 1990.

5 Bhattacharya says: "*Lokayata* does not mean materialism or the Charvaka system

quotation which reproduces his line of argument against the Vaidikas:

> If you object that, if there be no such thing as happiness in a future world, then how should men of experienced wisdom engage in the *agnihotra* and other sacrifices, which can only be performed with great expenditure of money and bodily fatigue. Your objection cannot be accepted as any proof to the contrary, since the *agnihotra*, etc., are only useful as means of livelihood: for the Veda is tainted by three faults of untruth, self-contradiction, and tautology; then again the impostors who call themselves Vaidic pundits are mutually destructive, as the authority of the Jnan-Kanda is overthrown by those who maintain the authority of the Karma-Kanda and those who maintain the authority of the Jnan-Kanda reject that of the Karma-Kanda; and lastly, the three Vedas themselves are only the incoherent rhapsodies of knaves, and to this effect

---

of philosophy (also known as Barhaspatya-mata or Lokayata-mata) in Buddhist Sanskrit. It stands for ... 'a technical logical science'. A comparison with Pali will prove the validity of this rendering. In all Pali commentaries, dictionaries, etc, *lokayatam* is always glossed as *vitandasattham* or *vitandavadasattham*, the science of disputation. This was the original meaning of the word ... Only later, but not much earlier than the fourth century CE, *lokayata* came to mean materialism (as it is used in Vatsyayana's *Kamasutra* (1.2.25–30)). What was common to the older Lokayatikas and the new Charvaka materialists was perhaps disputatiousness: nothing was sacred to them" (2011b, 195). Denigration of the Lokayata school abound in Brahmanic texts. In the 100th part of 'Ayodhya Kanda' of the *Ramayana* we hear Rama himself speaking dismissively of the Lokayatas. According to him, those belonging to the Lokayata party are guilty of (i) disparaging the Vedas, and, (ii) engaging in *Vitandashastra,* the art of disputation. Logic or disputation was heavily frowned upon by the *Manusmriti* 2.9: "The Veda (*shruti*) should be known as the revealed canon and the teachings of dharma (*smriti*) as the tradition." 2.10 says: "Any twice-born man who disregards these two because he relies on the teachings of logic (*hetusastra*) should be excommunicated by virtuous people as a *nastika* and a reviler of the Veda (*Veda-nindaka*)." The word *Lokayata/Loukayatic* occurs four times in Sankara's commentary on the *Brahma Sutra/Vedanta Sutra*. Though a past-master in disputations, Sankara makes his attitude towards those who follow the argumentative Lokayata path abundantly clear at the very beginning of his treatise. Explicating on *Brahma Sutra* I.1.1 he begins: "Unlearned people and the Lokayatics are of the opinion...." (see George Thibaut, tr. 1890, 14). In his commentary on the *Bhagavad Gita* 16.8, Sankara asserts that those who believe that the world is godless and desire is the sole cause of creation of beings are the (godforsaken) Lokayatics.

> runs the popular saying: "The Agnihotra, the three Vedas, the ascetic, three staves, and smearing oneself with ashes," Brahaspati says, "these are but means of livelihood for those who have no manliness nor sense."[6]

Brahaspati is another example of the same school of thought. Brahaspati was far more bold and militant in his opposition to the Vedas than the Charvakas.[7] As reported by Madhavacharya, Brahaspati argued:

> There is no heaven, no final liberation, nor any soul in another world;
>
> Nor do the actions of the four castes, orders etc., produce any real effect.
>
> The Agnihotra, the three Vedas, the ascetic's three staves and smearing one's self with ashes,
>
> Were made by Nature as the livelihood of those destitute of knowledge and manliness.
>
> If a beast slain in the Jyotishtoma rite will itself go to heaven, why then does not the sacrificer forthwith offer his own father?
>
> If the Sraddha produces gratification to beings who are dead,
>
> Then here, too, in the case of travellers when they start, it is needless to give provisions for the journey.
>
> If beings in heaven are gratified by our offering the Sraddha here,
>
> Then why not give the food down below to those who are standing on the housetop?

---

6 Ambedkar is quoting from E.B. Cowell and A.E. Gough's 1882 translation of the *Sarva-Darsana-Samgraha*, 4.

7 Brahaspati—not to be confused with the mythical Vedic rishi who figures as a rapist, among other things, and is discussed in Riddle No. 23—is a legendary figure considered the original founder of the Charvaka school, as well as the author of the *Brahaspati Sutra*, the lost doctrine of the school of which only fragments remain. It is unclear what Ambedkar meant about him being more militant than the Charvakas. "By the eighth century the two names, Charvaka and Lokayata, along with another, Barhaspatya (relating to Brahaspati, the mythical guru of the gods) are used interchangeably to signify materialism" (Bhattacharya 2011a).

While life remains let a man live happily, let him feed on ghee even though he runs in debt;

When once the body becomes ashes, how can it ever return again?

If he who departs from the body goes to another world,

How is that he comes not back again, restless for love of his kindred?

Hence it is only as a means of livelihood that Brahmans have established here.

All these ceremonies are for the dead,—there is no other fruit anywhere.

The three authors of the Vedas were buffoons, knaves and demons.

All the well-known formulas of the pundits Jarphari, Turphari, etc.

And all the obscene rites for the queen commanded in the Aswamedha,

These were invented by buffoons, and so all the various kinds of presents to the priests,

While the eating of flesh was similarly commanded by night-prowling demons.[8]

If the opinions of the Charvaka and Brahaspati are not accepted, there is plenty of other evidence. That evidence is recorded in the books of the various schools of philosophy such as the Nyaya, Vaishashikha, Purva and Uttara Mimamsa.[9] It must be said to the credit of the authors of the textbooks of these philosophies that, before proceeding to defend the authority of the Vedas, they have been very careful to set out the case of their

8 Cowell and Gough 1882, 10–11.

9 Orthodox Hinduism has six schools of philosophy: Nyaya, Vaiseshika, Samkhya, Yoga, Mimamsa and Vedanta. Uttara Mimamsa is another name for the Vedanta school, and Purva a prefix for the Mimamsa. According to Bhattacharya, the six systems referred to the pro-Vedic or *astika* systems only; the Buddhist, Jain and Charvaka systems were called *nastika* (negativist) because they did not accept the infallibility of the Vedas (2011b, 165).

opponents who were opposed to the authority of the Vedas.[10] This fact enables us to prove two things: (1) That there was a school of thought which was opposed to recognize the Vedas as books of authority; (2) That they were a respectable group of people whose opinions the defenders of the authority of the Vedas were bound to consider. I reproduce below the case of the opponents as set out in the Nyaya and the Purva Mimamsa.[11]

Gotama, the author of the Nyaya system of philosophy,[12] was an upholder of the doctrine of the authority of the Vedas. He has

---

10 Owing to colonial pedagogy, *nastika* is undertsood to imply 'atheist', the person who disbelieves the existence of God. The word 'atheist' however derives from the Greek *atheos,* meaning, 'without gods'. Building on Panini's aphorism, *'asti-nasti-distang matih'* (Panini, 4.4.60, *Ashtadhyayi,* Tr. Sumitra M. Katre 1989, 495), the grammarian Patanjali opines that *'astika* is he who believes it exists' and *'nastika* is he who does not believe it exists'. Since neither Panini nor Patanjali impute any specific meaning to the 'object of inquiry' by the article 'it', the two terms are relativistic in nature. That 'it' may refer to 'the validity of the Vedas', 'God/gods', 'atman', 'after-life', 'karmaphala' or for that matter anything. So, when deploying the two terms it is crucial to remember that their profiles, in place of being always-already filled with an available meaning, keep changing in correspondence to the object they signal. That the word 'atheist', whose significance is absolute in nature in Greek and Christian discourses, cannot be freely exchanged by the relativistic *nastika* is well borne out by the different positions the different schools of Indian philosophy take in relation to gods/God. The Sramanas, besides being *nastika* apropos the validity of the Vedas, reject the notion of 'Creator' or 'Prime Mover', i.e., they are also *nastika* apropos God. What is more interesting is that out of the six orthodox schools that are *astika* in relation to the validity of Vedas, two staunchly deny the notion of the 'Prime Mover' or the 'Original Maker', two are ambiguous about it and two accept it. Each one is *astika* as far as the Veda goes, the adherents of Samkhya and Purva Mimamsa were *nastika*, Vaiseshika and Nyaya were vaguely *astika,* Yoga and Vedanta were *astika* in reference to God. (The annotators owe this note to Sibaji Bandyopadhyay.)

11 The *Purva Mimamsa Sutras* consist of a systematically ordered collection of approximately 2,745 short statements, also referred to individually as sutra. For a full translation of the *Purva Mimamsa Sutras* with commentary, see Ganganath Jha 1942; see also Benson 2010 and Clooney 1990.

12 With origins in the ancient tradition of debate *(vada),* the Nyaya school, which took shape between third century BCE and first century CE, developed theories of logic, methodology and epistemology in a vast corpus of literature. The Nyaya system believes knowledge can be gained through four means: perception, inference, comparison and word. For more on the Nyaya school, see Vattanky 2003. On Buddhism and Nyaya, see chapter 5 of Siderits 2007.

summarized the arguments of his opponents in Sutra 57,[13] which reads as follows:

> "The Veda has no authority, since it has the defects of falsehood, self-contradiction, and tautology."[14] That verbal evidence, which is distinct from such as relates to visible objects, i.e., the Veda, has no authority. Why? Because it has the defects of falsehood etc.
>
> Of these defects, that of falsehood is established by the fact that we sometimes observe that no fruit results from performing the sacrifice for a son, or the like. "Self-contradiction" is a discrepancy between a former and a later declaration. Thus the Veda says, "he sacrifices when the sun is risen; he sacrifices when the sun is not yet risen; he sacrifices" [I cannot explain the next words.]
>
> "A tawny (dog?) carries away the oblation of him who sacrifices after the Sun has risen; a brindled [dog?] carries off the oblation of him who sacrifices before the sun has risen; and both of these two carry off the oblation of him who sacrifices."… Now here there is a contradiction between the words which enjoin sacrifices, and the words which intimate by censure that those sacrifices will occasion disastrous results. Again, the Veda has no authority, owing to its "tautology," as where it is said, "he repeats the first thrice, he repeats the last thrice." For as the lastness ultimately coincides with [?] the firstness and as there is a triple repetition of the words, this sentence is tautological. Now since these particular sentences have no authority, the entire Veda will be proved by these specimens to stand in the same predicament, since all its other parts have the same author, or are of the same character, as these portions.

---

13 The earliest text of the Nyaya school is the *Nyaya Sutra* of Akspada Gotama, whose identity and date has never been established. The final form of the *Nyaya Sutra* is dated between the second and fourth centuries CE. Ambedkar is citing Muir's translation of Sutra 57, 1870, Vol 3, 113. For a more recent translation, see Ganganath Jha 1999.

14 This is the only quotation from Sutra 57. The rest is an explanation and commentary by Muir 1870, Vol 3, 113.

Coming to Jaimini. He summarises the views of the opponents of the Vedas in the first parts of Sutras 28 and 32 of his *Purva Mimamsa*. Sutra 28 says:

> It is also objected that the Vedas cannot be eternal, because we observe that persons, who are not eternal, but subject to birth and death, are mentioned in them. Thus it is said in the Veda "Babara Pravahani desired," "Kusurvinda Auddalaki desired." Now, as the sentences of the Veda, in which they are mentioned, could not have existed before these persons were born, it is clear that these sentences had a beginning, and being thus non-eternal, they are proved to be of human composition.[15]

Sutra 32 says:

> It is asked how the Veda can constitute proof of duty when it contains such incoherent nonsense as the following: "An old ox, in blanket and slippers, is standing at the door and singing benedictions. A Brahman female, desirous of offspring, asks, "Pray O King, what is the meaning of intercourse on the day of the new moon?" or the following: "the cows celebrated this sacrifice."[16]

This is also the view of Yaska, the author of *Nirukta*,[17] who says:

> [Of the four kinds of verses specified in the preceding section],[18] (a) those which address a god as absent, (b) those which address him as present, and (c) those which address

15 Muir 1870, Vol 3, 77.

16 Muir 1870, Vol 3, 80. Ambedkar doesn't quote the sutra itself, but rather Muir's commentary preceding it. The sutra goes: *Krite va viniyogah syat karmanah sambandhat*. "The passages to which objection is taken may be applicable to the duty to be performed, from the relation in which they stand to the ceremony."

17 Yaska was a grammarian and a sage, said to be Panini's predecessor in the fifth to sixth century BCE, also believed to be author of the *Nirukta*, commentaries that consist of explanations and interpretations of difficult words in Vedic hymns. The *Nirukta* has three parts—*Naighantuka*, a collection of synonymous words; *Naigama*, a collection of words peculiar to the Vedas; and the *Daivata*, words related to deities and sacrifices (Cush et al 2012, 1029). All of these are followed by Yaska's commentary. For a translation of *Nirukta*, see Sarup 1967.

18 These parentheses appear as such in Muir.

> the worshippers as present and the god as absent, are the most numerous, while (d) those which refer to the speaker himself are rare. It happens also that a god is praised without any blessing being invoked, as in the hymn (RV i. 32).[19] "I declare the heroic deeds of Indra" etc. Again, blessings are invoked without any praise being offered, as in the words, "May I see well with my eyes, be resplendent in my face, and hear well with my ears". This frequently occurs in the Adhvaryava (Yajur) Veda, and in the sacrificial formulae. Then again we find oaths and curses as in the words (RV vii. 104, 15), "May I die today, if I am a Yatudhana," etc. Further, we observe the desire to describe some particular state of things, as in the verse (RV x. 129, 2), "Death was not then, nor immortality," etc. Then there is lamentation, arising out of a certain state of thing, as in the verse (RV x. 95, 14), "The beautiful god will disappear and never return," etc. Again we have blame and praise, as in the words (RV x. 117, 6), "The man who eats alone, sins alone," etc. So, too, in the hymn to dice (RV x. 34, 13) there is a censure upon dice, and a commendation of agriculture. Thus the objects for which the hymns were seen by the rishis were very various.[20]

To quote the words of Yaska again: "Each particular hymn has for its deity the god to whom the *rishi*, seeking to obtain any object of desire which he longs for, addresses his prayer."[21]

If this is not enough to prove that there is no ethical or spiritual value in the Vedas, further evidence could be added.

As to morality there is hardly any discussion about it in the *Rig Veda*. Nor does the *Rig Veda* contain elevating examples of moral life.[22] Three illustrations of cases on the other side may

---

19 All such references to the *Rig Veda* in this quote are inserted by Muir, with mandala, recitation and hymn/sukta number.

20 Muir, 1870, Vol 3, 211–2.

21 Muir, 1870, Vol 3, 211.

22 Morality is an important concern for Ambedkar. He attacks Hinduism often for lacking in morality and finds that Buddhism, which he later embraced, is grounded

well be given. The first is the conversation between Yama and Yami who were brother and sister.[23]

1. (Yami speaks). I invite my friend to friendship, having come o'er the vast and desert ocean; may Vedhas,[24] after reflecting, place in the earth the offspring (of thee) the father, endowed with excellent qualities.

2. (Yama speaks). Thy friend desires not this friendship, for although of one origin, she is of a different form; the hero sons of the great Asura (are) the upholders of heaven, enjoying vast renown.

3. (Yami speaks). The immortals take pleasure in (a union) like this which is forbidden to every mortal; let thy mind then concur with mine, and as the progenitor (of all) was the husband (of his daughter), do thou enjoy my person.

4. (Yama speaks). We have not done what was done formerly; for how can we who speak truth, utter now that

---

in morality and ethics. In AoC 13.1: "A Hindu's public is his caste. His responsibility is only to his caste. His loyalty is restricted only to his caste. Virtue has become caste-ridden, and morality has become caste-bound" (2014, 259). In 13.2: "The capacity to appreciate merits in a man, apart from his caste, does not exist in a Hindu. There is appreciation of virtue, but only when the man is a fellow caste-man" (259). In 20.1: "You cannot build anything on the foundations of caste. You cannot build up a nation, you cannot build up a morality" (283). In 22.16: "How are you going to break up caste, if people are not free to consider whether it accords with morality? The wall built around caste is impregnable, and the material of which it is built contains none of the combustible stuff of reason and morality" (303) Further at 22.17: "...you have got to apply the dynamite to the Vedas and the shastras, which deny any part to reason; to the Vedas and shastras, which deny any part to morality. You must destroy the religion of the shrutis and the smritis" (303–4). At 24.3: "the priestly class among Hindus is subject neither to law nor to morality. It recognises no duties. It knows only of rights and privileges. It is a pest which divinity seems to have let loose on the masses for their mental and moral degradation" (309–10).

23 Sukta 10.10. Ambedkar is quoting from Wilson 1854, Vol 6, 20–4; the parentheses for Yama and Yami are from the original. This famous hymn from the tenth mandala of the *Rig Veda* presents a tense dialogue between a pair of twins, the male Yama and the female Yami, who become the first mortals. Yami urges her twin brother to have sex with her, so that they can procreate and continue their line. Yama rejects her advances, outraged at the thought of incest and fearful of punishment from divine moral guardians (Jamison and Brereton 2014, 1381).

24 As spelt by Wilson.

which is untrue? Gandharva (the sun) was in the watery (firmament), and the water was his bride. She is our common parent, hence our near affinity.

5. (Yami speaks). The divine omniform generator Twashtri, the progenitor, made us two husband and wife, even in the womb; none frustrate his undertaking; earth and heaven are conscious of this our (union).

6. (Yama speaks). Who knows anything of this (his) first day (of existence)? Who has beheld it? Who has here revealed it? The dwelling of Mitra and of Varuna is vast. What sayest thou, who punishest men with hell?

7. (Yami speaks). The desire of Yama hath approached me Yami, to lie with him in the same bed; I will abandon my person as a wife to her husband; let us exert ourselves in union like the two wheels of a wagon.

8. (Yama speaks). The spies of the Gods, which wander upon earth, never stop, never close their eyes. Associate quickly, destructress, with some other than with me, and exert yourselves in union, like the two wheels of a wagon.

9. (Yami speaks). To him (Yama) let every worshipper sacrifice both day and night, on him let the eye of the Sun repeatedly rise; (for him may) the kindred pair (day and night unite) with heaven and earth. Yami will adhere to the non-affinity of Yama.

10. (Yama speaks). The subsequent ages will come, when sisters will choose one who is not a brother (as a husband); therefore, auspicious one, choose another husband than me, and make thine arm a pillow for thy mate.

11. (Yami speaks). Is he a brother whose sister has no lord? Is she a sister (whose brother) misfortune approaches? Overcome by desire, I strongly urge this one request; unite thy person with mine.

12. (Yama speaks). I will not unite my person with thine; they call him who approaches a sister, a sinner. Enjoy pleasure with some other than me; thy brother, auspicious one, has no such desire.

13. (Yami speaks). Alas, Yama, thou art feeble; we understand not thy mind or thy heart. Some other female embraces thee as a girth a horse, or as a creeper a tree.

14. (Yama speaks). Do thou, Yami, embrace another; and let another embrace thee as a creeper a tree; seek his affection, let him seek thine; and make a happy union.

From *Rig Veda* 10.162:[25]

1. May Agni, the destroyer of the *Rakshasas*, consenting to our prayer, drive hence (the evil spirit) who (in the form of) sickness assails thine embryo, who, as the disease *durnaman*, assails thy womb.

2. May Agni, concurring in our prayer, destroy the cannibal who, as sickness, assails thine embryo, who, as the disease *durnaman*, assails thy womb.

3. May we exterminate from hence (the evil spirit) who destroys the impregnating energy, the germ as it settles, the moving embryo, who seeks to destroy (the babe) when born.

4. May we exterminate from hence (the evil spirit), who separates thy thighs, who lies between husband and wife, who entering thy womb, devours (the seeds).

5. May we exterminate from hence (the evil spirit), who in the form of brother, husband, or paramour, approaches thee, and seeks to destroy thy offspring.

6. May we exterminate from hence (the evil spirit) who, having beguiled thee by sleep or darkness, approaches thee, and seeks to destroy thy offspring.

25 This line has been introduced here for clarity since the shift from the Yama–Yami dialogue to the new sukta is not indicated in BAWS. Sukta 10.162—translated variously as "Prayer to Avert Abortion" (Wilson Vol 6, 391), "Against Miscarriage" (Jamison and Brereton 2014, 1643) and "To Protect the Embryo" (Doniger 1981, 292)—consists of a charm meant to deflect harm from embryos. Notably, in verse 5, masquerading as a brother seems to give intimate access to a pregnant woman, and is reminiscent of the conversation between Yama and Yami (Jamison and Brereton 2014, 1644). See Riddle No. 23 (196n49) and the discussion on *niyoga* (201–2) and Indra (208) for more instances of rape, the post-facto legitimacy of incest, sex with a guru's wife and its subsequent proscription by lawmakers.

Take some of the hymns or prayers that are to be found in the *Rig Veda*. The following are a few of them:[26]

1. Oh! God Vayu, how very beautiful you are. We have prepared the Somarasa (an intoxicating drink) with spices. Pray come and drink it and grant us our prayers. 1.2.1.

2. Oh! God Indra. Bring ye wealth for our protection. Let the wealth that you bring make us happy be increasing and everlasting and help us to kill our enemies. 1.8.1.

3. Oh! ye people whenever you are performing your yajna, fail not to praise the Gods Indra and Agni. Advance their position and sing their praises in the Gayatri Meter. 1.21.2.

4. Oh! ye Agni, please bring the wives of the Gods and Twashta who are eager to come and drink Soma. 1.22.9.

5. We pray that the Gods' wives come to us with all available wings and with all happiness. 1.22.11.

6. I am praying the wives of Indra, Varuna and Agni to come to my place to drink Soma. 1.22.12

7. Oh! Varuna, we are supplicating before you to remove your anger. Oh! ye Asura, you are all wise, relieve us from our sins. 1.24.14.

8. Our Somarasa has been prepared by women who have churned it backward and forward. Oh! ye Indra we pray you to come and drink this Soma. 1.28.3.

9. Your enemies who do not make any offering to you may disappear and let your followers who do prosper. Oh ! Indra give us best cows and best horses and make us famous in the world. 1.29.4.

10. Oh! Agni save us from Rakshasas, from cunning enemies, from those who hate us and want to kill us. 1.36.15.

11. Oh! Indra, you are a hero. Come and drink the Soma we have prepared and be ready to give us wealth. Loot the wealth of those who do not make you any offering and give

---

26 It has not been possible to establish the translation Ambedkar is quoting from. He has—until this point—quoted from H.H. Wilson's 1850–1888 six-volume translation of the *Rig Veda*. However, the numbers of these hymns and their basic content and import are consistent with Wilson's as well as other contemporary translations.

the same to us. 1.81.8–9.

12. Oh! Indra, drink this Soma which is the best, giving immortality and most intoxicating. 1.84.4.

13. Oh! Adityas, you come to give us your blessings. You give us victory in war. You are wealthy. You are charitable. Just as a chariot is pulled through a difficult path in the same way you pull us through our dangers. 1.106.2.

14. Oh! ye Marutas...your followers are singing your praises. Be pleased to come and sit on the grass-cushion prepared for you for the purpose of drinking Soma. 7.57.1–2.

15. Oh! ye Mitra-Varuna we have offered you worship in the yajna. Be pleased to accept it and save us from all dangers. 7.60.12.

These are only a few verses out of a large bundle which form the *Rig Veda*. But there can be no doubt that this sample, small as it is, is true to bulk.

I may state that I have deliberately omitted a good many obscene passages to be found in the *Rig Veda* and *Yajur Veda*. Those who have any curiosity in the matter might look up the conversation between Surya and Pushan in *Rig Veda* 10.85.37[27] and between Indra and Indrani in *Rig Veda* 10.86.6.[28] A further obscenity will also be found in the Ashvamedha section of the *Yajur Veda*.[29]

Leaving these obscenities aside and confining oneself to the prayer portion of the *Rig Veda*, can anyone say that these are morally or spiritually elevating prayers?

---

27 "Pushan, inspire her who is most auspicious, in whom men may sow seed, who most affectionately may be devoted to us, and in whom animated by desire we may beget progeny" (Wilson Vol 6, 229–30).

28 "There is no woman more amiable than I am, nor one who bears fairer sons than I; nor one more tractable, nor one more ardent; Indra is above all the world" (Wilson Vol 6, 233).

29 In some of the more well-known translations of the Ashvamedha in the Black or Krishna *Yajur Veda*, the "obscene" parts were removed altogether. Ambedkar details the ritual later in Riddle No. 23, especially 194–5.

As to philosophy, there is nothing of it in the *Rig Veda*. As Prof Wilson[30] observes there is in the *Rig Veda*, which is the stock Veda, scarcely any indication or doctrinal or philosophical speculation, no allusion to the later notions of the several schools, nor is there any hint of metempsychosis, or of the doctrine intimately allied to it, of the repeated renovation of the world.[31] The Vedas may be useful as a source of information regarding the social life of the Aryans. As a picture of primitive life, it is full of curiosity but there is nothing elevating. There are more vices and a few virtues.

II

We may now turn to the *Atharva Veda* and examine its contents. The best I can do is to present the following extracts from the table of contents of the *Atharva Veda*.[32]

> Book I. Charms to cure diseases and possession by demons of disease (*bhaishagyani*).

30 Horace Hayman Wilson (1786–1860) was an English Orientalist who first came to India as an assistant-surgeon for the East India Company. After developing a deep interest in the ancient texts of the subcontinent, he was appointed secretary of the Asiatic Society of Bengal in 1811. His earliest translations and works included Kalidasa's *Meghaduta* in 1813, a Sanskrit–English dictionary in 1819, and *Select Specimens of the Theatre of the Hindus*, a survey of Indian drama, as well as the translation of six plays in 1827. His was the first complete translation of the *Rig Veda*, published between 1850 and 1888 in six volumes.

31 Wilson Vol 3, xiii.

32 Ambedkar here lists 209 items from the table of contents of the *Atharva Veda* (taken from Bloomfield 1897) as proof of its own faults and as proof of how ridiculously oriented toward magic and faith these "Vedic chants" are. Since his list fills many pages, we have retained here thirty of the most representative and ludicrous charms and prayers listed by him. In the 209 he lists, seven deal with charms and cures for various fevers; three are to control "excessive discharges" from the body; seven are charms for securing the love of a woman; three for the love of man and so on. According to Witzel (2003, 76), this feature of the *Atharva Veda* is in stark contrast to the other Vedas, even as Ambedkar shows below that the *Rig Veda* does have a few references to charms and spells.

v, 22. Charm against *takman* (fever) and related diseases.

vi, 44. Charm against excessive discharges from the body.

i, 3. Charm against constipation and retention of urine.

i, 24. Leprosy cured by a dark plant.

vi, 83. Charm for curing scrofulous sores called *apakit*.

vi, 109. The pepper-corn as a cure for wounds.

ii, 31. Charm against worms.

vii, 56. Charm against the poison of serpents, scorpions and insects.

vi, 16. Charm against ophthalmia.

vi, 136. Charm with the plant *nitatni* to promote the growth of hair.

iv, 4. Charm to promote virility.

Book III. Imprecations against demons, sorcerers and enemies (*abhikarikani* and *krityapratiharanani*)

i, 16. Charm with lead, against demons and sorcerers.

Book IV. Charms pertaining to women (*strikarmani*)

vi, 11. Charm for obtaining a son (*pumsavanam*).[33]

vii, 35. An incantation to make a woman sterile.

vi, 17. Charm to prevent miscarriage.

i, 11. Charm for easy parturition.

i, 34. Charm with licorice, to secure the love of a woman.

vi, 130. Charm to arouse the passionate love of a man.

vi, 77. Charm to cause the return of a truant woman.

vi, 18. Charm to allay jealousy.

iii, 18. Charm of a woman against a rival or co-wife.

vi, 138. Charm for depriving a man of his virility.

vi, 140. Expiation for the irregular appearance of the first pair of teeth.

33 The *pumsavanam* rite seems like the Vedic equivalent of a sex selection ritual. Hélène Stork says, "The desire for a male child is so strong in Hindu society that brahminical rites to this effect are introduced even into medical texts. One example is the 'male-producing' (*pumsavanam*) rite, the aim of which is to grant the family sons. Provided it is practised during the first two months of pregnancy (that is, before the manifestation of the sex of the foetus), this rite is believed to be capable of reversing the sex of the child" (1992, 92). Stork goes on describe the rituals in detail.

Book V. Charms pertaining to royalty (*ragakarmani*)

i, 19. Battle-charm against arrow-wounds.

Book VII. Charms to secure prosperity in house, field, cattle, business, gambling and kindred matters.

iv, 38. A Prayer for success in gambling.

B. Prayer to secure the return of calves that have strayed to a distance.

vii, 9. Charm for finding lost property.

Book VIII. Charms in expiation of sin and defilement.

vi, 29. Charm against ominous pigeons and owls.

vii, 64. Expiation when one is defiled by a black bird of omen.

vi, 46. Exorcism of evil dreams.

III

It will thus be seen that the *Atharva Veda* is nothing but a collection of sorcery, black magic and medicine. Three-fourths of it is full of sorcery and black magic. It must not however be assumed that it is only the *Atharva Veda* which contains black magic and sorcery. The *Rig Veda* is not altogether free from it. There are in it mantras relating to black magic and sorcery. I give below three suktas which deal with this matter:

Sukta XVII (CXLV)

The deity, or rather the aim, of the hymn is the getting rid of a rival wife; the Rishi is Indrani, the metre of the last verse is Pankati, of the rest Anushtubh.[34]

1. I dig up this most potent medicinal creeper, by which (a wife) destroys a rival wife, by which she secures to herself her husband.

2. O (plant) with up-turned leaves, auspicious, sent by the Gods, powerful, remove my rival and make my husband mine alone.

34 This is from Wilson's introduction to the sukta.

3. Excellent (plant), may I too be excellent, excellent amongst the excellent, and may she who is my rival be vile amongst the vile.

4. I will not even utter her name, no (woman) takes pleasure in that person; may we remove the other rival wife to a distance.

5. I am triumphing, thou art triumphant; we two being powerful will triumph over my rival.

6. I make thee the triumphant (herb) my pillow, I support thee with that more triumphant (pillow); let thy mind hasten to me as a cow to her calf, let it speed on its way like water.[35]

Sukta IV (CLV)

The deity of verses 1 and 4 is the averting of misfortune (*Alakshmighna*), of verses 2 and 3 Brahmanaspati, and of verse 5 the Viswadevas; the *Rishi* is Sirimbitha, the son of Bharadwaja, the metre is *Anushtubh*.

1. Miserable, ill-favoured, deformed ever-railing (goddess), go to thy mountain; with these exploits of Sirimbitha we scare thee away.

2. May she be scared away from this (world), scared away from the next (world), the destructress of all embryos; sharp-horned Brihaspati approach, driving away Distress.

3. The wood which floats by the sea-shore far off, remote from man, seize that, (O goddess), hard to destroy, and therewith go to a distant shore.

4. Utterers of discordant sounds, when swiftly moving you departed, all the enemies of Indra were slain, disappearing like bubbles.

5. These (Viswadevas) have brought back the (stolen) cattle; they have built up the fire; they have provided food for the Gods. Who will overcome them?[36]

---

35 Wilson Vol 6, 376–7. Sukta XVII is 10.145 in the *mandala* scheme of organising the text.

36 10.155. Wilson Vol 6, 385–6.

Sukta XII (CLXIII)

The deity is the cure of phthisis: the Rishi is Vivrihan, the son of Kasyapa, the metre is *Anushtubh*.

1. I banish disease from thine eyes, from thy head, from thy nose, from thy ears, from thy chin, from thy brain, from thy tongue.

2. I banish disease from thy neck, from thy sinews, from thy bones, from thy joints, from thy upper arms, from thy shoulders, and from thy fore-arms.

3. I banish disease from thine entrails, from thy anus, from thine abdomen, and from thy heart, from thy kidneys, from thy liver, from thy (other) viscera.

4. I banish disease from thy thighs, from thy knees, from thy heels, from thy toes, from thy loins, from thy buttocks, from thy private parts.

5. I banish disease from thy urethra, from thy bladder, from thy hair, from thy nails, from thy whole person.

6. I banish disease from each limb, from each hair, from each joint where it is generated, from thy whole person.[37]

Enough has been extracted from the Vedas to show that they contain nothing that can be said to be spiritually or morally elevating. Neither the subject matter nor contents of the Vedas justify the infallibility with which they have been invested. Why then did the Brahmans struggle so hard to clothe them with sanctity and infallibility?

37 10.163. Wilson Vol 6, 392–3.

Riddle No. 13

The Riddle of Ahimsa[1]

Anyone who compares the habits and social practices of the latter-day Hindus with those of the ancient Aryans will find a tremendous change almost amounting to a social revolution.

The Aryans were a race of gamblers. Gambling was developed to a science in the very early days of the Aryan civilization, so much so that they had even devised certain technical terms. The Hindus used the words Krita, Treta, Dwapara and Kali as the names of the four Yugas or periods into which historical times are divided. As a matter of fact, originally these are the names of the dices used by the Aryans at gambling.[2] The luckiest

1 The BAWS editors write: "The original Table of Contents shows Riddle No. 13 as 'How the Brahmans who were once cow-killers became the worshippers of the Cow?' This chapter is not found in the papers. However, few pages entitled 'Riddle of Ahimsa' have been found. The Riddle has been placed here as it seems to deal with the same topic. This chapter consisting of ten typed pages is obviously incomplete as the remaining text is missing."

2 According to Zimmer (1972, 13–15), Krita, the perfect participle of the verb *kri*, to do, means "done, made, accomplished, perfect". This is the throw of dice that wins the jackpot. The idea of total, or totality, is associated with the number four; thus 'four square' signifies 'totality'. Krita Yuga, the first of the ages, is the perfect, 'four-quartered' yuga where each of the four varnas adheres to its dharma. "The brahmins are established in saintliness. Kings and feudal chiefs act according to the ideals of truly royal conduct. The peasants and townsfolk are devoted to husbandry and the crafts. The lower, servile classes abide lawfully in submission." The Treta Yuga is named after the dice cast three, during which, "the universal body, as well as the body of human society, is sustained by only three fourths of its total virtue.

dice was called Krita and the unluckiest was called Kali. Treta and Dwapara were intermediate between them. Not only was gambling well developed among the ancient Aryans but the stakes were very high. Gambling with high stakes has been known elsewhere. But they are nothing compared with those which are known to have been offered by the Aryans. Kingdoms and even their wives were offered by them as stakes at gambling. King Nala staked his kingdom and lost it.[3] The Pandavas went much beyond. They not only staked their kingdom they also staked their wife Draupadi and lost both.[4] Among the Aryans gambling was not the game of the rich. It was a vice of the many.[5] So widespread was gambling among the ancient Aryans that the burden of all the writers of the Dharma Sutras (Shastras?)[6] was

---

The modes of life proper to the four castes have begun to lapse into decay." The Dwapara Yuga stands for "the dice-cast of the duad", during which "only two of the four quarters of Dharma are still effective in the manifest world; the others have been irrecoverably lost. The cow of ethical order, instead of firmly standing on four legs, or resting safely on three, now balances on two." And lastly, "Kali means the worst of anything; also, 'strife, quarrel, dissension, war, battle' (being related to *kal-aha*, 'strife, quarrel'). In the dice-play, kali is the losing throw. During the Kali Yuga, man and his world are at their very worst." See Riddle No. 23 in this volume where Ambedkar returns to this question; especially notes 2–4 on p. 180–1. See also Doniger (2009, 57–8).

3 In the Aranya Parva (Book of the Forest) of the *Mahabharata*, King Nala gambles away his kingdom during a *swayamvara* (groom-choosing) for princess Damayanti and is exiled. He eventually returns, gains back his kingdom and his love. The love story of Nala and Damayanti is told to Yudhishtira after his own gambling mistakes haunt him. See Debroy (2010, Vol 2, 271–98).

4 In the second of eighteen books of the *Mahabharata*, Sabha Parva or Book of the Assembly Hall, the Pandava brothers play a game of dice against Duryodhana, the chief antagonist of the epic. In the game, the eldest Pandava, Yudhishtira, loses first his kingdom, his brothers, himself, and finally their shared wife Draupadi. See Debroy (2010, Vol 2, 69–102).

5 Speaking of administration and political organization among the Aryan tribes, Thapar says, "Later sources mention a more elaborate group surrounding the king: the charioteer, the treasurer, the steward, and the superintendent of dicing. The latter is not surprising, considering the love of gambling among both royalty and commoners" (1990/1996b, 32).

6 The Dharmasutras are the earliest literature of dharma, in prose form, which

to impress upon the king the urgency of controlling it by state authorities under stringent laws.[7]

The relation of the sexes among the Aryans were of a loose sort. There was a time when they did not know marriage as a permanent tie between a man and a woman. This is evident from the *Mahabharata* where Kunti, the wife of Pandu, refers to this in her reply to Pandu's exhortation to go to produce children from someone else.[8] There was a time when the Aryans did not observe the rule of prohibited degrees in their sex relations.

---

were succeeded by the Dharmashastras in verse form. The Dharmasutras deal with topics such as the sources of dharma, *upanayana*, Veda study, the ashramas, food, purity, means of livelihood, marriage, succession of property, the dharma of women, penances, punishments and duties of a king (Cush et al 2012, 188–9). The Dharmashastras, on the other hand, do not belong to a specific Vedic school and are not linked with particular ritual traditions. They look at ritual in the broadest sense (Cush et al 2012, 186), and include treatises on jurisprudence, grammar, astronomy, etc. In order to ensure acceptance, these works were given divine origin and the names of ancient sages; hence the Manavadharmashastra or the *Manusmriti*, assigned to Manu, believed to be the first mortal king.

7 See, for instance, *Manusmriti*: "Gambling and betting let the king exclude from his realm: those two vices cause the destruction of the kingdom of princes. Gambling and betting amount to open theft; the king shall always exert himself in suppressing both (of them) … On every man who addicts himself to that (vice) either secretly or openly, the king may inflict punishment according to his discretion" (IX 221–2, 228; Bühler 1886, 380–81). In *Arthashastra*, Book VIII, Section 3, Kautilya discusses four vices associated with "hunting", "gambling", "women" and "drink" (see Bandyopadhyay 2014, 3–28, where he also discusses the intimate connection between Four Ages and the throws of dice). Disagreeing with earlier commentators in the matter of rank in the hierarchy of vices, Kautilya considers gambling more harmful than hunting and drinking, but less calamitous than 'woman-mongering'. The reason he gives is: while there is a chance, though very slim, that a gambler may reform himself, womanizing is beyond cure. In support of his thesis he resorts to the *Mahabharata*: he compares and contrasts the dice-besotted Yudhishtira with the reformed gambler Nala (see Bandyopadhyay 2014, 3–28).

8 In the *Mahabharata*'s Sambhava Parva, Pandu, the king of Hastinapur, and the father of the Pandavas, could not bear children because of a curse on him by the Rishi Kindama that would kill him and his wives if he were to make advances. Therefore, he asks Kunti to bear him children, which she does: "Through Dharma, Yudhishtira. Through Marut, Bhima. Through Shakra, Arjuna. Pandu was pleased and said, 'Your co-wife doesn't have children either. Let the right offspring also be fathered on her'. Kunti agreed and Nakula and Sahadeva were then fathered on Madri through the Ashvins" (Debroy 2010, Vol 1, 251).

There are cases among them of brother cohabiting with sister, son with mother, father with daughter and grandfather with granddaughter. There was a communism in women. It was a simple communism where many men shared a woman and no one had a private property in, or exclusive right over, a woman. In such a communism the woman was called Ganika, belonging to many.[9] There was also a regulated form of communism in women among the Aryans. In this the woman was shared among a group of men but the day of each was fixed and the woman was called Warangana, one whose days are fixed. Prostitution flourished and had taken the worst form. Nowhere else have prostitutes consented to submit to sexual intercourse in public.[10] But the practice existed among the ancient Aryans. Bestiality also prevailed among the ancient Aryans and among those who were guilty of it are to be reckoned some of the most reverend Rishis.[11]

The ancient Aryans were also a race of drunkards. Wine formed a most essential part of their religion. The Vedic gods drank wine. The divine wine was called Soma. Since the gods of the Aryans drank wine, the Aryans had no scruples in the matter of drinking. Indeed to drink it was a part of an Aryan's religious duty. There were so many Soma sacrifices among the ancient Aryans that there were hardly any days when Soma was not drunk. Soma was restricted to only the three upper classes, namely the Brahmans, the Kshatriyas and the Vaishyas. That

9 Kautilya's *Arthashastra*, a treatise on statecraft dated between the second century BCE and third century CE, lists *ganika* as one of several kinds of prostitutes, and dedicates an entire chapter to the *ganikadhyaksa*, or the Superintendent of Courtesans, and the rules for women in this profession. For details, see Jaiswal (2001, 53–5).

10 See also Riddle No. 23, pp. 205–6.

11 Among the supernatural powers promised to those practising yogic disciplines includes being able to turn into an animal in order to have sex with animals and "experience sex in its totality". See Miletski 2005 (10–11) for more examples.

does not mean the Shudras were abstainers. Who were denied Soma drank Sura, which was ordinary, unconsecrated wine sold in the market.

Not only were the male Aryans addicted to drinking but the females also indulged in drinking. The *Kaushitaki Grihyasutra* I. 11–12[12] advises that four or eight women who are not widowed after having been regaled with wine and food should be called to dance for four times on the night previous to the wedding ceremony.[13] This habit of drinking intoxicating liquor was not confined to the non-Brahman women. Even Brahman women were addicted to it. That drinking was not regarded as a sin; it was not even a vice, it was quite a respectable practice. The *Rig Veda* says: "Worshipping the sun before drinking madira (wine)".[14]

The *Yajur Veda* says: "Oh, Deva Soma! being strengthened and invigorated by Sura (wine), by thy pure spirit, please the Devas; give juicy food to the sacrificer and vigour to Brahmanas and Kshatriyas."[15]

The *Mantara Brahmana*[16] says: "By which women have

---

12 The Grihyasutras are a group of texts in Sanskrit that describe rituals performed around the household (*grihya*) fire by the head of the family, and are dated between 600 and 300 BCE. The rituals are prescribed for all the Dwija or 'twice-born' classes. There are two types of *grihya* rituals—consecration rites for important occasions, and rituals that accompany festivals, performances and particular occasions.

13 See Oldenberg 1886, Vol 1, 31–2.

14 Ambedkar likely uses this fragmentary quote from P.V. Kane's edition of *History of Dharmasastra: Ancient and Mediæval Religious and Civil Law in India*, a five-volume work. The first four volumes were published between 1930 and 1953, which Ambedkar could access. Ambedkar often refers to Kane's works in his writings on history.

15 The source is likely to be Kane again. The verse Ambedkar cites also appears in a recent edition of Gaurinath Bhattacharya Shastri's work on Tantra (2002, 343). Ambedkar could possibly be citing from an earlier edition of Shastri's work on Tantra which we have not been able to trace.

16 The Brahmanas are texts containing commentaries on the four Vedas. The *Mantara Brahmana* is part of the *Chandogya Brahmana*, a commentary on the *Sama Veda*.

been made enjoyable by men, and by which water has been transformed into wine (for the enjoyment of men), etc."[17]

That Rama and Sita both drank wine is admitted by the *Ramayana*. Uttara Kanda says: "Like Indra in the case (of his wife) Shachi, Ramachandra saw that Sita drank purified honey called wine. Servants brought for Ramachandra meat and sweet fruit."[18]

So did Krishna and Arjuna. The Udyoga Parva of the *Mahabharata* says:[19]

> Arjuna and Shrikrishna drinking wine made from honey and being sweet-scented and garlanded, wearing splendid clothes and ornaments, sat on a golden throne studded with various jewels. I saw Shrikrishna's feet on Arjuna's lap, and Arjuna's feet on Draupadi and Satyabhama's lap.[20]

The greatest change that has taken place is in the diet. The present-day Hindus are very particular about their diet. There are twofold limitations on commensality. A Hindu will not eat food cooked by a non-Hindu. A Hindu will not eat food cooked

---

17 Shastri 2002, 343.

18 It is not clear which translation of the *Ramayana* Ambedkar is citing. From Griffith 1870–1874, 519: "The winter is past and the pleasant spring-time is come, and Rama and Sita sit together in the shade of the Asoka trees happy as Indra and Sachi when they drink in Paradise the nectar of the Gods." The Uttara Kanda is believed to be a later addition to the core seven books of the *Ramayana*, evident from its different style, language and outlook (Cush et al 2012, 668).

19 When citing the same passages in Riddle No. 23, Ambedkar inserts "Sanjaya says:" here.

20 Section LIX of the Udyog Parva, the fifth book in the *Mahabharata*. It is not clear which translation Ambedkar is using. The Critical Edition of the Mahabharata was published by the Bhandarkar Oriental Research Institute in 1966, ten years after Ambedkar's demise. From Ganguli 1883–1896: "There I beheld those chastisers of foes, exhilarated with Bassia wine, their bodies adorned with garlands of flowers. Attired in excellent robes and adorned with celestial ornaments, they sat on a golden dais, decked with numerous gems, and covered over with carpets of diverse texture and hue. And I beheld Kesava's feet resting upon Arjuna's lap while those of the high-souled Arjuna rested upon the laps of Krishna and Satyabhama." http://www.sacred-texts.com/hin/m05/m05059.htm, accessed 29 February 2016.

even by a Hindu unless he is a Brahman or a man of his caste. The Hindu is not only particular on the question of whose food he should eat, he is also particular to what he should eat. From the point of view of diet Hindus may be divided into two main classes.

(1) Those who are vegetarians.

(2) Those who are non-vegetarians.

The non-vegetarians again fall into several sub-divisions:

a) Those who will eat all kinds of flesh and fish.

b) Those who will eat only fish.

Those who will eat flesh are sub-divided into the following categories:

(i) Those who will eat the flesh of any animal except the cow.[21]

(ii) Those who will eat the flesh of any animal including that of the cow.

(iii) Those who will eat flesh but not of a cow (whether dead or slaughtered) nor of chicken.

Classifying the Hindu population from the point of view of its diet, the Brahmans are divided into two classes (1) Pancha Gauda and (2) Pancha Dravida.[22]

Of these, Pancha Dravidas are completely vegetarian. The Pancha Gaudas, with the exception of one section namely Gauda Saraswatas, are also completely vegetarian. The Untouchables, who are at the other end of Hindu society, are non-vegetarian. They eat meat, not merely of goats and fowls but also of the

---

21 Readers keen on Ambedkar's views on untouchability and the dead cow may consult Chapters 11 to 14 of Ambedkar's 1948 work *The Untouchables: Who Were They and Why They Became Untouchables?* reprinted in BAWS Vol 7 (1990).

22 The Brahmans are divided into ten main territorial divisions, five associated with the north and five with the south. The northern group consists of Saraswat, Gauda, Kannauj, Maithil and Utkal Brahmans, and the southern group comprises Maharashtra, Andhra, Dravida, Karnataka and Malabar Brahmans.

cow, irrespective whether it is dead or slaughtered. The non-Brahmans, who are midway between the Brahmans and the Untouchables, have different ways. Some like the Brahmans are vegetarians. The rest unlike the Brahmans are non-vegetarians. All of them are alike in one thing, namely that all of them are opposed to eating the cow's flesh.

There is one other aspect which needs to be mentioned. It is the question of killing an animal for purposes of food. On this, the Hindu mind is more or less united. No Hindu will kill an animal, not even for food. Except for a small caste known as Khatiks, there are no butchers among the Hindus.[23] Even the Untouchables will not kill. He eats the flesh of a dead cow. But he will not kill a cow. In India today the butcher is a Musalman and any Hindu who wants to kill an animal for his food has to seek the services of a Musalman. Every Hindu believes in Ahimsa.

When did vegetarianism come into India? When did Ahimsa become an established belief?[24] There are Hindus who do

23 In Chapter 2 of his 1948 work *The Untouchables* (BAWS Vol 7, 1990), Ambedkar lists the communities considered Untouchable by Hindus, in which Khatik is featured under Bengal, United Provinces, Punjab and Central Provinces. The Khatiks, associated with butchering and leatherwork, are usually classified as a Scheduled Caste across various parts of North India.

24 Chapters 11–14 of *The Untouchables* deal extensively with these questions, where Ambedkar, at one point, says: "[T]here was a time when the Brahmans were the greatest beef-eaters. Although the non-Brahmans did eat beef they could not have had it every day. The cow was a costly animal and the non-Brahmans could ill afford to slaughter it just for food. He only did it on special occasion when his religious duty or personal interest to propitiate a deity compelled him to do. But the case with the Brahman was different. He was a priest. In a period overridden by ritualism there was hardly a day on which there was no cow sacrifice to which the Brahman was not invited by some non-Brahman. For the Brahman every day was a beef-steak day. The Brahmans were therefore the greatest beef-eaters. The Yajna of the Brahmans was nothing but the killing of innocent animals carried on in the name of religion with pomp and ceremony with an attempt to enshroud it in mystery with a view to conceal their appetite for beef" (BAWS Vol 7, 1990, 334). For a history of vegetarianism in the Indian subcontinent, see Alsdorf 2010, where he discusses Gandhi's role but makes no mention of Ambedkar or untouchability.

not understand the propriety of this question. They hold that vegetarianism and Ahimsa are not new things in India.[25]

The evidence in support of the contention that the ancient Aryans, the ancestors of present-day Hindus, were not only meat-eaters but beef-eaters is really overwhelming. As evidence in support of this view it is enough to draw attention to the following facts. They are quite indisputable.

Take the case of Madhuparka.[26] Among ancient Aryans there was a well-established procedure of reception to be given to a guest known as Madhuparka, the detailed descriptions regarding which will be found in the various Grihyasutras. According to most of the Grihyasutras there are six persons who deserve Madhuparka. Namely (1) Ritvij or the Brahman called to perform a sacrifice, (2) Acharya, the teacher, (3) the Bridegroom, (4) the King, (5) the Snatak, the student who has just finished his studies at the Gurukul and (6) any person who is dear to the host.[27] Some add Atithi to this list. Except in the case

25 The conceptual network involving ahimsa is the contribution of the Brahman-baiting/hating Sramanas, pre-eminently, the Jains and the Buddhists. In pre-Buddhist and even in post-Buddhist texts aligned to the Brahmanical tradition, the mention of ahimsa is at best stray and cursory. Even Gandhi was forced to concede this. He wrote in the English introduction to his Gujarati *Gita*: 'It may be freely admitted that the *Gita* was not written to establish *Ahimsa*' (Gandhi 2009, xxii). For an analysis of Gandhi's approach to the *Gita*, see Bandyopadhyay 2016, 123–44. According to Bandyopadhyay (2016, 267–307), many scholars, including the orthodox Orientalist S. Radhakrishnan, have "freely admitted" that the *Mahabharata* is a "product" of a set of compromises between the contending camps of the Brahmans and the Sramanas. This partly explains the sudden appearance of the category called *anrsamsya* (pronounced *aan ri shum sya*, 'non-cruelty' or 'leniency') in the epic. Functioning as an obtrusive middle term, 'non-cruelty' attempts to unhinge the himsa–ahimsa binary. Bandyopadhyay says it is both significant and strange that *anrsamsya* vanishes from the scene of writing after the *Mahabharata*.

26 Literally 'Madhuparka' is a honey mixture offered to a revered guest.

27 George Bühler provides a similar list in the Max Müller-edited fifty-volume series Sacred Books of the East (1895–1910) to which Ambedkar often refers. A similar list is found under *Gautama Dharmasutra* in Volume 1 of Bühler (1879, 205): "27. When an officiating priest, his teacher, his father-in-law, paternal or maternal uncles visit (him), a Madhuparka (or honey-mixture must be offered to them). 28. (If they have

of the Ritvij, King and Acharya, Madhuparka is to be offered to the rest once in a year. To the Ritvij, King and Acharya it is to be offered each time they come. The procedure consisted first in washing by the host the feet of his guest, then the offer of the Madhuparka and the drinking of it by the guest accompanied by certain mantras.

What were the components of the Madhuparka? Madhuparka literally means a ceremony in which honey is shed or poured on the hand of a person. This is what Madhuparka was in its beginning. But in course [of time], its ingredients grew and included much more than honey. At one time it included three ingredients—curds, honey, and butter. There was a time when it was made of five things, curds, honey, ghee, yava and barley. Then it came to be a mixture of nine items. The *Kaushika Sutra*[28] speaks of nine kinds of mixtures, viz. *Brahma* (honey and curds), *Aindra* (of *payasa), Saumya* (curds and ghee), *Mausala* (saine and ghee, this being used only in *Sautramani* and *Rajasuya* sacrifices), *Varuna* (water and ghee), *Sravana* (sesame oil and ghee), *Parivrajaka* (sesame oil and oil cake). Then we come to the time of the *Manava Grihyasutra*,[29] which says that the Veda declares that the Madhuparka must not be without flesh and so it recommends that if the cow is let loose, goat's meat or *payasa* (rice cooked in milk) may be offered; the *Hir gr.* i.13.14[30] says

---

been once honoured in this manner, the ceremony need be) repeated (only) after a year. 29. (But) on (the occasion of) a sacrifice and of the wedding (a Madhuparka must be offered, though) less than a year (has passed since the last visit of the persons thus honoured). 30. And to a king who is a Srotriya (a Madhuparka must be offered as often as he comes), 31. (But to a king) who is not a Srotriya a seat and water."

28 The *Kaushika Sutra* is the Grihyasutra for the *Atharva Veda*.

29 The *Manava Grihyasutra* is one of the Grihyasutras for the Krishna *Yajur Veda*.

30 The *Hiranyakesi Grihyasutra* is also connected to the Krishna *Yajur Veda*. Oldenberg 1886, Vol 2, 174, 1.13.14: "If (the cow) is let loose, a meal is prepared with other meat, and he announces it (to the guest) in the words 'It is ready!'"

that other meat should be offered; *Baud. gr.* (1.2.51–54) says[31] that when the cow is let off, the flesh of a goat or ram may be offered or some forest flesh (of a deer etc) may be offered, as there can be no Madhuparka without flesh, or if one is unable to offer flesh one may cook ground grains. But in the final stage, flesh became the most essential part of Madhuparka.[32] In fact some of the Grihyasutras go to the length of saying that there can be no Madhuparka without flesh. This they base upon an express injunction contained in the *Rig Veda* (VIII.101.5) which says, "Let the Madhuparka not be without flesh".[33]

---

31 The *Baudhayana Grihyasutra* belongs to the Krishna *Yajur Veda* and is among the earliest texts of the *sutra* genre, c. eighth to seventh centuries BCE. However, this quote could not be found in either Olivelle 1999 or Bühler 1879.

32 According to D.N. Jha (2009, 33–4): "The killing of the kine to honour guests seems to have been prevalent from earlier times. The *Rig Veda* (X.68.3) mentions the word *atithinir*, which has been interpreted as 'cows fit for guests' and refers to at least one Vedic hero, *Atithigva*, meaning literally 'slaying cows for guests'. The cow was also killed on festive occasions like marriage. A Rig Vedic passage, for instance, refers to the slaughter of a cow on the occasion of marriage and, later, in the *Aitareya Brahmana*, we are told, that 'if the ruler of men comes as a guest or anyone else deserving of honour comes, people kill a bull or a cow'. The word *madhuparka*, however, is first referred to by the *Jaiminiya Upanisad-Brahmana* and discussed at length in several Grihyasutras. It was performed in honour of special guests such as the teacher, the priest, a *snataka*, father-in-law, paternal and maternal uncles, a friend and a king. Their reception not only included the offering of a mixture of curds and honey (whence the term *madhuparka* was derived) but, more importantly, of a cow that was either immolated or let loose according to their wishes, through other meat. Several Grihyasutras describe *madhuparka* independently as well as part of the marriage ceremonies in which a cow was slain more than once in honour of guests. Panini, therefore, uses the term *goghna* for a guest. The Grihyasutras also attest to the use of the hide of the bull or the cow in domestic rituals like the *simantonnayana* (the parting of the hair of the woman upwards) ceremony performed in the fourth month of pregnancy and the *upanayana* (investiture ceremony preceding the beginning of one's studenthood). Cattle, in fact, seem to have been killed even on what would appear to many of us to be flimsy grounds."

33 This quotation Ambedkar attributes to the *Rig Veda* has been taken from the *Ashvalayana Grihyasutra* 1.24.32–33: "Having murmured, 'The mother of the Rudras, the daughter of the Vasus, (he says) 'Om, let her loose,' if he chooses to let her loose. Let the Madhuparka not be without flesh" (Oldenberg 1886, Vol 1, 199–200). *Rig Veda* 8.101.15 does not talk about the Madhuparka: "(She who is) the mother of the Rudras, the daughter of the Vasus, the sister of the Adityas, the

Flesh-eating was thus quite common. From the Brahmans to the Shudras everybody ate meat. In the Dharmasutras numerous rules are given about the flesh of beasts and birds and about fishes. Gaut. 17.27–31,[34] Ap.Dh.S. 1.5.17.35,[35] Vas.Dh.S. 14.39–40,[36] Yaj. 1.177,[37] Vishnu Dh.S. 51.6,[38] Sankha (quoted by

---

home of ambrosia—I have spoken to men of understanding—kill not *her*, the sinless inviolate cow" (Wilson, Vol 5, 210). In another translation: "Mother of the Rudras, daughter of the Vasus, sister of the Adityas, navel of immortality—I now proclaim to observant people: do not smite the blameless cow—Aditi" (Jamison and Brereton 2014, 1213).

34 The *Gautama Dharmasutra* 17.22–38 deals with 'forbidden food'. It begins with these injunctions: "It is forbidden to drink the milk of a cow, a goat, or a buffalo, during the first ten days after it gives birth; the milk of sheep, camels, and one-hoofed animals under any circumstances" and goes on to say, "Birds that feed by thrusting their beaks or scratching with their feet and that do not have webbed feet may be eaten, as also fish that are not grotesque" (Olivelle 1999, 109).

35 This is likely a typographical error either in Ambedkar's original papers or has been introduced by BAWS. It is *Apastambha Dharmasutra* 1.17.9 that deals with rules of eating (for a Brahman). The Dharmasutras often reference each other: "If, while he is eating, he is touched by a Sudra, he should stop eating. He shall not eat seated alongside ignoble people; or in a place where, while the group is eating, one of them may get up and give away his leftovers or sip water (A 1.3.27n.); or where people insult him when they give food; or food that men or other filthy creatures have smelt. He should not eat on a boat or a terrace. Let him eat sitting on a specially prepared area of the floor" (Olivelle 1999, 27). Ambedkar likely referred to Bühler's 1879 edition of the Dharmasutras.

36 Olivelle says the *Vasishtha Dharmasutra* has been associated with the *Rig Veda*. The section Ambedkar refers to, 14.39–40 (Olivelle 1999, 287–8) again lists dos and don'ts regarding food: "If someone eats garlic, onions, mushrooms, Grnjana onions, Sleshmantaka fruits, tree resins, or red juices flowing from incisions on tree barks (G 17.33 n.), he should perform the very arduous penance … Among animals with five claws, the porcupine, hedgehog, hare, tortoise, and Godha monitor lizard may be eaten (A 1.17.37 n.), as also, among domestic animals, those that have teeth in only one jaw, with the exception of the camel". Crucially, verse 46 says: "It is stated in the Veda of the Vajasaneyins that the milch cow and the draught ox are pure and can be eaten."

37 The reference is to *Yajnavalkyasmriti* 1.177, which according to Olivelle (2008, 363) lists the five-nailed animals than can be eaten; they are porcupine, iguana, tortoise, hedgehog and rabbit/hare. The same list is cited in the *Ramayana's* Kishkinda Kanda (17.39) as well, where Vali lists them to Rama, which Ambedkar cites next.

38 One of the latest books in the tradition, the *Vishnu Dharmasutra* borrows heavily from the earlier Dharmashastra texts—*Manusmriti, Yajnavalkyasmriti, Naradasmriti* and the *Bhagavad Gita*. 51.6: "If a man has (unawares) eaten meat of a five-toed

Apararka p. 1167),[39] *Ramayana* (Kiskindha 17.39),[40] *Markandeya Purana* (35.2–4)[41] prescribe that one should avoid the flesh of all five-nailed animals except of porcupine, hare, *svavidh* (a boar of hedgehog), iguana, rhinoceros and tortoise (some of these works omit the rhinoceros). Gautama adds that one should also avoid the flesh of all animals with two rows of teeth in the two jaws, of hairy animals, of hairless animals (like snakes), of village cocks and hogs and of cows and bulls. *Ap.Dh.S.* 1.5.17. 29–31 first forbids the flesh of animals with one hoof only, of camels, of *gavaya* (gayal), of the village hog, of the *sarabha* and of cows, but adds the exception that the flesh of milch cows and of bulls may be eaten as the Vajasaneyaka declares the flesh of these to be pure.[42] *Ap.Dh.S.* 1.2.5–15 forbids the use of flesh to a teacher of the Veda in the ...[43]

(Incomplete. Further text missing)

---

animal, with the exception of the hare, the porcupine, the iguana, the rhinoceros, and the tortoise, he must fast for seven days" (Jolly 1880, 163).

39 Apararka is said to have been a logician of the twelfth century. According to Sures Chandra Banerji (1989, 13), he is also called Aparaditya, and may have been a "Silahara king born in the family of Jimutavahana of the Vidyadhara race". He is the author of a comprehensive commentary, *Apararka-yajnavalkya-dharmasastra-nibadha*, popularly known as *Apararka*, on the *Yajnavalkyasmriti*.

40 See Griffith 1895, 345.

41 One of the eighteen major Puranic texts, the *Markandeya Purana* is constructed as a dialogue between sage Markandeya and Jaimini (see 66n1 in Riddle No. 6). See also 35.2–4 in Pargiter 1904, 181.

42 This reference is actually from the *Vasishtha Dharmasutra*, not *Apastambha*. In 14.39–45, the animals Ambedkar lists are given. See Olivelle 1999, 287–8.

43 This seems to be misattributed, since *Apastambha Dharmasutra* 1.2.5 onwards deals with "Failure to be Initatiated" and "Residency" (see Olivelle 1999, 4).

Riddle No. 14

From Ahimsa Back to Himsa[1]

"From Himsa to Ahimsa" is only a part of the story of Ahimsa. There is another part of the story which can only be described under the heading "From Ahimsa back to Himsa". The second part of the story will be clear if only one were to note the religious practices of the Tantras and Tantrism to which a reference has already been made.[2]

The essentials of Tantrik worship are the five Makars.[3] These five Makars consist of:

---

1 The editors of BAWS begin this section with the note: "The chapter seems to be a continuation of the previous chapter on 'Ahimsa'. There are six typed pages with few corrections and having the title written by the author himself."

2 'Tantrism'—as a single, coherent entity—is, like 'Hinduism', now largely considered an invention of nineteenth-century scholarship (see Urban 1999). Scholars have struggled to define it as a cogent school of thought. But it is clear that all strands of Tantric worship were marked by a rejection of orthodox Vedic rules and notions. Other characteristics include special forms of physical discipline, such as kundalini yoga, being at once theistic and nondualistic, using symbolic diagrams such as yantras or mandalas, and prescribing the use of prohibited substances such as wine, meat and sexual intercourse (Lorenzen 2002, 25). A narrow definition would consider Tantric only those religious phenomena associated directly with the Sanskrit texts Tantras, Samhitas and Agamas, making the social base of Tantric religion literate and upper caste. However, a broader definition adds a range of popular beliefs and practices, including the Sakta and Hatha Yoga traditions, where the texts, when there were any, were in vernacular languages. Another aspect of Tantra is Buddhism. An entire school of Buddhist thought, Vajrayana, is about Tantra, but oddly Ambedkar does not discuss this. For a recent work that brings us up to date with the historiography around Tantra and Buddhism, giving an account of different competing origin theories, see Wedemeyer 2014.

3 The Panchamakara are the five 'substances' used in Tantric rituals.

1. The drinking of wine and liquors of various kinds (Madya)
2. The eating of meat (Mansa)
3. The eating of fish (Matsya)
4. The eating of parched or fried grain (Mudra)
5. The sexual union (Maithuna)[4]

It is unnecessary to say at this stage anything about Maithuna or sexual intercourse having been made an element of religious worship.[5] It is sufficient to take note of Madya and Mansa.

> With regard to the first four of these acts, the Tantras prescribe twelve sorts of liquors, three sorts of wine, and three sorts of meat. Pulastya, one of the ancient sages who is the supposed author of certain law-books,[6] also enumerates twelve kinds of liquors, as follows: 1. Liquor extracted from the bread fruit (*panasa*), called Jack-liquor; 2. from grapes (*draksha*); 3. from date-palm (*kharjuri*); 4. from common palm (*tali*), or toddy; 5. from coconut (*narikela*); 6. from sugarcane (*ikshu*); 7. from Madhavika plant; 8. long-pepper liquor (*saira*); 9. soap-berry liquor (*arishta*); 10. Honey-liquor (*madhuka*);[7] 11. a kind of rum or liquor prepared from molasses, etc. (called Gaudi, or

4 Sir John Woodroffe (see note 11 to this riddle), in the introduction to his translation of *Mahanirvana Tantra,* says: "All the elements or their substitutes are purified and consecrated, and then, with the appropriate ritual, the first four are consumed, such consumption being followed by *lata-sadhana* or its symbolic equivalent. The Tantra prohibits indiscriminate use of the elements, which may be consumed or employed only after purification (*sho-dhana)* and during worship according to the Tantric ritual. Then, also, all excess is forbidden" (Woodroffe 1913).

5 Sexual practice is often considered the most distinctive feature of Hindu Tantra. What can be considered the most 'extreme' sexual acts within Tantrism were limited to a small circle of elite practitioners, called the Kaula, and included, among other things, the ingestion of various bodily fluids. For a comprehensive analysis of Tantric sex in the South Asian context, see D.G. White 2003.

6 According to the Bühler edition of *Manusmriti* (1.34–35) Pulastya was one of the rishis who were the 'mind-born sons' of Vishnu, along with Marici, Atri, Angira, Pulaha, Kratu, Bhrgu, Vasishtha, Pracetas and Narada. He is considered the father of Ravana and his brethren, and therefore an ancestor of the Rakshasas (Wilson 1864, 10 and 100).

7 As in the original. The BAWS edition says: "10. liquor from the Bassia Latifola (madhuka)".

> sometimes Maireya); 12. arrack, or liquor prepared from rice and other grain (*sura* or *varuni*, or *paishti*).

Besides the above twelve kinds of spirituous drink others are frequently mentioned, for example, Tanka, made from wood-apple, Koli, made from the jujube; and Kadambari; the last being the favourite beverage of Bala-Rama.

The meat may be that of birds, beasts, or fish. The parched grain is eaten, like dry biscuit, as a relish with the wine and spirituous liquors. The drinking of each kind of drink is supposed to be attended with its own peculiar merit and advantage. Thus one liquor gives salvation, another learning, another power, another wealth, another destroys enemies, another cures diseases, another removes sin, another purifies the soul.[8]

The Tantrik worship had gone deep into Bengal. Referring to his own experience Rajendralal Mitra[9] says:

> I knew a highly respectable widow lady, connected with one of the most distinguished families in Calcutta, who belonged to the Kaula sect, and had survived the 75th anniversary of her birthday, who never said her prayers (and she did so regularly every morning and evening) without touching the point of her tongue with a tooth-pick dipped in a phial of arrack, and sprinkling a few drops of the liquor on the flowers which she offered to her god. I doubt very much if she had ever drunk a wine-glassful of arrack at once in all her life, and certain it is that she never had any idea of the pleasures of drinking; but, as a faithful Kaula, she felt herself in duty bound to observe the mandates of her religion with the greatest scrupulousness. That thousands of others do so, I have every reason to believe. In some parts of Bengal, where

---

8 Ambedkar is excerpting this from Sir Monier Monier-Williams' 1883 work, *Brahmanism and Hinduism*, 192–3.

9 [Rajendralal Mitra — *Indo-Aryans* Vol. pp. 405–6.] Rajendralal Mitra (1823/24–1891) was the first Indologist of Indian origin, whose work *Indo-Aryans*, published in 1881 in two volumes, is a collection of essays on India from the Vedic times.

> arrack is not easily accessible, such female votaries prepare a substitute by dropping the milk of a coconut in a bell-metal pot, or milk in a copper vessel, and drink a few drops of the same. Men are, however, not so abstemious, and the Tantras ordain a daily allowance of five cupsful, the cup being so made as to contain five *tolas*, or two ounces, i.e. they are permitted to take ten ounces or about a pint of arrack daily.[10]

This Tantrik worship was not confined to the small corner of Bengal. As is pointed out by Mahamahopadhyaya Jadaveshwara Tarkaratna:

> Just as the Bengalis of the higher castes are divided into Shaktas, Vaishnavas, and Shaivas, so it is with the peoples of Kamarupa, Mithila, Utkala, and Kalinga, and the Kashmirian pandits. The Shakti Mantra, Shiva Mantra and Vishnu Mantra are each Tantrik. Amongst Dakshinatyas, Mahamahopadhyaya Subramanya Shastri, and many others, are Shaktas. The late Mahamahopadhyaya Rama Mishra Shastri. Bhagavatacharya. and many others, were and are Vaishnavas. Mahamahopadhyaya Shivakumara Shastri, and a number of others are Shaivas. In Vrindavana there are many Shaktas as well as Vaishnava Brahmanas. Though amongst the higher castes in Maharashtra and other Southern Indian countries. Shaivas and Vaishnavas are more numerous than Shaktas. Followers of the Pashupata and Jangama cults are Shaivas whereas those of Madhavacharya and Ramanujacharya are Vaishnavas. Many in the North-West are initiated in the Rama-Mantra which is to be found only in the Tantra. It is still more remarkable that according to this author, the pandas of Shri Purushottama are all Shaktas, and the priests of Kamakhya Devi are all Vaishnavas.[11]

10 Mitra 1881, Vol 1, 405–6. In a chapter titled "Spirituous Drinks in Ancient India", Mitra details how different Hindu texts dealt with the issue of alcohol and drinking. The Kaula sect—who Mitra calls "the most ardent followers of the Sakta Tantras"—are said to partake of alcohol as one of the Panchamakara in closed-room worship of the Devi (Mitra 1881, Vol 1, 405). It is in that context that he talks of the widow and the continuing presence of liquor in modern daily ritual, even if in small doses.

11 [Quoted by Avalon in his *Principles of Tantra* Part I. Introduction p. xxxviii.] Arthur

Although it is not possible to give the exact date when the Tantras and Tantra worship came into existence, there is no doubt that their date is after Manu.[12] This fact makes the rise of the Tantra worship a matter of great surprise. The Tantras not only lifted the prohibition enacted by Manu against wine and flesh but they made drinking and flesh-eating articles of faith.

The surprising thing is the part that the Brahmans have played in furthering the Tantras and Tantra worship. The Tantras had no respect for the Vedas. The Tantrikas said that the Vedas were like a common woman open to all but that the Tantra was like a high-born woman kept secluded. The Tantra was never repudiated by the Brahmans. On the other hand they recognized it as a fifth Veda. So orthodox a Brahman as Kulluka Bhatt, the celebrated commentator on *Manusmriti,* says that *shruti* is of two kinds, Vaidik and Tantrik.[13] Not only did the

---

Avalon was the pseudonym of Sir John George Woodroffe (1865–1936), an English Orientalist who published many works on yoga and Tantra. In his public life, he was a judge on the court of Calcutta and a well-respected authority on Indian law; but in his other life as Arthur Avalon, he became one of the most influential and widely read scholars on Tantra, and played a leading role in rehabilitating Tantra from its earlier status as debased, irrational and superstitious (Urban 1999, 124). Though he himself used 'Saktism' or 'Tantrasastra' over 'Tantrism', the credit for popularizing it as a category in the Western mind goes to him. He is credited also with sanitising and domesticating the more 'offensive' elements in Tantric texts.

12 While some components of Tantric belief can be traced back much earlier, the 'complex as a whole' is not documented before fifth/sixth century CE. According to Lorenzen, the phenomenon was primarily northern, although it had some following in parts of the south. The earliest clear datable evidence of Tantric religion can be narrowed down to four Sanskrit texts of the seventh century CE: Banabhatta's *Kadambari* and *Harsacharita,* Mahendravarman's *Mattavilasa* and Dandin's *Dasakumaracharita* (Lorenzen 2002, 26). The *Manusmriti* is considered the oldest of the verse Dharmashastras, with its date of composition between 200 BCE and 200 CE (Rocher 2003, 110), making it at least four hundred years older than the Tantric texts.

13 While commenting on the *Manusmriti,* the medieval commentator Kulluka Bhatt juxtaposes *vaidik* and *tantric* as two forms of revelation (*shruti ca dvidvidha vaidiki tantriki ca).* The Hindu texts are divided into two kinds—*smriti* (memory, tradition) and *shruti* (hearing, revelation). For Padoux (2002, 18), the fact that Kulluka Bhatt refers to both Tantric and Vedic texts as *shruti* is important, even though those

Brahmans not repudiate the Tantras but actually promoted the Tantrik worship.

The *Matrika Bheda Tantra*[14] makes Shiva address his wife Parvati as follows:

> O sweet-speaking goddess, the salvation of Brahmans depends on drinking wine. I impart to you, a great truth, O mountain-born, (when I say) that the Brahman who attends to drinking and its accompaniments, forthwith becomes a Siva. Even as water mixes with water, and metal amalgamates with metal; even as the confined space in a pitcher merges into the great body of surrounding space on the destruction of the confining vessel, and air commingles with air, so does dear one, a Brahman melt into Brahma, the great soul.
>
> There is not the least doubt about this, O mountain-born. Similitude with the divinity and other forms of liberation are designed for Kshatriyas and others; but true knowledge can never be acquired, goddess dear, without drinking wine; therefore should Brahmans always drink. No one becomes a Brahman by repeating the Gayatri, the mother of the Vedas; he is called a Brahman only when he has knowledge of Brahma. The ambrosia of the gods is their Brahma, and on earth it is arrack; and because one attains through it the condition of a god (*suratva*), therefore is arrack called *sura*.[15]

Why did the Brahmans repudiate father Manu and start drinking liquor and flesh-eating again which Manu had stopped?[16] This is a riddle.

---

within as well as outside the Tantric tradition made a distinction between the two. This is evident when one considers the Vedic elements present in Tantric traditions, and vice versa.

14 *Matrika Bheda Tantra* is an alchemical Tantra text of Saivite extraction associated with Gorakhnath and the Natha Siddhas of the eleventh century in eastern India.

15 Mitra 1881, Vol 1, 408–9. There were omissions either Ambedkar or the BAWS editors possibly made in quoting this from Mitra; these have been added here.

16 This last sentence seems problematic. *Manusmriti* 5.55 reads: "He whose *meat* in this world do I eat will in the other world *me eat.*" In the note to the verse the translators write: "This translation of this much-quoted verse is based on that

of Charles Lansman, who attempted to capture the Sanskrit pun: meat is called *mamsa* because he (*sa*) eats me (*mam*)." A similar word-play is to be found in the *Mahabharata*'s Anushasana Parva 117/34 (Critical Edition), where Bhishma says to Yudhishtira: "Me (*mang*) he (*swa*) has eaten in the last life, therefore, I shall eat him—this is the meaning of *mangsa* (meat)." English translation: "Since he hath eaten me, I shall eat him in return—even this, O Bharata, constitutes the character as *Mansa* of Mansa" (K.M. Ganguli 2004, 243). In the note to the verse the translator writes: "*Mansa* is flesh. This verse explains the etymology of the word, *Mam* (me) *sa*: *Me he eateth,* therefore, I shall eat him. The words following *Me he* should be supplied in order to get at the meaning." The *Satapatha Brahmana* 12.9.11 states: "Whatever a man consumes in this world, that (food), in return, consumes him in yonder world" (tr. Eggeling 2002, 260). Nevertheless, in 5.56, Manu explicitly says: "There is nothing wrong in eating meat (*mangsa-bhaksan*), nor in drinking wine, nor in sexual union, for this is how living beings engage in life" (tr. Doniger and Smith 1991). According to Bandyopadhyay (2016, 281–3), who discusses this in tandem with Walter Benjamin's essay "Critique of Violence", the act of dressing up himsa as ahimsa is perhaps most transparent in the *Manusmriti* 5.39 and 5.44. In 5.39 Manu says, "...killing in sacrifice is not killing"; and in 5.44, "The violence ... sanctioned by the Veda and regulated by official restraints—that is known as nonviolence."

Riddle No. 16

The Four Varnas: Are the Brahmans Sure of their Origin?[1]

It is the cardinal faith of every Hindu that the Hindu social order is a divine order. The prescriptions of this divine order are three. First, society is permanently divided into four classes namely (1) Brahmans, (2) Kshatriyas, (3) Vaishyas and (4) Shudras.[2] Second, the four classes in point of their mutual status are linked together in an order of graded inequality. The Brahmans are at the head and above all others. The Kshatriyas below the Brahmans but above the Vaishyas and the Shudras. The Vaishyas below the Brahmans and the Kshatriyas but above the Shudras and the Shudras below all. Third, the occupations of the four classes are fixed. The occupation of the Brahmans is to acquire learning and to teach. The occupation of the Kshatriyas is to fight, that of the Vaishyas to trade and that of the Shudras to serve as menials to the other three classes above him. This is called by the Hindus

1 The editors of BAWS write: "This is a 33-page typed script having all necessary corrections and additions incorporated by the author. There are two concluding pages written by the author himself. All the pages of the chapter are loose sheets tagged together with a title page in the handwriting of the author."

2 This Riddle has much in common with *Who Were the Shudras?* (BAWS Vol 7, 1990). The first chapter of the book written in 1946 is in fact called "The Riddle of the Shudras" and extensively discusses the Purusha Sukta hymn and other Dharmasutras compared with it. Much in the present riddle also figures in Chapter 2, "The Brahmanic theory of the origin of the Shudras".

the Varna Vyavastha.[3] It is the very soul of Hinduism. Without Varna Vyavastha there is nothing else in Hinduism to distinguish it from other religions.[4] That being so, it is only proper that an enquiry should be made into the origin of this varna system.

For an explanation of its origin, we must have recourse to what the ancient Hindu literature has to say on the subject.

I

It would be better to collect together in the first place the views expressed in the Vedas.

The subject is referred to in the *Rig Veda* in the ninetieth hymn of the tenth book.[5] It runs as follows:

> 1. Purusha has a thousand heads, a thousand eyes, a thousand feet. On every side enveloping the earth, he overpassed (it) by a space of ten fingers.
>
> 2. Purusha himself is this whole (universe), whatever has been and whatever shall be. He is also the lord of immortality since (or, when) by food he expands.
>
> 3. Such is his greatness, and Purusha is superior to this. All existences are a quarter of him; and three-fourths of him are that which is immortal in the sky.
>
> 4. With three quarters Purusha mounted upwards. A quarter of him was again produced here. He was then diffused everywhere over things which eat and things which do not eat.
>
> 5. From him was born Viraj, and from Viraj, Purusha. When born, he extended beyond the earth, both behind and before.
>
> 6. When the Gods performed a sacrifice with Purusha as

---

3 The editors of BAWS/Ambedkar use the term *Vevastha* as it perhaps is spoken. Since in his other published works such as AoC, Ambedkar sticks to the more Sanskritic *Vyavastha*, we have changed it to Vyavastha here.

4 Ambedkar discusses the present-day implications of the *chaturvarna* system extensively in AoC 2014, 263–78.

5 See 56n13 to the introduction. Ambedkar is citing this translation from Muir 1868, Vol 1, 9.

the oblation, the spring was its butter, the summer its fuel, and the autumn its (accompanying) offering.

7. This victim Purusha, born in the beginning, they immolated on the sacrificial grass. With him the gods, the Sadhyas, and the rishis sacrificed.

8. From that universal sacrifice were provided curds and butter. It formed those aerial (creatures) and animals both wild and tame.

9. From the universal sacrifice sprang the *rich* and *saman* verses, the *metres* and the *yajush*.

10. From it sprang horses, and all animals with two rows of teeth; kine sprang from it; from it goats and sheep.

11. When (the gods) divided Purusha, into how many parts did they cut him up? What was his mouth? What arms (had he)? What (two objects) are said (to have been) his thighs and feet?

12. The Brahman was his mouth; the Rajanya was made his arms; the being (called) the Vaisya, he was his thighs; the Sudra sprang from his feet.

13. The moon sprang from his soul (*manas*), the sun from his eye, Indra and Agni from his mouth, and Vayu from his breath.

14. From his navel arose the air, from his head the sky, from his feet the earth, from his ear the (four) quarters; in this manner (the gods) formed the worlds.

15. When the gods, performing sacrifice, bound Purusha as a victim, there were seven sticks (struck up) for it (around the fire), and thrice seven pieces of fuel were made.

16. With sacrifice the gods performed the sacrifice. These were the earliest rites. These great powers have sought the sky, where are the former Sadhyas, gods.[6]

This hymn is known by its general name Purusha Sukta and is supposed to embody the official doctrine of varna.

6 While this is from Muir, elsewhere Ambedkar also uses Wilson's 1850–1888 six-volume translation of the *Rig Veda*. For 10.90 in Wilson, see Vol 6, 249–54.

How far do the other Vedas support this theory?[7] The *Sama Veda* has not incorporated the Purusha Sukta among its hymns. Nor does it give any other explanation of the varna. The *Yajur Veda* has two branches—the White *Yajur Veda* and the Black *Yajur Veda*.[8] The Black *Yajur Veda* is known to have three Samhitas or collection of mantras,[9] the *Kathaka Samhita*, the *Maitriyani Samhita* and *Taittiriya Samhita*.

The White *Yajur Veda* has only one Samhita, which is known as *Vajasaneya Samhita*. The *Maitriyani Samhita* and the *Kathaka Samhita* of the Black *Yajur Veda* do not make any reference to the Purusha Sukta of the *Rig Veda*; nor do they attempt to give any other explanation of the origin of the varna system. It is only *Taittiriya Samhita*[10] of the Black *Yajur Veda* and the *Vajasaneya Samhita* of the White *Yajur Veda* that have spoken something relating to the varna system.

The *Vajasaneya Samhita*[11] contains one explanation of the origin of the varna system. The *Taittiriya Samhita* on the other hand contains two explanations. There are two things to be

---

7 Charting the history of the Purusha Sukta, Meera Visvanathan (2011, 148) says sections of the Sukta occur, almost verbatim, not only in the *Atharva Veda*, but also in the *Panchavimsha Brahmana*, the *Vajasaneya Samhita* and the *Taittiriya Aranyaka*.

8 On the various recensions of the samhitas of the *Yajur Veda*, see also Riddle No. 23, 195n44.

9 Ambedkar uses both Sanhita and Samhita in this work, and since Samhita is more often used in all scholarly literature, we have retained it.

10 Samhita is a "collection of hymns addressed to various Devatas in nature. These songs are in the form of mantras" (*Puranic Encyclopedia*, Mani 1975, 679).

11 On *Vajasaneya*, says the *Puranic Encyclopedia* (820): "A religion or religious book (scripture). At the end of Kaliyuga, people will become thieves and lose all good qualities, and moreover fifteen branches of the Veda Vajasaneya alone will be accepted as Regulations of Life (Agni Purana, Chapter 16)." Vajasaneyi refers to a group of priests: "Priest Yajnavalkya was one of the disciples of *Yajur Veda* group of Vyasa. Of the line of disciples, Yajnavalkya had fifteen disciples. They were called Vajasaneyins or Vajasaneyas. The Yajus collection received from the god Sun were divided into fifteen groups by Yajnavalkya and given to each of his disciples. From that day onwards, his disciples became famous by the name Vajasaneyas."

noted about these two explanations contained in the *Taittiriya Samhita*. The first is that these two do not agree with each other in the least; they are quite different. The second is that one of them agrees completely with that contained in the *Vajasaneya Samhita* of the White *Yajur Veda*.

The explanation contained in the *Vajasaneya Samhita* which tallies with the second[12] explanation given by the *Taittiriya Samhita* (IV.3.10.1) reads as follows:

> He lauded with one. Living beings were formed: Prajapati was the ruler. He lauded with three: the Brahman was created: Brahmanaspati was the ruler. He lauded with five: existing things were created: Brahamanaspati was the ruler. He lauded with seven: the seven rishis were created: Dhatri was the ruler. He lauded with nine: the Fathers were created: Aditi was the ruler. He lauded with eleven: the seasons were created: the Artavas were the rulers. He lauded with thirteen: the months were created: the year was the ruler. He lauded with fifteen: the Kshattra (the Kshattriya) was created: Indra was the ruler. He lauded with seventeen: animals were created: Brihaspati was the ruler. He lauded with nineteen: the Sudra and the Arya (Vaisya) were created: day and night were the rulers. He lauded with twenty-one: animals with undivided hoofs were created: Varuna was the ruler. He lauded with twenty-three: small animals were created: Pushan was the ruler. He lauded with twenty-five: wild animals were created: Vayu was the ruler (compare R.V. x. 90, 8).[13] He lauded with twenty-seven: heaven and earth separated: Vasus, Rudras, and Adityas separated after them: they were the rulers. He lauded with twenty-nine: trees were created: Soma was the ruler. He lauded with thirty-one: living beings were created:

---

12 [Khanda IV, Prapathaka III Verses X following--]. Ambedkar's note here is incomplete.

13 Muir's original insertion. *Rig Veda* 10.90.8, as seen above, goes: "From that universal sacrifice were provided curds and butter. It formed those aerial (creatures) and animals both wild and tame."

The first and second halves of the month were the rulers. He lauded with thirty-one: existing things were tranquilized: Prajapati Parameshthin was the ruler.[14]

Here it should be noted that not only is there no unanimity between the *Rig Veda* and the *Yajur Veda* but there is no agreement between the two Samhitas of the *Yajur Veda* on so important a subject as the origin of the varnas.

The following is the text of the *Taittiriya Samhita* which may be taken as an independent explanation:[15]

He (the Vratya) became filled with passions thence sprang the Rajanya.[16]

Let the king to whose house the Vratya who knows this, comes as a guest, cause him to be respected as superior to himself. So doing he does no injury to his royal rank, or to his realm. From him arose the Brahman and the Kshattra (Kshatriya). They said, "Into whom shall we enter, etc".[17]

Let us turn to the *Atharva Veda*. The *Atharva Veda* has also two explanations to give. It incorporates the Purusha Sukta though the order of the verses varies from the order in which they stand in the *Rig Veda*. What is however important to note is that the *Atharva Veda* is not content with the Purusha Sukta. It offers other explanations also. One such explanation reads as follows:[18]

The Brahman was born the first, with ten heads and ten faces. He first drank the soma; he made poison powerless.

The Gods were afraid of the Rajanya when he was in

---

14 Muir 1868, Vol 1, 18–9.

15 In the BAWS edition, this paragraph and the quotation that follow seem wrongly placed in terms of the logic of argument. Here, we have moved it two paragraphs below. It is not clear if the error was Ambedkar's or of the editors of BAWS.

16 This is in fact from *Atharva Veda*, 15.8.1. Ambedkar is using here Muir's translation (1868, Vol 1, 22).

17 *Atharva Veda*, 15.9.1. Muir 1868, Vol 1, 22.

18 [Muir's Sanskrit Texts Vol. I pp. 21–2.] Muir says this is from *Taittiriya Samhita*. Ambedkar cites this same verse in *Who Were the Shudras?* (BAWS Vol 7, 1990, 38) and gives the source as "T.S., ii.4.13.1".

> the womb. They bound him with bonds when he was in the womb. Consequently this Rajanya is born bound. If he were born unbound he would go on slaying his enemies. In regard to whatever Rajanya any one desires that he should born unbound, and should go on slaying his enemies, let him offer for him this Aindra-Barhaspatya oblation. A Rajanya has the character of Indra, and a Brahman is Brihaspati. It is through the Brahman that anyone releases the Rajanya from his bond. The golden bond, a gift, manifestly releases from the bond that fetters him.

The other explanation speaks of people being descended from Manu and is to be found referred to in the following passages:[19]

> Prayers and hymns were formerly congregated in the Indra, in the ceremony which Atharvan, father Manu, and Dadhyanch celebrated. I.80.16
>
> Whatever prosperity or succour father Manu obtained by sacrifices, may we gain all that under thy guidance, O Rudra. I.114.2
>
> Those pure remedies of yours, O Maruts, those which are most auspicious, ye vigorous gods, those which are beneficent, those which our father Manu chose, those, and the blessing and succour of Rudra, I desire. II.33.13
>
> That ancient friend hath been equipped with the powers of the mighty (gods). Father Manu has prepared hymns to him, as portals of success to the gods. VIII.52.1
>
> Sacrifice is Manu, our protecting father. X.100.5
>
> Do ye (gods) deliver, protect, and intercede for us; do not lead us far away from the paternal path of Manu. VIII.30.3
>
> He (Agni) who abides among the offspring of Manu as the invoker (of the gods), is even the lord of these riches. I.68.4
>
> Agni, together with the gods, and the children of Manush, celebrating a multiform sacrifice with hymns, etc. III.3.6
>
> Ye gods, Vajas, and Ribhukshans, come to our sacrifice by the path travelled by the gods, that ye, pleasing deities,

19 [Muir's Sanskrit Texts Vol. I pp. 162–5.]

> may institute a sacrifice among these people of Manush on auspicious days. IV.37.1
>
> The people of Manush praise in the sacrifices Agni the invoker. VI.14.2
>
> Whenever Agni, lord of the people, kindled, abides gratified among the people of Manush, he repels all Rakshasas. VIII.23.13.

Stopping for a moment to take stock, so to say, of the position, it is quite clear that there is no unanimity among the Vedas on the origin of the four varnas. None of the other Vedas agree with the *Rig Veda* that the Brahman was created from the mouth of the Prajapati, the Kshatriyas from his arms, the Vaishyas from his thighs and the Shudras from his feet.

II

Let us now turn to the writings called the Brahmanas[20] and see what they have to say on this question. The explanation given by the *Satapatha Brahmana* is as follows:[21]

> (Uttering) "*bhuh*", Prajapati generated this earth. (Uttering) "*bhuvah*" he generated the air, and (uttering) "*svah*", he generated the sky. This universe is co-extensive with these worlds. (The fire) is placed with the whole. Saying "*bhuh*", Prajapati generated the Brahman; (saying) "*bhuvah*" he generated the Kshattra; (and saying) "*svah*", he generated the Vis. The fire is placed with the whole, (saying) "*bhuh*", Prajapati generated himself; (saying) "*bhuvah*" he generated

20 The Brahmanas are prose texts attached to each Veda and form a part of *shruti* literature. While the Srautasutras and Grihyasutras describe ritual, the Brahmanas discuss why a particular ritual is performed, sometimes with mythological tales meant to bolster the status of the rituals (Witzel 2003, 82). The earliest Brahmana texts are perhaps the interspersed explanations of mantras in the Samhita text of the Black *Yajur Veda*. In the other Vedas, the Brahmanas are separate from the mantras. The *Satapatha Brahmana* of the White *Yajur Veda* is the longest collection. Over time, the Black *Yajur Veda* also developed a separate collection, the *Taittiriya Brahmana* (Cush et al 2012, 118).

21 [Muir Sanskrit Texts Vol. I p.17.]

offspring; (saying) "*svah*", he generated animals. This world is so much as self, offspring, and animals. (The fire) is placed with the whole.[22]

The *Satapatha Brahmana* also gives another explanation. It reads as follows:[23]

23. Brahma (here, according to the Commentator, existing in the form of Agni, and representing the Brahman caste)[24] was formerly this (universe), one only. Being one, it did not develop. It energetically created an excellent form, the Kshattra, viz., those among the gods who are powers (*kshattrani*), Indra, Varuna, Soma Rudra, Parjanya, Yama, Mrityu, Isana. Hence nothing is superior to the Kshattra. Therefore the Brahman sits below the Kshattriya at the Rajasuya-sacrifice; he confers that glory on the Kshattra (the royal power). This, the Brahma, is the source of the Kshattra; hence, although the king attains supremacy, he at the end resorts to the Brahma as his source. Whoever destroys him (the Brahman) destroys his own source. He becomes most miserable, as one who has injured a superior.

24. He did not develop. He created the Vis—viz, those classes of gods who are designated by troops, Vasus, Rudras, Adityas, Visvadevas, Maruts,

25. He did not develop. He created the Sudra class, Pushan. This earth is Pushan; for she nourishes all that exists.

26. He did not develop. He energetically created an excellent form, Justice (Dharma). This is the ruler (*kshattra*) of the ruler (*kshattra*), namely justice. Hence nothing is superior to justice. Therefore the weaker seeks (to overcome) the stronger by justice, as by a king. This justice is truth. In consequence they say of a man who speaks truth, "he speaks

---

22 The *Satapatha Brahmana* survives in two recensions, the Madhyandina Sakha and the Kanva Sakha. Julius Eggeling translated the former in 1882 for the Sacred Books of the East series (Vol 12). Muir translates from this recension as well.

23 [Muir Sanskrit Texts Vol. I p.20.]

24 Insertion by Muir in the original.

justice;" or of a man who is uttering justice, "he speaks truth." For this is both of these.

27. This is the Brahma, Kshattra, Vis, and Sudra. Through Agni it became Brahma among the gods, the Brahman among men, through the (divine) Kshatriya a (human) Kshattriya, through the (divine) Vaisya a (human) Vaisya, through the (divine) Sudra a (human) Sudra. Wherefore it is in Agni among the gods and in a Brahman among men, that they seek after an abode.

The *Taittiriya Brahmana*[25] offers three explanations. The first is in the following terms:[26]

This entire (universe) has been created by Brahma. Men say that the Vaisya class was produced from rich-verses. They say that the *Yajur Veda* is the womb from which the Kshattriya was born. The *Sama Veda* is the source from which the Brahmans sprang. This word the ancients declared to the ancients.

The second says: "The Brahman caste is sprung from the gods; the Sudra from the Asuras."[27]

The third is as follows:[28]

Let him at his will milk out with a wooden dish. But let not a Sudra milk it out. For this Sudra has sprung from non-existence. They say that which a Sudra milks out is no oblation. Let not a Sudra milk out the Agnihotra. For they do not purify that. When that passes beyond the filter, then it is an oblation.

Again looking at the testimony of the Brahmanas, how far do they support the Purusha Sukta? Not one of them do.

---

25 The *Taittiriya Brahmana,* associated with the Black *Yajur Veda,* is distinct from the *Taittiriya Samhita*. Ambedkar thus far cited from the latter.

26 [Muir I p. 17.]

27 [Muir's Sanskrit Texts Vol 1 p. 21]

28 [Ibid p. 21.]

III

The next thing would be to see what the Smritis have to offer [as] explanation of the origin of the varna system. It is worthwhile to take note of them. This is what Manu has to say on the subject.[29]

> I.8 He (the self-existent) having felt desire, and willing to create various living beings from his own body, first created the waters, and threw into them a seed. 9. That seed became a golden egg, of lustre equal to the sun; in it he himself was born as a Brahma, the parent of all the worlds. 10. The waters are called *narah,* for they are sprung from Nara; and as they were his first sphere of motion he is therefore called Narayana. 11. Produced from the imperceptible, eternal, existent and non-existent cause, the male (*purusha*) is celebrated in the world as Brahma. 12. After dwelling for a year in the egg, the glorious being, himself, by his own contemplation, split it in twain.
>
> I. 31. That the worlds might be peopled, he caused the Brahman, the Kshattriya, the Vaisya, and the Sudra to issue from his mouth, his arms, his thighs, and his feet. 32. Having divided his own body into two parts, the lord (Brahma became), with the half of male (purusha), and with the half, a female; and in her he created Viraj. 33. Know, O most excellent twice-born men, that I, whom that male, (Purusha) Viraj, himself created, am the creator of all this world.
>
> 34. Desiring to produce living creatures, I performed very arduous devotion and first created ten Maharshis (great rishis), lords of living beings, 35. viz., Marichi, Atri, Angiras, Pulastya, Pulaha, Kratu, Prachetas, Vasishtha, Bhrigu, and Narada. 36. They, endowed with great energy, created other seven Manus, gods, and abodes of gods, and Maharshis of boundless might; 37. Yakshas, Rakshases, Pisachas, Gandharvas, Apsaras, Asuras, Nagas, Serpents, great birds, and the different classes of Pitris; 38. lightnings, thunderbolts, clouds, portentous atmospheric sounds, comets, and various luminaries; 39. Kinnars, apes, fishes, different sorts of birds,

29 [Ibid pp. 36–7.]

> cattle, deer, men, beasts with two rows of teeth; 40. small and large reptiles mouths; lice, flies, fleas, all gadflies, and gnats, and motionless things of different sorts. 41. Thus by my appointment, and by the force of devotion, was all this world both motionless and moving, created by those great beings, according to the (previous) actions of each creature.

There is also another view expressed by Manu in his Smriti as to the basic reasons for dividing men into four classes:[30]

> XII.39 I shall now declare succinctly in order the states which the soul reaches by means of each of these qualities. 40. Souls endowed with the *sattva* quality attain to godhead; those having the *rajas* quality become men; whilst those characterized by *tamas* always become beasts—such is the threefold destination... 43. Elephants, horses, Sudras and contemptible Mlechhas, lions, tigers, and boars form the middle dark condition... 46. Kings, Kshattriyas, a King's priests (*purohitah*), and men whose chief occupation is the war of words, compose the middle condition of passion... 48. Devotees, ascetics, Brahmans, the deities borne on aerial cars, constellations, and Daityas, constitute the lowest condition of goodness. 49. Sacrificing priests, rishis, Gods, the Vedas, the celestial luminaries, years, the fathers, the Sadhyas, form the second condition of goodness. 50. Brahma, the creators, righteousness, the Great one *(mahat)*, the Unapparent One *(avyakta)*, compose the highest condition of goodness.

Manu, of course, agrees with the *Rig Veda*. But his view is of no use for comparison. It is not original. He is merely repeating the *Rig Veda*.

IV

It will be interesting to compare with these views those contained in the *Ramayana* and the *Mahabharata*. The *Ramayana* says that the four varnas are the offspring of Manu, the daughter

30 [Muir's Sanskrit Texts Vol I p. 41.]

of Daksha and the wife of Kasyapa.[31]

> Listen while I declare to you from the commencement all the Prajapatis (lord of creatures) who came into existence in the earliest time. Kardama was the first, then Vokrita, Sesha, Samsraya, the energetic Bahuputra, Sthanu, Marichi, Atri, the strong Kratu, Pulastya, Angiras, Prachetas, Pulaha, Daksha, then Vivasvat, Arishtanemi, and the glorious Kasyapa, who was the last. The Prajapati Daksha is famed to have had sixty daughters. Of these Kasyapa took in marriage eight elegant maidens, Aditi, Diti, Danu, Kalaka, Tamra, Krodhavasa, Manu and Anala. Kasyapa, pleased, then said to these maids, "ye shall bring forth sons like me, preservers of the three worlds." Aditi, Diti, Danu and Kalaka assented; but the others did not agree. Thirty-three gods were born by Aditi, the Adilyas, Vasus, Rudras, and the two Asvins.
>
> Manu (wife) of Kasyapa, produced men—Brahmans, Kshattriyas, Vaisyas, and Sudras. 'Brahmans were born from the mouth, Kshattriyas from the breast, Vaisyas from the thighs, and Sudras from the feet,' So says the Veda. Anala gave birth to all trees with pure fruits.[32]

Strange, very strange that Valmiki should have credited the creation of the four varnas to Kasyapa instead of to Prajapati. His knowledge was evidently based only on hearsay. It is clear he did not know what the Vedas had said.

Now the *Mahabharata* gives four different explanations in four different places. The first runs as follows:

> Born all with splendour, like that of great rishis, the ten sons of Prachetas, reputed to have been virtuous and holy; and by them the glorious beings were formerly burnt up by fire springing from their mouths. From them was born Daksha Prachetas, and from Daksha, the Parent of the world (were produced), these creatures. Cohabiting with Virini, the Muni Daksha

31 [Muir's Sanskrit Texts Vol 1 pp. 116–7.]

32 This is from Book II of the *Ramayana*, Ayodhya Kanda, 110, 6–14 and 29–31.

> begot a thousand sons like himself, famous for their religious observances, to whom Narada taught the doctrine of final liberation, the unequalled knowledge of the Sankhya. Desirous of creating offspring, the Prajapati Daksha next formed fifty daughters of whom he gave ten to Dharma, thirteen to Kasyapa, and twenty-seven, devoted to the regulation of time, to Indu (Soma)... On Dakshayani, the most excellent of his thirteen wives, Kasyapa, the son of Marichi, begot the Adityas, headed by Indra and distinguished by their energy, and also Vivasvat. To Vivasvat was born a son, the mighty Yama Vaivasvata. To Martanda (i.e.Vivasvat, the Sun) was born the wise and mighty Manu, and also the renowned Yama, his (Manu's) younger brother. Righteous was this wise Manu, on whom a race was founded. Hence this (family) of men became known as the race of Manu. Brahmans, Kshattriyas, and other men sprang from this Manu. From him, o king, came the Brahman conjoined with the Kshattriya.[33]

The theory propounded here is very much the same as that contained in the *Ramayana* with this difference, namely, that the *Mahabharata* makes Manu the progenitor of the four varnas, and secondly it does not say that the four varnas were born from the different parts of Manu.

The second explanation[34] given by the *Mahabharata* follows what is given in the Purusha Sukta of the *Rig Veda*. It reads thus:

> The King should appoint to be his royal priest a man who will protect the good, and restrain the wicked. On this subject they relate this following ancient story of a conversation between Pururavas the son of Ila, and Matarisvan (Vayu, the wind god). Pururavas said: "You must explain to me whence the Brahman, and whence the (other) three castes were produced, and whence the superiority (of the first) arises." Matarisvan answered: "The Brahman was created from Brahma's mouth,

33 Muir 1868, Vol 1, 125–6. This is from Book 1, Adi Parva, verses 3128 and 3135.

34 [Muir's Vol I p.] Ambedkar's citation is incomplete; see the following note for the correct reference.

> the Kshatriya from his arms, the Vaisya from his thighs, while for the purpose of serving these three castes was produced the fourth class, the Sudra, fashioned from his feet. The Brahman, as soon as born, becomes the lord of all beings upon the earth, for the purpose of protecting the treasure of righteousness. Then (the creator) constituted the Kshattriya the controller of the earth, a second Yama to bear the rod, for the satisfaction of the people. And it was Brahma's ordinance that the Vaisya should sustain these three classes with money and grain, and that the Sudra should serve them." The son of Ila then enquired: "Tell me, Vayu, to whom the earth, with its wealth, rightfully belongs, to the Brahman or the Kshattriya?" Vayu replied: "All this, whatever exists in the world is the Brahman's property by right of primogeniture; this is known to those who are skilled in the laws of duty. It is his own which the Brahman eats, puts on, and bestows. He is the chief of all the castes, the first-born and the most excellent. Just as a woman when she has lost her (first) husband, takes her brother in law for a second; so the Brahman is thy first resource in calamity; afterwards another may arise."[35]

The third view is expounded in the Shanti Parva[36] of the *Mahabharata*:[37]

> Bhrigu replied: "Brahma thus formerly created the Prajapatis, Brahmanic, penetrated by his own energy, and in splendour equalling the sun and fire. The lord then formed truth, righteousness austere fervour, and the eternal veda (or sacred science), virtuous practice, and purity for (the attainment of) heaven. He also formed the gods, Danavas, Gandharvas, Daityas, Asuras, Maharagas, Yakshas, Rakshasas, Nagas, Pisachas, and men, Brahmans, Kshatriyas, Vaisyas, and Sudras, as well as all other classes (*varnah*) of beings. The colour

35 Muir 1868, Vol 1, 128–9. From Book 12, Shanti Parva, verses 2749–55.

36 Shanti Parva is the twelfth and longest of the eighteen books of the *Mahabharata*. Several parts of the Parva are considered later interpolations (see Brockington 1998, 18–28, 120–7). Chapters 188 and 189 deal with Bhrigu's theory of varna.

37 [Ibid pp. 139–40.]

> (*varna*) of the Brahmans was white; that of the Kshattriyas red; that of the Vaishyas yellow, and that of the Sudras black." Bharadvaja here rejoins: "If the caste (*varna*) of the four classes is distinguished by their colour (*varna*), then a confusion of all the castes is observable. Desire, anger, fear, cupidity, grief, apprehension, hunger, fatigue, prevail over us all: by what then, is caste discriminated? Sweat, urine, excrement, phlegm, bile and blood (are common to all); the bodies of all decay; by what then is caste discriminated? There are innumerable kinds of things moving and stationary; how is the class (*varna)* of these various objects to be determined?" Bhrigu replies: "There is no difference of castes..."[38]

The fourth explanation is also contained in the same Shanti Parva.[39] It says:

---

38 From Shanti Parva, verses 6930–9. In this context, two more works may be cited—one Brahmanical, and the other Buddhist. The first, *Vajrasuchika Upanishad,* belonging to the *Sama Veda,* puts forward this thesis: although the view that "the Brahamna is the chief among [the four] castes is in accord with the Vedic texts and is affirmed by the Smritis", there is still the scope to raise the question, "Who is, verily, the Brahamna?" (verse 2). It then proceeds to systematically demolish Brahamna's claim of superiority on the grounds of *jiva* or "individual self", "body", "birth", "knowledge", "work", "performance of religious duties" (verses 3–8). Finally, in verse 9 the Upanishad declares: "Then, who, verily is the Brahamna? He who, after directly perceiving, like the amalaka fruit in the palm of one's hand, the Self, without a second, devoid of distinctions of birth, attribute and action..." (see Radhakrishnan 1998, 933–8). In his note to verse 9, Radhakrishnan says: "It is valuable to recall the teachings of this Upanishad which repudiates the system that consecrates inequalities and hardens contingent differences into inviolable divisions" (938). In the *Majjhima Nikaya,* section 2.147, the Buddha is shown disputing with the Brahamna scholar Assalayana, a youth of sixteen, who has been deputed by the (mostly ignorant) Brahamnas of Savatthi to defend the Brahmanical order. The Buddha mocks as well as negates the ideas of purity and impurity so dear to Brahmanism: "First, Assalayana, you based your claim on birth, then you gave up birth for learning, and finally you have come round to my way of thinking, that all four castes are equally pure." What is absolutely startling is this text transmutes the notion of four-some *rank* into the notion of two-some *class* and opens up a space for interrogating the monolithic Brahmanical hierarchy in terms of haves and have-nots; it also speaks of the possibility of social mobility. At one point the Buddha says: "Have you ever heard that in the lands of the Greeks and Kambojas and other peoples on the borders there are only two classes, masters and slaves, and a master can become a slave and vice versa?" (in Embree 1991, 140–1).

39 The following quote is from verses 6950–5, and seems to be a continuation of the

> Bharadvaja again enquires: "What is that in virtue of which a man is a Brahman, a Kshattriya, a Vaisya, or a Sudra; tell me, o most eloquent Brahman rishi." Bhrigu replies: "He who is pure, consecrated by the natal and other ceremonies, who has completely studied the Veda, lives in the practice of the six ceremonies, performs perfectly the rites of purification, who eats the remains of oblations, is attached to his religious teacher, is constant in religious observances, and devoted to truth—is called a Brahman. He in whom are seen truth, liberality inoffensiveness, harmlessness, modesty, compassion, and austere fervour—is declared to be a Brahman. He who practises the duty arising out of the kingly office, who is addicted to the study of the Veda, and who delights in giving and receiving—is called a Kshattriya. He who readily occupies himself with cattle, who is devoted to agriculture and acquisition, who is pure, and is perfect in the study of the Veda—is denominated a Vaisya. He who is habitually addicted to all kinds of food, performs all kinds of work, who is unclean, who has abandoned the Veda, and does not practise pure observances—is traditionally called a Sudra. And this (which I have stated) is the mark of a Sudra, and it is not found in a Brahman: (such) a Sudra will remain a Sudra, while the Brahman (who so acts) will be no Brahman.[40]

Except in one place, the *Mahabharata* gives no support to the Rig Vedic origin of the varna system.

---

conversation between Bhrigu and Bharadvaja in the previously quoted verses. In the part Ambedkar omits—verses 6940 to 6949—Bhrigu goes on to say "...this world, having been at first created by Brahma entirely Brahmanic, became (afterwards) separated into castes in consequence of works. Those Brahmans (lit. twice-born man), who were fond of sensual pleasure, fiery, irascible, prone to violence, who had forsaken their duty, and were red-limbed, fell into the condition of Kshattriyas. Those Brahmans, who derived their livelihood from kine, who were yellow, who subsisted by agriculture, and who neglected to practice their duties, entered into the state of Vaisyas. Those Brahmans who were addicted to mischief and falsehood, who were covetous, who lived by all kinds of work, who were black and had fallen from purity, sank into the condition of Sudras."

40 Muir 1868, Vol 1, 141.

V

Let us inquire what the Puranas have to say on the origin of the varna system.

To begin with the *Vishnu Purana*.[41] There are three theories propounded in the *Vishnu Purana* on the origin of the *chaturvarna* According to one, the origin is to be ascribed to Manu. Says the *Vishnu Purana*:[42]

> Before the mundane egg existed the divine Brahma Hiranyagarbha, the eternal originator of all worlds, who was the form of essence of Brahma, who consists of the divine Vishnu, who again is identical with the Rik, Yajush, Saman and Atharva Vedas. From Brahma's right thumb was born the Prajapati Daksha; Daksha had a daughter Aditi; from her was born Vivasvat; and from him sprang Manu. Manu had sons called Ikshvaku, Nriga, Dhrishta, Saryati, Narishanta, Pramsu, Nabhagandishta, Karusha and Prishadhra.[43]
>
> From Karusha the Karushas, Kshattriyas of great power, were descended.[44]
>
> Nabhaga, the son of Nedishta, became a Vaisya.[45]

This explanation is incomplete. It only explains the origin of Kshatriyas and Vaishyas. It does not explain the origin of Brahmans and Shudras.[46]

---

41 The *Vishnu Purana* is one of the eighteen Mahapurana texts dating from the early centuries of the Common Era (Cush et al 2012, 634). The *Vishnu Purana* takes the form of a conversation between the maharishi Parashara and his disciple Maitreya, and includes some of the best-known stories of the corpus, including the avatars of Vishnu, cosmogony myths and genealogies and stories of legendary kings.

42 [Muir I pp. 220–1.] Ambedkar cites the same passage in *Who Were the Shudras?* (BAWS Vol 7, 1990, 95).

43 *Vishnu Purana* IV.1.4.

44 *Vishnu Purana* IV.1.13, in Muir 1868, Vol 1, 222.

45 *Vishnu Purana* IV.1.9 in Muir 1868, Vol 1, 222.

46 Muir translates one crucial sentence here from the *Vishnu Purana* that Ambedkar does not cite. It reads,"Prishadhra became a Shudra in consequence of his having killed his religious preceptor's cow" (Muir 1868, Vol 1, 221). This indicates that the *Vishnu Purana* does have one line about the origin of the Shudra. Muir then goes on

There is also another and a different version in the *Vishnu Purana*. It says:

> Desirous of a son, Manu sacrificed to Mitra and Varuna; but in consequence of a wrong invocation through an irregularity of the hotri (priest) a daughter called Ila was born. Then through the favour of Mitra and Varuna she bore to Manu a son called Sudyumna. But being again changed into a female through the wrath of Isvara (Mahadeva) she wandered near the hermitage of Budha the son of Soma (the Moon); who becoming enamoured of her had by her a son called Pururavas. After his birth, the god who is formed of sacrifice of the Rik, Yajush, Saman, and Atharva Vedas, of all things, of mind, of nothing, he who is in the form of the sacrificial Male, was worshipped by the rishis of infinite splendour who desired that Sudyumna should recover his manhood. Through the fervour of this god Ila became again Sudyumna.
>
> According to the *Vishnu Purana*,[47] Atri was the son of Brahma, and the father of Soma (the Moon), whom Brahma installed as the sovereign of plants, Brahmans and stars. After celebrating the Rajasuya sacrifice, Soma became intoxicated with pride, and carried off Tara (Star), the wife of Brihaspati, the preceptor of the gods, whom, although admonished and entreated by Brahma, the gods, and rishis, he refused to restore. Soma's part was taken by Usanas; and Rudra, who had studied under Angiras, aided Brihaspati. A fierce conflict ensued between the two sides, supported respectively by the gods and the Daityas, etc. Brahma interposed, and compelled Soma to restore Tara to her husband. She had, however, in the meantime become pregnant and bore a son Budha (the planet Mercury), of whom, when strongly urged, she acknowledged Soma to be the father. Pururavas, as has been already mentioned, was the son of this Budha by Ila, the daughter of Manu

---

to quote another example from the *Harivamsa*.

47 Ambedkar is quoting verbatim from Muir 1868, Vol 1, 225–6. Muir himself is paraphrasing the *Vishnu Purana* from IV.6.2 onwards.

> … Pururavas had six sons, of whom the eldest was Ayus. Ayus had five sons: Nahusha, Kshattra-vriddha, Rambha, Raji, and Anenas…
>
> Kshattravriddha had a son Sunahotra, who had three sons, Kasa, Lesa, and Gritsamada. From the last sprang Saunaka, *who originated the system of four castes.*[48] Kasa had a son Kasiraia, of whom again Dirghatamas was the son as Dhanvantari was Dirghatamas.[49]

The third version ascribes the origin to Brahma. It says:[50]

> *VP* I.6.1 Maitreya[51] says: You have described to me the Arvaksrotas, or human creation; declare to me, o Brahman, in detail the manner in which Brahma formed it. 2. Tell me how and with what qualities, he created the castes, and what are traditionally reputed to be the functions of the Brahmans and others. Parasara replies: 3. When, true to his design, Brahma became desirous to create the world, creatures in whom goodness *(sattva)* prevailed sprang from his mouth; 4. others in whom passion *(rajas)* predominated came from his breast; other in whom both passion and darkness *(tamas)* were strong, proceeded from his thighs; 5. others he created from his feet, whose chief characteristic was darkness. Of these was composed the system of four castes, Brahmans, Kshatriyas, Vaisyas, and Sudras, who had respectively issued from his mouth, breast, thighs, and feet.

Herein the *Vishnu Purana* has given the Rig Vedic theory supported by the Sankhya philosophy.[52]

---

48 Italicised as such in BAWS, not in Muir. Perhaps based on Ambedkar's emphasis in the original MS.

49 Muir 1868, Vol 1, 225–6. The last paragraph is Muir citing an actual translation of *Vishnu Purana* IV.8.1, not paraphrased.

50 [Muir's Sanskrit Texts Vol 1 pp. 61–2.]

51 [The *Vishnu Purana* is cast in the form of a dialogue between Maitreya, the student who asks questions, and Rishi Parashara, who answers his questions.]

52 See Riddle No. 6, 70n9.

In the *Harivamsa*[53] are to be found two theories. One[54] upholds the theory of the origin of the varnas as being born from one of the descendents of Manu as the stock of descent than the one mentioned by the *Vishnu Purana*:

> The son of Gritsamada was Sunaka, from whom sprang the Saunakas, Brahmanas, Kshattriyas, Vaisyas, and Sudras.[55]
>
> Vitatha was the father of five sons, Suhotra, Suhotri, Gaya, Garga, and the great Kapila. Suhotra had two sons, the exalted Kasaka, and King Gritsamati. The sons of the latter were Brahmans, Kshattriyas and Vaisyas.[56]

The other version speaks of their being formed by Vishnu who sprang from Brahma and had become Prajapati Daksha and is as follows:[57]

> Janmejaya[58] says: I have heard, O Brahman the (description of the) Brahma Yuga, the first of the ages. I desire also to be accurately informed both summarily, and in detail, about the age of the Kshattriyas, with its numerous observances, illustrated as it was by sacrifice, and described, as it has been by men skilled in the art of narration. Vaisampayana replied: I shall describe to you that age revered for its sacrifices and distinguished for its various works of liberality, as well as for its people. Those Munis of a size of a thumb had been absorbed by the sun's rays. Following a rule of life leading to final[59] emancipation, practising unobstructed ceremonies,

---

53 The *Harivamsa* is considered both a supplement to the *Mahabharata* and a Purana (Rocher 1986, 81). Besides the lengthy legend of Krishna that it is known for, the *Harivamsa* contains other legends and myths, such as accounts of the incarnations of Vishnu. For more, see Brockington 1998, 313–44.

54 [Muir's Sanskrit Texts Vol. 1 p. 227.]

55 The quote is from the *Harivamsa*, section 29, verse 1520, according to Muir.

56 *Harivamsa*, section 32, verse 1732.

57 [Muir's Vol. 1 pp. 152–3.]

58 [The *Harivamsa* is a dialogue between Janmejaya and Vaisampayana.]

59 "Those Munis of a size of a thumb had been absorbed by the sun's rays. Following a rule of life leading to final…" This part of the sentence is missing in the BAWS

both in action and in abstinence from action constantly intent upon Brahma, united to Brahman as the highest object,—Brahmans glorious and sanctified in their conduct, leading a life of continence, disciplined by the knowledge of Brahma,—Brahmans complete in their observances, perfect in knowledge, and contemplative,—when at the end of a thousand yugas, their majesty was full, these Munis became involved in the dissolution of the world. Then Vishnu sprung from Brahma, removed beyond the sphere of sense, absorbed in contemplation, became the Prajapati Daksha, and formed numerous creatures. The Brahmans, beautiful (or, dear to Soma), were formed from an imperishable *(akshara),* the Kshattriyas from a perishable *(kshara),* element, the Vaisyas from alteration, the Sudras from a modification of smoke. While Vishnu was thinking upon the castes *(varnan),* Brahmans were formed with white, red, yellow, and blue colour (*varnaih*). Hence in the world men have become divided into castes, being of four descriptions, Brahmans, Kshattriyas, Vaisyas, and Sudras, one in form, distinct in their duties, two-footed, very wonderful, full of energy(?), skilled in expedients in all their occupations. Rites are declared to be prescribed by the Vedas for the three (highest) castes. By that contemplation practised by the being sprung from Brahma—by that practised in his character as Vishnu—the Lord Prachetasa (Daksha), i.e. Vishnu the great contemplator (*yogin*), passed through his wisdom and energy from that state of meditation into the sphere of works. Next the Sudras, produced from extinction, are destitute of rites. Hence they are not entitled to be admitted to the purificatory ceremonies, nor does sacred science belong to them. Just as the cloud of smoke which rises from the fire on the friction of the fuel, and is dissipated, is of no service in the sacrificial rite, so too the Sudras wandering over the earth, are altogether (useless for purposes of sacrifice) owing to their birth, their mode

---

edition. It has been inserted here from Muir.

> of life devoid of purity and their want of the observances prescribed in the Veda.[60]

The *Bhagavata Purana*[61] also has an explanation as to the origin of the varnas. It says:[62]

> At the end of many thousand years the living soul which resides in time, action, and natural quality gave life to that lifeless egg floating on the water. Purusha then having burst the egg, issued from it was a thousand thighs, feet, arms, eyes, faces and heads. With his members the sages fashion the worlds, the seven lower worlds with his loins etc, and the seven upper worlds with his groin, etc. The Brahman (was) the mouth of Purusha, the Kshattriya his arms, the Vaishya was born from the thighs, the Sudra from the feet of the divine being. The earth was formed from his feet, the air from his navel; the heaven by the heart, and the *maharloka* by the breast of the mighty one.

Lastly the *Vayu Purana*.[63] What does it say? It takes up the theory of Manu as the originator of the varna system. "The son of Gritsamada was Sunaka, from whom sprang Saunaka. In his family were born Brahmanas, Kshattriyas, Vaisya, and Sudras, twice-born men with various functions."[64]

VI

What a chaos! Why could the Brahmans not give a uniform and consistent explanation of the origin of the four varnas?

---

60 This long passage comprises verses 11808–11820 of the *Harivamsa*.

61 The *Bhagavata Purana* is one of the Mahapuranas. An immensely popular work with many commentaries and vernacular translations (Winternitz 1977, 555), it is considered both connected to and dependent on the content of the *Vishnu Purana*.

62 [Muir's Sanskrit Texts Vol. 1 p. 156.] Writes Muir before the translated quote from the *Bhagavata Purana*: "The first extract reproduces some of the ideas of the Purusha Sukta more closely than any of the accounts yet given."

63 Dedicated to the wind god Vayu, the *Vayu Pùrana* is generally recognized as one of the oldest and most authoritative Puranas (Rocher 1986, 245).

64 Muir 1868, Vol 1, 227.

On the issue of who created them, there is no uniformity. The *Rig Veda* says the four varnas were created by Prajapati. It does not mention which Prajapati. One would like to know which Prajapati it was who created the four varnas. For there are so many Prajapatis. But even on the point of creation by Prajapati, there is no agreement. One says they were created by Brahman. Another says they were created by Kassyapa. The third says they were created by Manu.

On the issue of how many varnas, the creator—whoever he was—created, again there is no uniformity. The *Rig Veda* says four varnas were created. But other authorities say only two varnas were created, some say Brahmans and Kshatriyas and some say Brahmans and Shudras.

On the issue of the relations intended by the creator for binding together the four varnas, the *Rig Veda* lays down the rule of graded inequality based on the importance of the part of the creation from which the particular varna was born. But the White *Yajur Veda* denies this theory of the *Rig Veda*. So also the Upanishads, *Ramayana*, *Mahabharata* and Puranas. Indeed the *Harivamsa* goes to the length of saying that the Shudras are twice-born.[65]

This chaos seems to be the result of concoction of the theory of *chaturvarna*, which the Brahmans quietly smuggled[66] into the *Rig Veda*, contrary to established traditions.

What was the purpose, what was the motive of the Brahmans who concocted this theory?

---

65 Ambedkar is inferring this from the *Harivamsa* verse he cites earlier. See 125n53.

66 The word printed in the BAWS edition here, 'singled', is in all likeliness a typographical error. Ambedkar most likely meant 'smuggled', and we have replaced it thus.

Riddle No. 17

The Four Ashramas: The Why and How about them[1]

The division of society into four orders called varnas is not the only peculiar feature of Hindu society. What is called Ashrama Dharma is another. There is however one point of difference between the two. The Varna Dharma is a theory of the organization of society. The Ashrama Dharma, on the other hand, is a theory of regulating the life of an individual.

Ashrama Dharma divides the life of an individual into four stages (1) Brahmacharya, (2) Grahasthashrama, (3) Vanaprastha and (4) Sannyasa. The state of Brahmacharya has both *de jure* and *de facto* connotations in that it means an unmarried state of life. Its *de jure* connotation means the stage of study under a teacher. Grahasthashrama is the stage of a householder, a stage of a married family life. The stage of Sannyasa is a stage of renunciation of civic rights and responsibilities. It is a stage of civic death. The stage of Vanaprastha is in between Grahasthashrama and Sannyasa. It is a stage in which one belongs to society but is bound to live away from society. As the name implies, it prescribes dwelling in the forest.

The Hindus believe that this institution of Ashrama Dharma is as vital as that of the Varna Dharma for the well-being of

1 The BAWS editors write: "This is an eighteen-page Manuscript. This is the typed first copy with a title written in the author's handwriting."

society. They call the two by a joint name of Varnashrama Dharma as though they were one and integral. The two together form the steel-frame of Hindu society.[2]

To begin with, it would be better to have a full understanding of the Ashrama Dharma before inquiring into its origin and its purpose and its peculiarities. The best source for an exposition of the Ashrama system is the *Manusmriti* from which the following relevant extracts are reproduced:

> In the eighth year after conception, one should perform the initiation (*upanayana*) of a Brahmana, in the eleventh after conception (that) of a Kshatriya, but in the twelfth that of a Vaisya.[3]
>
> A twice-born man who, not having studied the Veda, applies himself to other (and worldly study), soon falls, even while living, to the condition of a Sudra and his descendants (after him).[4]
>
> The vow of the three Vedas under a teacher must be kept for thirty-six years or for half that time, or for a quarter, or until the (student) has perfectly learnt them.
>
> Who has studied in due order the three Vedas, or two, or even one only, without breaking the (rule of) studentship, shall enter the order of householders.[5]
>
> The student, the householder, the hermit, and the ascetic, these (constitute) four separate orders, which all spring from

---

2 Sociologist G.S. Ghurye said in 1964, "Varnasramadharma, duties of castes and asramas, is almost another name for Hinduism" (cited in Olivelle 1993, 3). Gandhi defended Varnashrama and called it a "gift of Hinduism to mankind" though he lamented that the varna system was not being followed in purity, marred by notions of inferiority and superiority. His writings on this subject were put together by his acolyte, Anand T. Hingorani (see Gandhi 1965). On how this ashrama theory is connected to the four-varna idea to produce the complex of varnashrama as Sanatana Dharma (Eternal Law), see Notes 2 and 5 to the Introduction.

3 [Manu Smriti Chapter II 36.] All the extracts from the *Manusmriti* in this Riddle are from Bühler's 1886 translation.

4 [Ibid., II 168.]

5 [Ibid., III 1–2.]

(the order of) householders.

But all (or) even (any of) these orders, assumed successively in accordance with the Institutes (of the sacred law), lead the Brahmana who acts by the preceding (rules) to the highest state.

And in accordance with the precepts of the Veda and of the Smriti, the housekeeper is declared to be superior to all of them; for he supports the other three.[6]

A twice-born Snataka,[7] who has thus lived according to the law in the order of householders, may, taking a firm resolution and keeping his organs in subjection, dwell in the forest, duly (observing the rules given below).

When a householder sees his (skin) wrinkled and (his hair) white, and the sons of his sons, then he may resort to the forest.[8]

But having thus passed the third part of (a man's natural term of) life in the forest, he may live as an ascetic during the fourth part of his existence, after abandoning all attachment to worldly objects.

He who after passing from order to order, after offering sacrifices and subduing his senses, becomes tired with (giving alms and offerings of food), an ascetic, gains bliss after death.

When he has paid the three debts, let him apply his mind to (the attainment of) final liberation; he who seeks it without having paid (his debts) sinks downwards.

Having studied the Vedas in accordance with the rule, having begat sons according to the sacred law, and having

6 [Ibid., VI 87–9.]

7 According to the Monier-Williams dictionary, *snataka* is a Brahman who, after performing the ceremonial lustrations required on finishing his studentship as a *brahmacharin* under a religious teacher, returns home and begins the second period of his life, as a *grihastha*. There are three kinds of *snataka—vidya* [one who has finished his studentship and completed his study of the Vedas], a *vrata* [who has completed the vows, such as fasting, continence etc., without the Vedas], and a *vidya-vrata* or *ubhaya snataka* [who has completed both Vedas and vows], the last being the highest.

8 [Ibid., VI 1–2.]

> offered sacrifices according to his ability, he may direct his mind to (the attainment of) final liberation.
>
> A twice-born man who seeks final liberation, without having studied the Vedas, without having begotten sons, and without having offered sacrifices, sinks downwards.[9]

From these rules it is clear that according to Manu, there are three features of the Ashrama Dharma. The first is that it is not open to Shudras and women. The second is Brahmacharya, which is compulsory, as is Grahasthashrama. Vanaprastha and Sannyasa are not compulsory. The third is that one must pass from one stage to another in the order in which they stand; namely first Brahmacharya, then Grahasthashrama, then Vanaprastha and lastly Sannyasa. No one can omit one and enter the next stage.

A cursory reflection on this system of stages, which may well be called a system of planned economy of the life of the individual, raises many questions. The first is, what forced Manu to have such a system of planned economy? Referring to the Vedas, the theory of stages in life is quite unknown.[10] The Vedas speak of

---

9 [Manu Smriti Chapter VI. 33–7.]

10 In continuation of 50n5 to the Introduction, on how varna and ashrama evolved along two different vectors: In not one of the four Vedas is there any injunction regarding the four 'Stages of Life' as one whole unit. Scholars (Thapar 1978, 65) are unanimous in agreeing that the prescription was first spelt out in *Jabala Upanishad*. "After completing the life of a student, let one become a householder; after completing the life of a householder let one become a forest dweller; after completing the life of a forest dweller, let one renounce" (verse 4). However, the very next sentence in the same verse says: "Otherwise, let one renounce even from the state of a student or from the state of a householder or from that of a forest dweller ... on whatever day he has the spirit of renunciation, that very day let him renounce" (see S. Radhakrishnan 1998, 896–7). Given the undecidedness in the 'original' pronouncement, it is not surprising that we meet with conflicting rulings apropos ashrama in different dharma texts. In his bid to rationalise the divergences, P.V. Kane in "Chapter VIII: Asrama", had proposed to divide the dharma texts into three clusters. Namely: (i) *badha*: proponents of this paradigm favour only one ashrama, that of the householder [cf. Gautama]; (ii) *bikalpa*: proponents of this paradigm grant the student the liberty to choose his next ashrama [cf. Vasishtha]; (iii) *samuchhai*: proponents of this paradigm insist upon following the four ashramas consecutively; they do not allow for the skipping of any of the four stages [cf. Manu] (Kane 1974, 424). One may conjecture that only after the bonding between the idea

Brahmachari. But there is nothing to show that Brahmacharya was regarded as the first and inescapable stage in life. Why did the Brahmans make Brahmacharya a compulsory stage in the life of an individual? This is the first riddle about the Ashrama Dharma.

The second question is why Manu made it obligatory to observe the order of sequence in the following of the different stages of life by the individual. Now there is no doubt that there was a time when it was open to a Brahmachari to enter any of the three Ashrams![11] He may become a Grahasthashrami or he may at once become a Sannyasi without becoming a Grahasthashrami.[12] Compare what the authors of the Dharmasutras have to say on the point. *Vasishtha Dharmasutra*[13] says:

> There are four orders viz. (that of) the student, (that of) the householder, (that of) the hermit, and (that of) the ascetic.
>
> A man who has studied one, two or three Vedas without violating the rules of studentship, *may enter any of these* (orders) *whichsoever he pleases*.

---

of varna and the idea of *samuchhaivadi ashrama* becomes firm that the complex varnashrama gets to be operative; and, the credit for this consolidation goes to Manu as Ambedkar avers.

11 Olivelle has shown (1993, 73–111) how the ashrama system originated as a "theological scheme" that presented four alternative paths of religious life, from which men could freely choose. They were also conceived as lifelong vocations and not temporary stages in one's life. So Ambedkar isn't completely wrong in questioning the contradictions in the system, given that they weren't meant to be steps on a linear life path. Over time, in what Olivelle calls the "classical phase" of the ashrama system—best inscribed in *Manusmriti*, as Ambedkar notes—the four ashramas came to be regarded as the four ideals of the Brahmanical ethic, to be realised by *each* individual, where the ascetic life mode became an institution of old age (see Olivelle 1993, 131–60).

12 In fact, in the Dharmasutras, a distinction was made between *brahmacharin* (student) and *brahmacharya* (studentship), whereby the former was a temporary period of study for all adolescent boys, whereas the latter was an ashrama chosen for life. Therefore, it was even possible, according to the *Apastambha Dharmasutra*, to choose the student ashrama and remain a student for life (Olivelle 1993, 78).

13 [Ibid Chapter VII verses 1, 2, 3.] Ambedkar probably means that he's using Bühler's 1882 translation of the *Vasishtha Dharmasutra*. Both this and his translation of the *Manusmriti* were part of the SBE series.

Gautama Dharmasutra[14] says:

> Some (declare, that) he (who has studied the Veda) *may make his choice* (which) among the orders (he is going to enter.).
>
> The four orders are, (that of) the student (that of) the householder, (that) of the ascetic (*bhikshu*) (and that of) the hermit in the woods (*vaikhanasa*).

It is obvious from the views expressed by the Dharmasutras that there was a time when the married state was an optional state.[15] After Brahmacharya, one would straight enter the stage of Vanaprastha or Sannyasa. Why did Manu remove the option and make the married state an obligatory state,[16] why did he

---

14 [Ibid Chapter III verses 1 and 2.] From Bühler 1879, 190.

15 The Dharmasutras—*Apastambha, Gautama, Baudhayana, Vasishtha*—are dated from around 600 to 100 BCE (Olivelle 1999, xxxii). Though there is some debate about the date of the *Manusmriti*'s composition, it was probably around the second or third century CE (Olivelle 2005, 24–5).

16 Manu is exceedingly hostile to the very concept of 'renunciation' (Sannyasa). Firstly, Manu not only assigns it the fourth stage, he makes it virtually impossible for anyone to embrace it; secondly, in contradistinction to the democratic impulse organic to the Sramanic concept of the 'wanderer' or *parivrajaka*, Manu reserves the right for renunciation to the twice-born. "After he has lived in the householder's stage of life in accordance with rules ... a twice-born Vedic graduate should live in the forest ..." (6.1); "When a householder sees that that he is wrinkled and grey, and when he sees the children of his children, then he should take himself to the wilderness" (6.2); "Taking to the wilderness' means, the householder enters the third stage of life, the *vanaprastha*. The 'forest-dweller' or the *vanaprasthi* is entitled to take his wife along with him" (6.3). Only after spending the third part of his lifespan in accordance to the ordinances outlined in verses 6.5–32, (and provided he survives the ordeal), is the 'forest-dweller' allowed to move on to the fourth stage and take on the role of the 'renouncer'. Manu's depiction of his preferred 'renouncer' both departs from and mimics the picture of the Sramanic *parivrajaka*. Says Manu in verse 6.52: "With his hair, nails, and beard trimmed, carrying a bowl, a staff, and a water pot, he should wander constantly..." It is quite apparent that Manu takes far too many precautions to ensure that the renouncer or the Sannyasi is no better than an ineffectual doddering old man. Kautilya too shows remarkable hostility towards 'renunciation': "No man shall renounce his marital life to become an ascetic without providing for his wife and sons ... A man, who has passed the age of sexual activity can renounce family life, with the approval of judges, but if the judges do not approve, he shall be prevented from doing so" (Rangarajan 1992, 405). In addition, Kautilya forbids ascetics belonging to heretical sects (those other than Brahman *vanaprasthis*) to enter the country for the purpose of settlement (2.1.32 in Rangarajan 1992, 180). Technically, a Shudra is he who is simultaneously *included*

make the married state a condition precedent to the stage of hermit and the stage of hermit a condition precedent to the stage of a Sannyasa?[17]

After Grahasthashrama, there remain two stages to complete the round of life—Vanaprastha and Sannyasa. The question is why did Manu feel the necessity of dividing the life of the individual after Grahasthashrama into two stages? Why was the one stage of Sannyasa not enough?[18] The rules of regulating the life of the Vanaprastha and the Sannyasi as laid down in Manu are so alike that they give some point to the question.[19]

...

Comparing the Vanaprastha with Sannyasa and Grahasthashrama with Vanaprastha, one sees some very striking

---

in the varna system and *excluded* from the ashrama system. In Manu 1.91: "The Lord assigned only one activity to a servant [sudra]: serving these (other) classes [varnas] without resentment." Again, the proper dwija/twice-born renouncer is someone who has forfeited the right to be a member of a householder-centric community. Many scholars have argued that the double move of (grudging) incorporation of Sannyasa in the ashrama system and its domestication by allocating to it the fourth stage by *samuchhaivadis* like Manu was intended to blunt the political threat posed by the Sramanas (see Winternitz 1972, 232–3; T.W. Rhys Davids 2007, 216; Doniger and Smith 1991, xxxiv–v; Thapar 1978, 65). By placing his entire premium on the figure of the renouncer, the anti-Vedic, anti-Brahman Sramana—to borrow from Engels—had hit out at the very foundations of family, private property and the state. To counter this threat, the wily Brahmans were compelled to usher in a second wave of Brahmanism. It was during this wave that the Brahman began to pay lip-service to ahimsa and Sannyasa and took to cow-worshipping and vegetarianism. (The annotators owe this note to Sibaji Bandyopadhyay.)

17 The original meaning of the term 'ashrama' referred to the life of a Brahman who epitomized Vedic religious living (Olivelle 1993, 35). Importantly, the ideal and typical religious life within Vedic ideology was that of a married householder.

18 Olivelle echoes Ambedkar in this: "The anomaly of having two *asramas* relating to old age and the centrality of the ideal of liberation *(moksa)* with which renunciation was closely connected may have contributed to the third *asrama's* eventually becoming obsolete" (1993, 132).

19 To reinforce his point, Ambedkar here provides a very long table running to over six pages, derived from chapter 4 of Bühler's *Manusmriti,* that juxtaposes Manu's injunctions and prescriptions for the two ashramas: Vanaprastha (verses 3 to 29) and Sannyasa (verses 38 to 60 and 80 to 85). See the original in BAWS Vol 4, 1987a, 208–13.

resemblances between them. Comparing Vanaprastha with Sannyasa , there are only a few differences in the modes of life prescribed for them. Firstly a Vanaprastha does not abandon his wife or his rights over his property. But a Sannyasi must abandon both. Secondly, a Vanaprastha can have a fixed dwelling although it must be in a forest. But a Sannyasi cannot have a fixed dwelling, not even in a forest. He must keep on wandering from place to place. Thirdly, a Sannyasi is debarred from expounding the Shastras while the Vanaprastha is not expressly placed under such a disability. As for the rest, their mode of life is identical.

The resemblance between Grahasthashrama and Vanaprastha is also very close. The Vanaprasthi is a Grahasthashrami for all essential purposes. Like the Grahasthashrami, he continues to be a married man. Like the Grahasthashrami, he continues to be the owner of his property. Like the Grahasthashrami, he does not renounce the world and like the Grahasthashrami, he follows the Vedic religion. The only points of difference between the Vanaprasthi and the Grahasthashrami are three: (1) the Grahasthashrami is not bound to observe abstinence in his food and clothing to which a Vanaprasthi is subject; (2) the Grahasthashrami dwells in the midst of society while the Vanaprasthi is required to live in a forest; (3) the Vanaprasthi is free to study the Vedanta while the Grahasthashrami is confined to the study of the Vedas. As for the rest, their modes of life are identical.

With regard to these close resemblances between Grahasthashrama and Vanaprastha, and between Vanaprastha and Sannyasa , it is difficult to understand why Manu recognized this third ashrama of Vanaprastha in between Grahasthashrama and Sannyasa, as an ashrama distinct and separate from both. As a matter of fact, there could be only three ashramas: (1) Bramhacharya, (2) Grahasthashrama and (3) Sannyasa. This seems to be also the view of Shankaracharya, who in his *Brahma*

Sutra,[20] in defending the validity of Sannyasa against the Purva Mimamsa School, speaks only of three ashramas.[21]

Where did Manu get this idea of Vanaprastha ashrama? What is his source? As has been pointed out above, Grahasthashrama was not the next compulsory stage of life after Brahmacharya. A Brahmachari may at once become Sannyasi without entering the stage of Grahasthashrama. But there was also another line of life which a Brahmachari, who did not wish to marry immediately, could adopt, namely to become Aranas or Aranamanas.[22] They were Brahmacharis who wished to continue the life of study without marrying. These Aranas lived in hermitages in forests outside the villages or centres of population. The forests where these Arana ascetics lived were called Aranyas and the philosophical works of these Aranas were called Aranyakas. It is obvious that Manu's Vanaprastha is the original Arana with two differences: (1) he has compelled Arana to enter the marital state and (2) the Arana stage, instead of being the second stage, is prescribed as the third stage. The whole scheme of Manu rests on the principle that marriage is compulsory. A Brahmachari, if he wishes to become a Sannyasi, must become a Vanaprastha

---

20 In his commentary Swami Sivananda (1949/2009, 454), when referring to verse III.4.32, mentions only three ashramas: "The present Sutra declares that since these duties are en joined on all who are in these Asramas or orders of life, viz., student-life, householder's life, and hermit life, one should observe them."

21 The *Brahma Sutra* was composed by Badarayana around the turn of the first millennium and is one of the foundational texts of the Vedanta school of philosophy, attempting to systematise various strands of the Upanishads (Radhakrishnan 1960, 21). Of the several surviving commentaries of the *Brahma Sutra*, the one by Sankara is considered the earliest, dating to the ninth century CE. For a complete translation of the *Brahma Sutra* with Sankara's commentary, see Thibaut 1890 & 1896. There are other instances as well in Sanskrit texts in which the third ashrama was skipped; see Olivelle 1993, 173.

22 [Radha Kumud Mookerjee—Ancient India Education p. 6.] Radha Kumud Mookerji (1884–1964) was an Indian historian. In his 1947 work *Ancient Indian Education: Brahmanical and Buddhist*, he writes about the Aranas, from where Ambedkar is paraphrasing.

and if he wishes to become a Vanaprastha, must become a Grasthashrami, i.e., he must marry. Manu made escape from marriage impossible. Why?[23]

23 In fact, Olivelle has argued that it is simply not possible to reduce the variety of modes of asceticism that then existed to just the two in the ashrama system (1993, 25).

Riddle No. 18

Manu's Madness or the Brahmanic Explanation of the Origin of the Mixed Castes[1]

A reader of the *Manusmriti* will find that Manu, for the purpose of his discussion, groups the various castes under certain specific heads namely (1) Aryan castes, (2) Non-Aryan castes, (3) Vratya castes, (4) Fallen castes and (5) Samkara castes.

By Aryan castes he means the four varnas, namely Brahman, Kshatriya, Vaishya and Shudra. In other words, Manu regards the system of *chaturvarna* to be the essence of Aryanism. By Non-Aryan castes he means those communities who do not accept the creed of *chaturvarna* and he cites the community called Dasyu as an illustration of those whom he regards as a Non-Aryan community.[2] By Vratyas he means those castes who were once believers in the *chaturvarna* but who had rebelled against it.

The list of Vratyas given by Manu includes the following castes:

1 The BAWS editors write: "This is about 20-page MS on the 'origin of the mixed castes'. Through the original typed MS several handwritten pages are inserted by the author and the text has been modified with several amendments pasted on the pages."

2 [Manu X. 45 This verse is significant for two reasons. Firstly, it shows Shudra as different from Dasyu. Secondly, it shows that a Shudra is an Arya.]

Vratya Brahmanas	*Vratya Kshatriyas*	*Vratya Vaishyas*
1. Bhrigga Kantaka	1. Jhalla	1. Sudhanvana
2. Avantya	2. Malla	2. Acharya
3. Vatadhana	3. Lacchavi	3. Karusha
4. Phushpada	4. Nata	4. Vijanman
5. Saikha	5. Karana	5. Maitra
	6. Khasa	6. Satvata
	7. Dravida	

In the list of "fallen castes", Manu includes those Kshatriyas who have become Shudras by reason of the disuse of Aryan rites and ceremonies and loss of services of the Brahman priests. They are enumerated by Manu as under:

1. Paundrakas
2. Cholas
3. Dravidas
4. Kambhojas
5. Yavanas
6. Sakas
7. Paradas
8. Pahlvas
9. Chinas
10. Kiratas
11. Daradas

By Samkara castes, Manu means castes the members of which are born of parents who do not belong to the same caste.

These mixed castes he divides into various categories (1) Progeny of different Aryan castes which he subdivides into two classes (a) *anuloma* and (b) *pratiloma*,[3] (2) Progeny of *anuloma* and

3 Endogamy is a preferred or prescribed practice of marrying within the defined kin-group, be it clan, lineage, village or social class. In the Hindu Brahmanical order, while marriage within the sub-caste is a rule, families and larger groups may negotiate a higher status for themselves by marrying their daughters 'upward' in the caste hierarchy. This practice is termed as hypergamy or *anuloma* system of

pratiloma castes and (3) Progeny of Non-Aryan and the Aryan *anuloma* and *pratiloma* castes.[4] Those included by Manu under the head of mixed castes are shown below under different categories:

PROGENY OF MIXED ARYAN CASTES

Father	*Mother*	*Progeny known as*	*Anuloma or Pratiloma*
Brahman	Kshatriya	?	
Brahman	Vaishya	Ambashta	Anuloma
Brahman	Shudra	Nishad (Parasava)	Anuloma
Kshatriya	Brahman	Suta	Pratiloma
Kshatriya	Vaishya	?	
Kshatriya	Brahman	Ugra	Anuloma
Vaishya	Brahman	Vaidehaka	Pratiloma
Vaishya	Kshatriya	Magadha	Pratiloma
Vaishya	Shudra	Karana	Anuloma
Shudra	Brahman	Chandala	Pratiloma
Shudra	Kshatriya	Ksattri	Pratiloma
Shudra	Vaishya	Ayogava	Pratiloma

marriage. It stands in contrast with hypogamy or *pratiloma* system of marriage, which is stigmatised because the bride's family is of superior status to that of the groom's. See Patricia Uberoi 1993, 230–1. Uma Chakravarti has described the development of these two forms of marriage as *Varnasamkara*, or the theory of mixed unions, which is based on hierarchical arrangement of a few 'base categories' that generate new categories through violation of preferred endogamous categories. Hybrid reproduction such as this, which is a consequence of the violation of endogamy, enabled varnas to become jatis and led to the development of the caste system. The caste system was thus organised by linking together reproduction, production, occupational specialization, and distinctive cultural and ritual practices. For hybrid reproduction and the development of the caste system, see Chakravarti 2003, 53–4.

4 The Brahmanical calculus of hatred looks down upon both hypergamy and hypogamy as against marriage between men and women belonging to the same rank. Obviously, even if hypergamy is partly condoned, hypogamy finds no saving grace. The offspring of hypogamous unions are especially despised, in direct proportion to the disparity between the ranks of the parents. Hence, the Chandala, said to be the offspring of a Shudra by a Brahman woman, is the lowest Untouchable.

Progeny of Aryan Castes with Anuloma–Pratiloma Castes

Father	Mother	Progeny known as
1. Brahman	Ugra	Avrita
2. Brahman	Ambashta	Abhira
3. Brahman	Abhira	Dhigvana
4. Shudra	Nishada	Kukutaka

Progeny of Mixed Marriages between Anuloma and Pratiloma Castes

Father	Mother	Progeny known as
1. Vaideha	Ayogava	Maitreyaka
2. Nishada	Ayogava	Margava (Das) Kaivarta
3. Nishada	Vaideha	Karavara
4. Vaidehaka	Ambashta	Vena
5. Vaidehaka	Karavara	Andhra
6. Vaidehaka	Nishada	Meda
7. Chandala	Vaideha	Pandusopaka
8. Nishada	Vaideha	Ahindaka
9. Chandala	Pukkassa	Sopaka
10. Chandala	Nishada	Antyavasin
11. Kshattari	Ugra	Swapaka

To Manu's list of Samkara (mixed) castes, additions have been made by his successors. Among these are the authors of *Usanasmriti*, *Baudhayanasmriti*, *Vasishthasmriti*,[5] *Yajnavalkyasmriti* and the *Suta Samhita*.[6]

5 These three are technically Dharmasutras, not *smritis*.

6 The following texts deal with the issues of mixes castes: *Gautama Dharmasutra*, *Baudhayana Dharmasutra*, *Vasishtha Dharmasutra*, *Vishnusmriti*, *Manusmriti*, *Yajnavalkyasmriti* and the *Arthashastra* (see Rocher 2012, 255–65). *Apastambha* is the only one of the Dharmasutras to not mention mixed castes.

Of these additions four have been made by the *Usanasmriti*. They are noted below:

Name of the mixed caste	*Father's caste*	*Mother's caste*
1. Pulaksa	Shudra	Kshatriya
2. Yekaj	Pulaksa	Vaishya
3. Charmakarka	Ayogava	Brahman
4. Venuka	Suta	Brahman

The following four are added by the *Baudhayanasmriti*:[7]

Name of the mixed caste	*Father's caste*	*Mother's caste*
1. Kshatriya	Kshatriya	Vaishya
2. Brahman	Brahman	Kshatriya
3. Vaina	Vaidehaka	Ambashta
4. Shvapaka	Ugra	Kshatriya

The *Vasishthasmriti*[8] adds one to the list of Manu, namely:

Name of the mixed caste	*Father's caste*	*Mother's caste*
Vaina	Shudra	Kshatriya

The *Yajnavalkyasmriti*[9] adds two new castes to Manu's list:

Name of the mixed caste	*Father's caste*	*Mother's caste*
1. Murdhavasika	Brahman	Kshatriya
2. Mahisya	Kshatriya	Vaishya

7 See 1.9.17 of the *Baudhayana Dharmasutra* in Bühler 1882, 197–8.

8 Mixed castes are discussed in Chapter 18 of the *Vasishtha Dharmasutra*. See Bühler 1882, 94–6.

9 The *Yajnavalkyasmriti* is one of the major Dharmasastric texts, hailed by Lingat (1973, 98) as "assuredly the best composed and appears to be the most homogeneous". In contrast to the *Manusmriti*, the tone of the *Yajnavalkyasmriti* is far more sober and concise.

The additions made by the author of the *Suta Samhita*[10] are on a vast scale. They number sixty-three castes.

Name of the mixed caste	*Father's caste*	*Mother's caste*
1. Ambashteya	Kshatriya	Vaishya
2. Urdhvanapita	Brahman	Vaishya
3. Katkar	Vaishya	Shudra
4. Kumbhkar	Brahman	Vaishya
5. Kunda	Brahman	Married Brahman
6. Golaka	Brahman	Brahman Widow
7. Chakri	Shudra	Vaishya
8. Daushanti	Kshatriya	Shudra
9. Daushantya	Kshatriya	Shudra
10. Pattanshali	Shudra	Brahman
11. Pulinda	Vaishya	Kshatriya
12. Bahyadas	Shudra	Brahman
13. Bhoja	Vaishya	Kshatriya
14. Mahikar	Vaishya	Vaishya
15. Manavika	Shudra	Shudra
16. Mleccha	Vaishya	Kshatriya
17. Shalika	Vaishya	Kshatriya
18. Shundika	Brahman	Shudra
19. Shulikha	Kshatriya	Shudra
20. Saparna	Brahman	Kshatriya
21. Agneyanartaka	Ambashta	Ambashta
22. Apitar	Brahman	Daushanti
23. Ashramaka	Dantakevala	Shudra
24. Udabandha	Sanaka	Kshatriya
25. Karana	Nata	Kshatriya
26. Karma	Karana	Kshatriya
27. Karmakar	Renuka	Kshatriya
28. Karmar	Mahishya	Karana

10 The *Suta Samhita* is the second of six parts of the *Skanda Purana*, the largest of the major Puranic texts. See Rocher 1986, 228. Rocher discusses the Samhita division of the texts, but doesn't discuss mixed castes for this Samhita.

Name of the mixed caste	*Father's caste*	*Mother's caste*
29. Kukkunda	Magadha	Shudra
30. Guhaka	Swapach	Brahman
31. Charmopajivan	Vaidehaka	Brahman
32. Chamakar	Ayogava	Brahmani
33. Charmajivi	Nishad	Karushi
34. Taksha	Mahishya	Karana
35. Takshavriti	Ugra	Brahman
36. Dantakavelaka	Chandala	Vaishya
37. Dasyu	Nishad	Ayogava
38. Drumila	Nishad	Kshatriya
39. Nata	Picchalla	Kshatriya
40. Napita	Nishad	Kshatriya
41. Niladivarnavikreta	Ayogava	Chirkari
42. Piccahalla	Malla	Kshatriya
43. Pingala	Brahman	Ayogava
44. Bhaglabdha	Daushanta	Brahmani
45. Bharusha	Sudhanva	Vaishya
46. Bhairava	Nishada	Shudra
47. Matanga	Vijanma	Vaishya
48. Madhuka	Vaidehaka	Ayogava
49. Matakar	Dasyu	Vaishya
50. Maitra	Vijanma	Vaishya
51. Rajaka	Vaideha	Brahman
52. Rathakar	Mahishya	Karana
53. Renuka	Napita	Brahman
54. Lohakar	Mahishya	Brahmani
55. Vardhaki	Mahishya	Brahmani
56. Varya	Sudhanva	Vaishya
57. Vijanma	Bharusha	Vaishya
58. Shilp	Mahishya	Karana
59. Shvapach	Chandala	Brahmani
60. Sanaka	Magadha	Kshatriya
61. Samudra	Takashavrati	Vaishya
62. Satvata	Vijanma	Vaishya
63. Sunishada	Nishad	Vaishya

Of the five categories of castes it is easy to understand the explanation given by Manu as regards the first four. But the same cannot be said in respect of his treatment of the fifth category, namely the Samkara (mixed) caste. There are various questions that begin to trouble the mind. In the first place Manu's list of mixed castes is a perfunctory list. It is not an exhaustive list, stating all the possibilities of Samkara.

In discussing the mixed castes born out of the mixture of the Aryan castes with the *anuloma–pratiloma* castes, Manu should have specified the names of castes which are the progeny of each of the four Aryan castes with each of the twelve *anuloma–pratiloma* castes. If he had done so we should have had a list of forty-eight resulting castes. As a matter of fact he states only the names of four castes of mixed marriages of this category.

In discussing the progeny of mixed marriages between *anuloma–pratiloma* castes, given the fact that we have twelve of them, Manu should have give the names of 144 resulting castes. As a matter of fact, Manu only gives a list of eleven castes. In the information of these eleven castes, Manu gives five possible combinations of five castes only. Of these, one (Vaideha) is outside the *anuloma–pratiloma* list. The cases of the eight are not considered at all.

His account of the Samkara castes born out the Non-Aryan and the Aryan castes is equally discrepant. We ought to have had first a list of castes resulting from a combination between the Non-Aryans with each of the four Aryan castes. We have none of them. Assuming that there was only one Non-Aryan caste—Dasyu—we ought to have had a list of twelve castes resulting from a conjugation of Dasyus with each of the *anuloma–pratiloma* castes. As a matter of fact we have in Manu only one conjugation.

In the discussion of this subject of mixed castes, Manu does not consider the conjugation between the Vratyas and the Aryan castes, the Vratyas and the *anuloma–pratiloma* castes, the Vratyas and the Non-Aryan castes.

Among these omissions by Manu there are some that are glaring as well as significant. Take the case of Samkara between Brahmans and Kshatriyas. He does not mention the caste born out of the Samkara between these two. Nor does he mention whether the Samkara caste begotten of these two was a *pratiloma* or *anuloma*. Why did Manu fail to deal with this question? Is it to be supposed that such a Samkara did not occur in his time? Or was he afraid to mention it? If so, of whom was he afraid?

Some of the names of the mixed castes mentioned by Manu and the other Smritikaras appear to be quite fictitious. For some of the communities mentioned as being of bastard origin have never been heard of before Manu. Nor does anyone know what has happened to them since. They are today non-existent without leaving any trace behind. Caste is an insoluble substance and once a caste is formed it maintains its separate existence, unless for any special reason it dies out. This can happen but to a few.

Who are the Ayogava, Dhigvana, Ugra, Pukkasa, Svapaka, Svapacha, Pandusopaka, Ahindaka, Bandika, Matta, Mahikar, Shalika, Shundika, Shulika Yekaj, Kukunda, to mention only a few? Where are they? What has happened to them?

Let us now proceed to compare Manu with the rest of Smritikaras. Are they unanimous on the origin of the various mixed castes referred to by them? Far from it. Compare the following cases.

Smriti	*Father's caste*	*Mother's caste*
	I. Ayogava	
1. Manu	Shudra	Vaishya
2. Aushanas	Vaishya	Kshatriya
3. Yajnavalkya	Shudra	Vaishya
4. Baudhayana	Vaishya	Kshatriya
5. Agni Purana	Shudra	Kshatriya

Smriti	*Father's caste*	*Mother's caste*
	II. Ugra	
1. Manu	Kshatriya	Shudra
2. Aushanas	Brahman	Shudra
3. Yajnavalkya	Kshatriya	Vaishya
4. Vasshtha	Kshatriya	Vaishya
5. Suta	Vaishya	Shudra
	III. Nishada	
1. Manu	Brahman	Shudra
2. Aushanas	Brahman	Shudra
3. Baudhayana	Brahman	Shudra
4. Yajnavalkya	Brahman	Shudra
5. Suta Samhita	Brahman	Vaishya
6. Suta Samhita	Brahman	Shudra
7. Vasishtha	Vaishya	Shudra
	IV. Pukkasa	
1. Manu	Nishada	Shudra
2. Brihad-Vishnu	Shudra	Kshatriya
3. Brihad-Vishnu	Vaishya	Kshatriya
	V. Magadha	
1. Manu	Vaishya	Kshatriya
2. Suta	Vaishya	Kshatriya
3. Baudhayana	Shudra	Vaishya
4. Yajnavalkya	Vaishya	Kshatriya
5. Brihad-Vishnu	Vaishya	Kshatriya
6. Brihad-Vishnu	Shudra	Kshatriya
7. Brihad-Vishnu	Vaishya	Brahman
	VI. Rathakar	
1. Aushanas	Kshatriya	Brahman
2. Baudhayana	Vaishya	Shudra
3. Suta	Kshatriya	Brahman
	VII. Vaidehaka	
1. Manu	Shudra	Vaishya
2. Manu	Vaishya	Brahman
3. Yajnavalkya	Vaishya	Brahman

If these different Smritikaras are dealing with facts about the origin and genesis of mixed castes mentioned above, how can such a wide difference of opinion can exist among them? The conjugation of two castes can logically produce a third mixed caste. But how does the conjugation of the same two castes produce a number of different castes? But this is exactly what Manu and his followers seem to be asserting. Consider the following cases:

I. Conjugation of Kshatriya father and Vaishya mother—
   1. Baudhayana says that the caste of the progeny is Kshatriya.
   2. Yajnavalkya says it is Mahishya.
   3. Suta says it is Ambashta.

II. Conjugation of Shudra father and Kshatriya mother—
   1. Manu says the progeny is Ksattri.
   2. Aushanas says it is Pullaksa.
   3. Vasishtha says it is Vaina.

III. Conjugation of Brahman father and Vaishya mother—
   1. Manu says that the progeny is called Ambashta.
   2. Suta once says it is called Urdhava Napita but again says it is called Kumbhakar.

IV. Conjugation of Vaishya father and Kshatriya mother—
   1. Manu says that the progeny is called Magadha.
   2. Suta states that (1) Bhoja, (2) Mleccha, (3) Shalik and (4) Pulinda are the progenies of this single conjugation.

V. Conjugation of Kshatriya father and Shudra mother—
   1. Manu says that the progeny is called Ugra.
   2. Suta says that (1) Daushantya, (2) Daushanti and (3) Shulika are the progenies of this single conjugation.

VI. Conjugation of Shudra father and Vaishya mother—
   1. Manu says the progeny is called Ayogava.
   2. Suta says the progeny is (1) Pattanshali and (2) Chakri.

Let us take up another question. Is Manu's explanation of the genesis of the mixed castes historically true?

To begin with the Abhira. According to Manu, the Abhiras are the bastards born of Brahman males and Ambashta females. What does history say about them? History says that the Abhiras (the corrupt form of which is Ahira) were pastoral tribes which inhabited the lower districts of the North-West as far as Sindh.[11] They were a ruling independent tribe and, according to the *Vishnu Purana*,[12] the Abhiras conquered Magadha and reigned there for several years.

The Ambashta,[13] says Manu, are the bastards born of Brahman male and Vaishya female. Patanjali speaks of Ambashtas as those who are the natives of a country called Ambashta. That the Ambashtas were an independent tribe is beyond dispute. The Ambashtas are mentioned by Megasthenes, the Greek ambassador at the court of Chandragupta Maurya,[14] as one of the tribes living in the Punjab who fought against Alexander when he invaded India. The Ambashtas are mentioned in the *Mahabharata*. They were reputed for their political system and for their bravery.

The Andhras,[15] says Manu, are bastards of second degree in

---

11 The Abhira, says Thapar (1978, 189n100), are nomadic herdsmen believed to have migrated with the Scythians/Sakas, and located in the lower Indus and Kathiawar region.

12 [Book IV Chapter 24.] See Wilson 1864–68, Vol 4, 201ff.

13 [For Ambashtas, see Jaiswal's (sic) *Hindu Polity–Part 1*, 73–4.] Ambedkar is drawing on the work of historian Kashi Prasad Jayaswal (1881–1937) known for his two-part *Hindu Polity: A Constitutional History of India in Hindu Times* (1918).

14 Megasthenes was a Greek ethnographer in the fourth century BCE, whose work *Indica* was one of the foremost writings on India in the ancient western world. Though the original book is lost, it survives as fragments in later Greek and Latin texts. He visited Pataliputra during the rule of Chandragupta Maurya, c. 340–297 BCE (Bosworth 1996, 113).

15 [For the Andhras, see *Early Dynasties of Andhradesa* by Bhavaraju Venkata Krishnarao. They are also called Satavahanas.] The full title of this book is *A History of the Early Dynasties of Andhradesa, c. 200–625 A.D.* (Krishnarao 1942).

so far as they are the progeny of Vaidehaka male and Karavara female, both of which belong to bastard castes. The testimony of history is quite different. The Andhras are a people who inhabited that part of the country which forms the eastern part of the Deccan Plateau. The Andhras are mentioned by Megasthenes. Pliny the Elder (77 A.D.)[16] refers to them as a powerful tribe enjoying paramount sway over their land in the Deccan, possessing numerous villages, thirty walled towns defended by moats and levers, and supplying their king with an immense army consisting of 1,00,000 infantry, 2,000 cavalry and 1,000 elephants.

According to Manu, the Magadhas[17] are bastards born of Vaishya male and Kshatriya female. Panini the grammarian gives quite a different derivation of 'Magadha'. According to him 'Magadha' means a person who comes from the country known as Magadha. Magadha corresponds roughly to the present Patna and Gaya districts of Bihar. The Magadhas have been mentioned as independent sovereign people right from the earliest times. They are first mentioned in the *Atharva Veda*. The famous Jarasandha was the king of Magadha, who was a contemporary of the Pandavas.

According to Manu, the Nishadas are the bastard caste born of Brahman males and Shudra females. History has quite a different tale to tell. The Nishadas were a native tribe with its own independent territory and its own kings. The *Ramayana* mentions Guha as the king of Nishadas, whose capital was Sringaverapura and who showed hospitality to Rama when he was undergoing exile in the forest.

As to the Vaidehaka, Manu says that they are the bastards

16 Gaius Plinuis Secundus (Pliny) was a Roman author in the first century CE whose *Historia Naturalis* became a model for all other encyclopedias.

17 [For the History of Magadha see Chapter IV *Ancient Indian Tribes* by B.C. Law.] Bimla Churn Law work was published in 1926 in Issue 12, Punjab Oriental Series.

born of Vaishya male and Brahman female. Etymologically Vaidehaka means a person who is a native of the country called Videha.[18] Ancient Videha corresponds to the modern districts of Champaran and Darbhanga in Bihar. The country and its people have been known to history from a very remote antiquity. The *Yajur Veda* mentions them. The *Ramayana* refers to them. Sita, the wife of Rama, is the daughter of Janaka, who was the king of Videha and whose capital was Mithila.

Many more cases could be examined. Those that have been are quite sufficient to show how Manu has perverted history and defamed the most respectable and powerful tribes into bastards. This wholesale bastardisation of huge communities by Manu did not apply to the Vratyas. But his successors carried the scheme further and bastardised the Vratyas also. Karna in Manu is Vratya. But the *Brahmavaivarta Purana*[19] makes them bastards and says that they are the progeny of a Vaishya father and Shudra mother. Paundraka in Manu is Vratya. But in the *Brahmavaivarta Purana*, he is a bastard born of a Vaishya father and a Chundi mother. Malla in Manu is Vartya. But in the *Brahmavaivarta Purana*, he is a bastard born of a Letta father and a Tibara mother. The Vharjjakautakas are Vratya Brahmans, according to Manu. But in the *Gautama Samhita*,[20] they are bastards born from a Brahman father and a Vaishya mother. The Yavanas were declared by Manu as Vratya Kshatriya. But in the *Gautama Samhita*, they are shown as bastards born of a Kshatriya father and a Shudra mother.

The Kiratas are, according to Manu, Vratya Kshatriya. But

18 [For the History of the Videha, see part II, Chapter 1 of *Kshatriya Clans in Buddhist India* by B.C. Law.] Law's *Kshatriya Clans in Buddhist India* was first published in 1922 and has been reissued (2005).

19 One of the eighteen major Puranic texts, the *Brahmavaivarta Purana* is considered one of the more recent Puranas, dating as late as the fifteenth–sixteenth centuries CE. It is said to be a work composed in Bengal (Rocher 1986, 163).

20 Ambedkar is referring to the *Gautama Dharmasutra*.

the *Ballalacharitta* makes them bastards born from a Vaishya father and a Brahman mother.[21]

It is quite clear that some of the communities mentioned by Manu as being bastard in origin—far from being bastard—were independent in origin, and yet Manu and the rest of the Smritikaras call them bastards. Why this madness on their part? Is there a method in their madness?

Having regard to all these considerations, it is a riddle why Manu raised the question of mixed castes at all and what he wanted to say about them. It is possible that Manu had realised that *chaturvarna* had failed and that the existence of a large number of castes—which could neither be described as Brahmans, Kshatriyas, Vaishyas or Shudras—was the best proof of the breakdown of the *chaturvarna* and that he was therefore called upon to explain how these castes who were outside the *chaturvarna* came into existence notwithstanding the rule of *chaturvarna*.

But did Manu realise how terrible the explanation he has given is? What does his explanation amount to?

What a reflection on the character of men and particularly of women! It is obvious that the unions of men and women must have been clandestine because [they are] prohibited by the rule of *chaturvarna*. Such clandestine unions could take place only here and there. They could not have taken place on a wholesale scale. But unless one assumes a wholesale state of promiscuity, how can one justify the origin of the Chandalas or Untouchables

---

21 According to the *Puranic Encyclopedia* (Mani 1975, 106), Ballala was the "son of a Vaisya named Kalyana. From childhood Ballala was an ardent devotee of Ganapati. When he was a child he used to gather pebbles and make a heap and then worship it, imagining it to be Ganesa (Ganapati). His parents did not like this. They tried their best to dissuade him from this habit. Once they tied him to a tree and gave him severe cuts. But their attempts were futile. One day an image of Ganapati arose in the place where the child used to worship. (Ganesa Purana 1: 2)." Sen (1942, 456) refers to "Anandabhatta's *Ballalacharita* written in the 16th century". The work is believed to be a history of King Ballalasena.

as given by Manu?

The caste of Chandala is said by Manu to be the progeny of illegitimate intercourse between a Shudra male and a Brahman female. Can this be true? It means that Brahman women must have been very lax in their morality and must have had special sexual attraction for the Shudra.[22] This is unbelievable.

So vast is the Chandala population that even if every Brahman female was a mistress of a Shudra, it could not account for the vast number of Chandalas in the country.

Did Manu realise that by propounding his theory of the origin of the mixed castes, he was assigning an ignoble origin to a vast number of the people of this country leading to their social and moral degradation? Why did he say that the castes were mixed in origin, when as a matter of fact they were independent in their existence?

---

22 [Megasthenes records that ancient Brahmans distrusted their wives and withheld metaphysical doctrine from women on the grounds that their 'natural' tendency to gossip would divulge rare knowledge to those who had no right to it, which probably refers to Shudras.] Ambedkar is citing Megasthenes via Max Müller who says: "Indians did not communicate their metaphysical doctrine to women; thinking that, if their wives understood these doctrines, and learned to be indifferent to pleasure and pain, and to consider life and death as the same, they would no longer continue to be slaves of others: or, if they failed to understand them, they would be talkative, and communicate their knowledge to those who had no right to it. This statement of the Greek author is fully borne out by the later Sanskrit authorities" (Müller 1859, 27).

Riddle no. 19

The Change from Paternity to Maternity: What did the Brahmans Wish to Gain by it?[1]

Mr Mayne,[2] in his treatise on Hindu law, has pointed out some anomalous features of the rules of kinships. He says:

> No part of the Hindu law is more anomalous than that which governs the family relations. Not only does there appear to be a complete break of continuity between the ancient system and that which now prevails, but the different parts of the ancient system appear in this respect to be in direct conflict with each other. We find a law of inheritance, which assumes the possibility of tracing male ancestors in an unbroken pedigree extending to fourteen generations; while, coupled with it, is a family law, in which several admitted forms of marriage are only euphemisms for seduction and rape, and in which twelve sorts of sons are recognised, the majority of whom have no blood relationship to their own father.[3]

The existence of this anomaly is a fact and will be quite clear to those who care to study the Hindu law of marriage and paternity.

---

1 The BAWS editors write: "This is an eleven-page chapter. Except the title of the chapter no other additions are found in the handwriting of the author."

2 John Dawson Mayne (1828–1917) was a British legal expert who practised law in the Madras Presidency before teaching law in England. He is best known as the author of the *Treatise on Hindu Law and Usage* (1878) that is widely sourced even today. The latest edition of the *Treatise* was published in 2008 with exhaustive commentary and case laws.

3 Mayne 1878, 49.

Hindu law recognises eight different forms of marriage, namely (1) *Brahma*, (2) *Daiva*, (3) *Arsha*, (4) *Prajapatya*, (5) *Asura*, (6) *Gandharva*, (7) *Rakshasa* and (8) *Paisacha*.[4]

The *Daiva* marriage consists of the giving of the daughter by father to the family priest attending a sacrifice at the time of the payment of the sacrificial fee and in lieu of it.

Arsha marriage is characterised by the fact that the bridegroom has to pay a price for the bride to the father of the bride.

The *Prajapatya* form of marriage is marked by the application of a man for a girl to be his wife and the granting of the application by the father of the girl. The difference between *Prajapatya* and *Brahma* marriage lies in the fact that in the latter, the gift of the daughter is made by the father voluntarily and does not have to be applied for. The fifth or the *Asura* form of marriage is that in which the bridegroom, having given as much wealth as he can afford to the father and paternal kinsmen, and to the girl herself, takes her as his wife. There is not much difference between *Arsha* and *Asura* forms of marriage. Both involve sale of the bride. The difference lies in this that in the *Arsha* form the price is fixed while in the *Asura* form it is not.

Gandharva marriage is a marriage by consent contracted from non-religious and sensual motives. Marriage by seizure of a maiden by force from her house while she weeps and calls for assistance after her kinsmen and friends have been slain in battle or wounded and their houses broken open, is the marriage styled *Rakshasa*.

Paisacha marriage is marriage by rape on a girl, either when she is asleep or flushed with strong liquor or disordered in her intellect.

4 The major distinguishing factors between these types of marriages, says Stephanie Jamison, are "the occasion and circumstances under which the bride comes into the groom's possession" (Jamison 1996, 210–11).

Hindu law recognised thirteen kinds of sons (1) *Aurasa*, (2) *Kshetraja*, (3) *Putrikaputra*, (4) *Kanina*, (5) *Gudhaja*, (6) *Punarbhava*, (7) *Sahodhaja*, (8) *Dattaka*, (9) *Kritrima*, (10) *Kritaka*, (11) *Apaviddha*, (12) *Svayamdatta* and (13) *Nishada*.

The *Aurasa* is a son begotten by a man himself upon his lawfully wedded wife.

Putrikaputra means a son born to a daughter. Its significance lies in the system under which a man who had a daughter but no son, could also have his daughter cohabit with a man selected or appointed by him. If a daughter gave birth to a son by such sexual intercourse, the son was called *Putrikaputra*. A man's right to compel his daughter to submit to sexual intercourse with a man of his choice in order to get a son for himself continued to exist even after the daughter was married. That is why a man was warned not to marry a girl who had no brothers.

Kshetraja literally means son of the field i.e., of the wife. In Hindu ideology the wife is likened to the field[5] and the husband is likened to the master of the field. Where the husband was dead, or alive but impotent, or incurably diseased, the brother or any other *sapinda* of the deceased was appointed by the family to procreate a son on the wife. The practice was called *niyoga* and the son so begotten was called *Keshetraja*.[6]

5 This ideology, however, seems linked to the advent of agriculture almost globally. According to Maria Mies (1986, 57) women in South Asia are seen as earth, field, furrow (*sita*) upon which men sow. Bina Agarwal's classic (1994) study says that though the plough itself developed from women's digging sticks, the advent of the plough marks the decline of the role of women in agriculture. Agarwal also discusses taboos around women wielding the plough (312–4).

6 The institution of *niyoga*, or levirate unions, finds mention in the *Rig Veda* but by the time of the Dharmashastras, it was made conditional on the absence of a son from the first husband, with the sanction of the family. Despite speaking of the *Kshetraja*, Manu generally condemned the practice, upholding instead perpetual widowhood, which would become the norm (Chakravarti 1995, 2251). See also Roy 1994, 6. An extensive discussion of *niyoga* can be found in Riddle No. 23, see especially 201n65.

If an unmarried daughter living in the house of her father has, through illicit intercourse, given birth to a son and if she subsequently was married, the son was called *Kanina*.

The *Gudhaja* was apparently a son born to a woman while the husband had access to her but it is suspected that he is born of an adulterous connection. As there is no proof by an irrefutable presumption, so to say, the husband is entitled to claim the son as his own. He is called *Gudhaja* because his birth is clouded in suspicion, *Gudha* meaning suspicion.

Sahodhaja is a son born to a woman who was pregnant at the time of her marriage. It is not certain whether he is the son of the husband who had access to the mother before marriage or whether it is the case of a son begotten by a person other than the husband. But it is the certain that the *Sahodhaja* is a son born to a pregnant maiden and claimed as his son by the man who marries her.

Punarbhava is the son of a woman who, abandoned by her husband and having lived with others, re-enters his family. It is also used to denote the son of a woman who leaves an impotent, outcaste, or a mad or diseased husband and takes another husband.

Parasava[7] is the son of a Brahman by his Shudra wife.

The rest of the sons are adopted sons as distinguished for those who were claimed as sons.

Dattaka is the son whom his father and mother give in adoption to another, whose son he then becomes.

Kratrima is a son adopted with the adoptee's consent only.

Kritaka is a son purchased from his parents.

---

7 [*Parasava* was also called *Nishada*. Jimutavahana differentiates between *Parasava* and *Nishada* by stating that *Parasava* is the son of a Brahman by an unmarried Shudra woman while *Nishada* is the son of a Brahman by his Shudra wife.] Jimutavahana was a twelfth-century scholar of religious treatises, most known for *Dayabhaga*, a work on laws of inheritance based on the *Yajnavalkyasmriti*, influential in the Bengal region even in the colonial period (Rocher 2002).

Apaviddha is a boy abandoned by his parents and is then taken in, adopted and reckoned as a son.

Svayamdatta is a boy bereft of parents, or abandoned by them, seeks a man's shelter and presents himself saying, "Let me become your son". When accepted, he becomes his son.

It will be noticed how true it is to say that many forms of marriage are only euphemisms for seduction and rape and how many of the sons have no blood relationship to their father. These different forms of marriage and different kinds of sons were recognised as lawful even up to the time of Manu and even the changes made by Manu are very minor. With regard to the forms of marriage, Manu[8] does not declare them to be illegal. All that he says is that of the eight forms, six—namely *Brahma, Daiva, Arsha, Prajapatya, Asura, Gandharva, Rakshasa* and *Paisacha*—are lawful for a Kshatriya, and that three—namely *Asura, Gandharva* and *Paisacha*—are lawful for a Vaishya and a Shudra.

Similarly he does not disaffiliate any of the twelve sons. On the contrary he recognises their kinship. The only change he makes is to alter the rules of inheritance by putting them into two classes (1) heirs and kinsmen and (2) kinsmen but not heirs. He says:

> 159. The legitimate son of the baby, the son begotten on a wife, the son adopted, the son made, the son secretly born and the son cast off (are) the six heirs and kinsmen.
>
> 160. The son of an unmarried damsel, the son received with the wife, the son bought, the son begotten on a remarried woman, the son self-given and the son of a Shudra female (are) the six (who are) not heirs, (but) kinsmen.
>
> 162. If the two heirs of one man be a legitimate son of

8 [Manu III.23.] In the following sentence, Ambedkar errs in mentioning six but incorrectly listing all eight forms of marriage for the Kshatriya. Bühler's edition says the first six forms "are lawful for a Brahman, the four last for a Kshatriya, and the same four, excepting the Rakshasa rite, for a Vaishya and a Shudra" in the same verse (III.23).

his body and a son begotten on his wife, each (of the two sons), to the exclusion of the other, shall take the estate of his (natural) father.

163. The legitimate son of the body alone (shall be) the owner of the paternal estate; but, in order to avoid harshness, let him allow maintenance to the rest.[9]

There is another part of the law of consanguinity which has undergone a profound change but which has hardly been noticed by anybody. It relates to the determination of the varna of the child. What is to be the varna of the child? Is it to be the father's varna or mother's varna? According to the law as it prevailed in the days before Manu, the varna of the child was determined by the varna of the father. The varna of the mother was of no account. A few illustrations will suffice to prove the thesis. [*See table on the next page.*]

What does Manu do? The changes made by Manu in the law of the child's varna are of a most revolutionary character. Manu lays down the following rules:

5. In all castes (varna) those (children) only which are begotten in the direct order on wedded wives, equal (in caste) and married as (virgins), are to be considered as belonging to the same caste (as their fathers).

6. Sons, begotten by twice-born men on wives of the next lower castes, they declare to be similar (to their fathers, but) blamed on account of the fault (inherent) in their mothers.

14. Those sons of the twice-born, begotten on wives of the next lower castes, who have been enumerated in due order, they call by the name Anantaras (belonging to the next lower caste) on account of the blemish (inherent) in their mothers.

41. Six sons, begotten (by Aryans) on women of equal and the next lower castes (Anantara), have the duties of twice-

9 [Manu IX, 159–60; 162–3; 359–60.] The page numbers refer to Bühler's 1886 translation.

Father		*Mother*		*Child*	
Name	*Varna*	*Name*	*Varna*	*Name*	*Varna*
1. Shantanu	Kshatriya	Ganga	Unknown	Bhishma	Kshatriya
2. Parashara	Brahman	Matsyagandha	Fisherman	Krishna Dwaya	Brahman
3. Vasishtha	Brahman	Akshamala	Payan		
4. Shantanu	Kshatriya	Matsyagandha	Fisherman	Vichitravirya	Kshatriya
5. Vishwamitra	Kshatriya	Menaka	Apsara	Shakuntala	Kshatriya
6. Yayati	Kshatriya	Devayani	Brahman	Yadu	Kshatriya
7. Yayati	Kshatriya	Sharmishtha	Asuri	Druhya	Kshatriya
8. Jarakaru	Brahman	Jaratkari	Naga	Asitika	Brahman

> born men: but all those born in consequence of a violation of the law are, as regards their duties, equal to Shudras.[10]

Manu distinguishes the following cases:

1. Where the father and mother belong to the same varna.
2. Where the mother belongs to a varna next lower to that of the father e.g. Brahman father and Kshatriya mother, Kshatriya father and Vaishya mother, Vaishya father and Shudra mother.
3. Where the mother belongs to a varna more than one degree lower to that of the father e.g. Brahman father and Vaishya or Shudra mother, Kshatriya father and Shudra mother.

In the first case the varna of the child is to be the varna of the father. In the second case also the varna of the child is to be the varna of the father. But in the third case the child is not to have the father's varna. Manu does not expressly say what is to be the varna of the child if it is not to be that of the father. But all the commentators of Manu—Medhatithi, Kalluka Bhatt, Narada and Nanda Pandit[11]—agree saying what, of course, is obvious, that in such cases the varna of the child shall be the varna of the mother. In short, Manu altered the law of the child's varna from that of *pitra-savarnya*—according to father's varna, to *matra-savarnya*—according to mother's varna.

This is a most revolutionary change. It is a pity few have

10 [Manu Chap. X, Verses 5, 6, 14 and 41, pp. 402–3, 404 and 412.]

11 Traditional commentary on Manu is invariably laudatory. Commentators typically attempt simplified paraphrasing and include examples that seek to clarify the original text. They simultaneously warn the readers against taking the verses literally. Among these, Kalluka Bhatt (also Bhatta), a fourteenth-century commentator and author of *Manavarthmuktavali*, seems to have deployed a text that differs considerably from texts used by earlier commentators. All but one among the European editions and all the Indian editions have used the text Kalluka seems to have preferred, according to Ketkar. Of the extant commentaries, Medhatithi's *Manubhashya* could be sourced from anywhere between ninth to eleventh centuries CE. Nanda Pandit is the author *Dattak Mimansa*; Narada's *Naradasmriti*, circa third century CE, is one of the earliest commentaries on the *Manusmriti*. See Ketkar 1998, 44–63.

realised that given the forms of marriage, kinds of sons, the permissibility of *anuloma* marriages and the theory of *pitra-savarnya*, the varna system, notwithstanding the desire of the Brahmans to make it a closed system, remained an open system. There were so many holes, so to say, in the varna system. Some of the forms of marriage had no relation to the theory of varna.[12]

Indeed they could not have. The *Rakshasa* and the *Paisacha* marriages were in all probability marriages in which the males belonged to the lower varnas and the females to the higher varnas. The law of sonship probably left many loopholes for the sons of Shudras to pass as children of Brahmans. Take for instance, sons such as *Gudhajas, Sahodhajas, Kaninas*. Who can say that they were not begotten by Shudra or Brahman, Kshatriya or Vaishya? Whatever doubts there may be about these, the *anuloma* system of marriage, which was sanctioned by law, combined with the law of *pitra-savarnya*, had the positive effect of keeping the varna system [fluid] by allowing the lower varnas to pass into the higher varna. A Shudra could not become a Brahman, a Kshatriya or a Vaishya. But the child of a Shudra woman could become a Vaishya if she was married to a Vaishya, a Kshatriya if she was married to a Kshatriya and even a Brahman if she was married to a Brahman. The elevation and the incorporation of the lower orders into the higher orders was positive and certain, though the way of doing it was indirect. This was one result of the old system. The other result was that a community of a varna was always a mixed and a composite community. A Brahman community might conceivably consist of children born of

---

12 In AoC 5.3, Ambedkar provokes with a question, "What harm could there be if a mixture of races and of blood was permitted to take place in India by intermarriages between different castes?" And in 20.5: "I am convinced that the real remedy is intermarriage. Fusion of blood can alone create the feeling of being kith and kin, and unless this feeling of kinship, of being kindred, becomes paramount, the separatist feeling—the feeling of being aliens—created by caste will not vanish" (2014, 238, 285).

Brahman women, Kshatriya women, Vaishya women and Shudra women—all entitled to the rights and privileges belonging to the Brahman community. A Kshatriya community may conceivably consist of children born of Kshatriya women, Vaishya women and Shudra women—all recognised as Kshatriya and entitled to the rights and privileges of the Kshatriya community. Similarly the Vaishya community may conceivably consist of children born of Vaishya women and Shudra women—all recognised as Vaishyas and entitled to the right and privileges of the Vaishya community.

The change made by Manu is opposed to some of the most fundamental notions of Hindu law. In the first place, it is opposed to the *Kshetra–Kshetraja* rule of Hindu law.[13] According to this rule, which deals with the question of property in a child, the owner of the child is the *de jure* husband of the mother and not the *de facto* father of the child. Manu is aware of this theory. He puts it in the following terms:

Thus men who have no marital property in women, but sow in the fields owned by others, may raise up fruit to the husbands, but the procreator can have no advantage from it. Unless there be a special agreement between the owners of the land and of the seed, the fruit belongs clearly to the landowner, for the receptacle is more important than the seed.[14]

It is on this that the right to the twelve kinds of sons is founded. This change was also opposed to the rule of *patria potestas*.[15] The

---

13 *Kshetra–Kshetraja* refers literally to the 'field' and the 'knower of the field'. In the *Bhagavad Gita*, Chapter 13, pertaining to Vibhaga Yoga, the (human) body is referred to as *Kshetra*/field and *Kshetraja* refers to the one (omnipresent/god) who knows the body/all bodies.

14 [Mayne, *Hindu Law*, p. 83.] The original footnote to Mayne is erroneous. Ambedkar is actually citing from Bühler's *Manusmriti*, IX: 51–2.

15 *Patria potestas* is a Latin phrase that literally means 'power of a father'—the authority which is lawfully exercised by the father over his children under Roman family law. Originally, this power implied absolute control over his children, including those

Hindu family is a patriarchal family, same as the Roman family. In both, the father possessed certain authority over members of the family. Manu is aware of this and recognised it in most ample terms. Defining the authority of the Hindu father, Manu says: "Three persons, a wife, a son, and a slave, are declared by law to have in general no wealth exclusively their own; the wealth which they may earn is regularly acquired for the man to whom they belong."

They belong to the head of the family—namely the father. Under the *patria potestas* the sons' earnings are the property of the father. The change in the law of paternity means a definite loss to the father.

Why did Manu change the law from *pitra-savarnya* to *matra-savarnya*?

adopted, and also the right to inflict capital punishment.

Riddle No. 22

Brahma is Not Dharma: What Good is Brahma?[1]

There are various forms of government known to history—monarchy, aristocracy and democracy, to which may be added dictatorship.

The most prevalent form of government at the present time is democracy. There is however no unanimity as to what constitutes democracy. When one examines the question, one finds that there are two views about it. One view is that democracy is a form of government. According to this view, where the government is chosen by the people that is where government is a representative government—there is democracy. According to this view democracy is just synonymous with representative government, which means adult suffrage and periodic elections.

According to another view, a democracy is more than a form of government. It is a form of the organization of society. There are two essential conditions which characterize a democratically constituted society. The first is the absence of stratification of society into classes. The second is a social habit on the part of individuals and groups which is ready for continuous readjustment or recognition of reciprocity of interests. As to the

1 The BAWS editors write: "This chapter consists [of] about 20 pages out of which first two pages and the concluding six are in the handwriting of the author. The rest are typed pages with all necessary modifications by Dr Ambedkar."

first, there can be no doubt that it is the most essential condition of democracy. As Prof. Dewey has observed:[2]

> A separation into a privileged and a subject-class prevents social endosmosis. The evils thereby affecting the superior class are less material and less perceptible, but equally real. Their culture tends to be sterile, to be turned back to feed on itself; their art becomes a showy display and artificial; their wealth luxurious; their knowledge overspecialized; their manners fastidious rather than humane.

Lack of the free and equitable intercourse which springs from a variety of shared interests makes intellectual stimulation unbalanced. Diversity of stimulation means novelty, and novelty means challenge to thought. The more activity is restricted to a few definite lines—as it is when there are rigid class lines preventing adequate interplay of experiences—the more action tends to become routine on the part of the class at a disadvantage, and capricious, aimless, and explosive on the part of the class having the materially fortunate position.

The second condition is equally necessary for a democratically constituted society.

The results of this lack of reciprocity of interests among groups and individuals produce anti-democratic results which have been well described by Prof. Dewey when he says:[3]

---

2 There's an in-text parenthetic note here in the BAWS edition that says: [Quotation referred to by the author is not recorded in the original MS from "Democracy and Education", by Dewey p. 98]. John Dewey (1859–1952) was a prominent American pragmatist philosopher, radical democrat and educational theorist who taught Ambedkar at Columbia University and influenced him deeply. In AoC, Ambedkar echoes and paraphrases Dewey extensively. According to Ạrun P. Mukherjee (2009, 347): "So deeply embedded is Dewey's thought in Ambedkar's consciousness that quite often his words flow through Ambedkar's discourse without quotation marks." The relevant portion from p. 98 of Dewey's 1916 work *Democracy and Education: An Introduction to the Philosophy of Education* has been inferred and incorporated into the main text here.

3 The in-text parenthetic note here in the BAWS edition says: [Quotation from "Democracy and Education" of page 99 referred to by the author is not recorded in

> The isolation and exclusiveness of a gang or clique brings its antisocial spirit into relief. But this same spirit is found wherever one group has interests "of its own" which shut it out from full interaction with other groups, so that its prevailing purpose is the protection of what it has got, instead of reorganization and progress through wider relationships. It marks nations in their isolation from one another; families which seclude their domestic concerns as if they had no connection with a larger life; schools when separated from the interest of home and community; the divisions of rich and poor; learned and unlearned. The essential point is that isolation makes for rigidity and formal institutionalizing of life, for static and selfish ideals within the group.

Of the two views about democracy there is no doubt that the first one is very superficial if not erroneous. There cannot be a democratic government unless the society for which it functions is democratic in its form and structure. Those who hold that democracy need be no more than a mere matter of elections seem to make three mistakes.

One mistake they make is to believe that government is something which is quite distinct and separate from society. As a matter of fact, government is not something which is distinct and separate from society. Government is one of the many institutions which society rears and to which it assigns the function of carrying out some of the duties which are necessary for collective social life.

The second mistake they make lies in their failure to realize that a government is to reflect the ultimate purposes, aims, objects and wishes of society and this can happen only where the society in which the government is rooted is democratic. If society is not democratic, government can never be. Where society is divided into two classes, the governing and the

the original MS.] The relevant portion has been inferred and incorporated here.

governed, the government is bound to be the government of the governing class.[4]

The third mistake they make is to forget that whether government would be good or bad, democratic or undemocratic depends to a large extent up on the instrumentalities particularly the civil service on which everywhere government has to depend for administering the law. It all depends upon the social milieu in which civil servants are nurtured. If the social milieu is undemocratic the government is bound to be undemocratic.

There is one other mistake which is responsible for the view that for democracy to function it is enough to have a democratic form of government. To realize this mistake it is necessary to have some idea of what is meant by good government.

Good government means good laws and good administration. This is the essence of good government. Nothing else can be. Now there cannot be good government in this sense if those who are invested with ruling power seek the advantage of their own class instead of the advantage of the whole people or of those who are downtrodden.

Whether the democratic form of government will result in good will depend upon the disposition of the individuals composing society. If the mental disposition of the individuals is democratic then the democratic form of government can be expected to result in good government. If not, a democratic form of government may easily become a dangerous form of

4 An echo of this—and Ambedkar's fears over a democratic government becoming undemocratic—can be found in Ambedkar's speech of 25 November 1949 to the Constituent Assembly, where he said: "On the 26th of January 1950, we are going to enter into a life of contradictions. In politics we will have equality and in social and economic life we will have inequality. In politics we will be recognizing the principle of one man one vote and one vote one value. In our social and economic life, we shall, by reason of our social and economic structure, continue to deny the principle of one man one value. How long shall we continue to live this life of contradictions?" http://parliamentofindia.nic.in/ls/debates/vol11p11.htm, accessed 17 March 2016.

government. If the individuals in a society are separated into classes, and the classes are isolated from one another and each individual feels that his loyalty to his class must come before his loyalty to everything else, and living in class compartments he becomes class conscious, [he is] bound to place the interests of his class above the interests of others[. He] uses his authority to pervert law and justice to promote the interests of his class and for this purpose systematically practises discrimination against persons who do not belong to his caste [class?] in every sphere of life—what can a democratic government [then] do?

In a society where classes clash and are charged with anti-social feelings and a spirit of aggressiveness, the government can hardly discharge its task of governing with justice and fair play. In such a society, government, even though it may in form be a government of the people and by the people, can never be a government for the people. It will be a government by a class for a class. A government for the people can be had only where the attitude of each individual is democratic, which means that each individual is prepared to treat every other individual as his equal and is prepared to give him the same liberty which he claims for himself. This democratic attitude of mind is the result of socialization of the individual in a democratic society. Democratic society is therefore a prerequisite of a democratic government. Democratic governments have toppled down largely due to the fact that the society for which they were set up was not democratic.[5]

Unfortunately to what extent the task of good government

5 Once again, this echoes Ambedkar's speech to the Constituent Assembly in 1949, where he says: "We must make our political democracy a social democracy as well. Political democracy cannot last unless there lies at the base of it social democracy. What does social democracy mean? It means a way of life which recognizes liberty, equality and fraternity as the principles of life. These principles of liberty, equality and fraternity are not to be treated as separate items in a trinity. They form a union of trinity in the sense that to divorce one from the other is to defeat the very purpose of democracy."

depends upon the mental and moral disposition of its subjects has seldom been realized. Democracy is more than a political machine. It is even more than a social system. It is an attitude of mind or a philosophy of life.

Some equate democracy with equality and liberty. Equality and liberty are no doubt the deepest concern of democracy. But the more important question is what sustains equality and liberty? Some would say that it is the law of the state which sustains equality and liberty. This is not a true answer. What sustains equality and liberty is fellow-feeling. What the French revolutionists called fraternity. The word fraternity is not an adequate expression. The proper term is what the Buddha called *maitri*.[6] Without fraternity, liberty would destroy equality and equality would destroy liberty. If in democracy, liberty does not destroy equality and equality does not destroy liberty, it is because at the basis of both there is fraternity. Fraternity is therefore the root of democracy.

The foregoing discussion is merely a preliminary to the main question. That question is—wherein lie the roots of fraternity without which democracy is not possible? Beyond dispute, it has its origin in religion.

---

6 *Maitri* is a key Buddhist concept which is translated as 'benevolence', 'loving kindness' and universal love. P. Lakshmi Narasu, a Tamil scholar of Buddhism says in *The Essence of Buddhism* (first published in 1907), that from *maitri* come *karuna* (compassion) and *mudita* (goodwill) (55). Ambedkar wrote a foreword to the third edition of Narasu's work in 1948 and published it himself. According to the scholar G. Aloysius, Ambedkar kept in his possession the manuscript of Narasu's unpublished last work, *Religion of the Modern Buddhist*. Aloysius traced this manuscript with Vasant Moon in 2000, when Moon was editor of the BAWS volumes, and republished it in 2002 with an introduction, where he says, "Ambedkar was so highly influenced by *The Essence of Buddhism* that he described it as the 'best book on Buddhism that has appeared so far'." Ambedkar was deeply influenced by the ideals of the French revolution—liberty, equality and fraternity—and from a very early stage, such as in his Mahad Satyagraha intervention (1923–1927), he constantly invoked these ideas. Later, he sought and found the equivalences of these very ideas in Buddhism. For Ambedkar's speeches at Mahad, see Teltumbde 2015.

In examining the possibilities of the origin of democracy or its functioning successfully, one must go to the religion of the people and ask—does it teach fraternity or does it not? If it does, the chances for a democratic government are great. If it does not, the chances are poor. Of course, other factors may affect the possibilities. But if fraternity is not there, there is nothing to build democracy on. Why did democracy not grow in India? That is the main question. The answer is quite simple. The Hindu religion does not teach fraternity. Instead it teaches division of society into classes or varnas and the maintenance of separate class consciousness. In such a system where is the room for democracy?

The Hindu social system is undemocratic not by accident. It is designed to be undemocratic. Its division of society into varnas and castes, and of castes and outcastes are not theories but are decrees. They are all barricades raised against democracy.

From this it would appear that the doctrine of fraternity was unknown to the Hindu religious and philosophic thought. But such a conclusion would not be warranted by the facts of history. The Hindu religious and philosophic thought gave rise to an idea which had greater potentialities for producing social democracy *than* the idea of fraternity. It is the doctrine of Brahmaism.[7]

---

7 [I have borrowed this term from Prof Hopkins' *The Epics of India*.] The reference here is to American Sanskritist Edward Washburn Hopkins' *The Great Epic of India: Character and Origin of the Mahabharata* (1902). Hopkins, who taught at Yale and was the author of such books as *Caste in Ancient India* (1881) and *Manu's Lawbook* (1884), says: "As Vedanta is commonly used of Sankara's interpretation, I employ Brahmaism to connote a belief in the All-soul without necessarily implying a concomitant doctrine of Illusion, Maya" (1902, 101n3). Hopkins, who uses the word 'Hindu' to refer to modern Hindus but avoids the descriptor 'Hinduism', identifies what he calls six 'approved epic systems': "(1) Vedism or orthodox Brahmanism; (2) atmanism or Brahmaism (properly Brahmanism, but this term connotes a different idea), that is, an idealistic interpretation of life; (3) Samkhya, the dualism spoken of above; (4) Yoga, the deistic interpretation of Samkhya; (5) Bhagavata or Pasupata, different but both sectarian interpretations of Yoga; (6) Vedanta or Illusion-idealism" (85–6). Hereon, Ambedkar improvises on Hopkins.

It would not be surprising if someone asked what is this Brahmaism? It is something new even to Hindus. The Hindus are familiar with Vedanta. They are familiar with Brahmanism. But they are certainly not familiar with Brahmaism. Before proceeding further a few words of explanation are necessary.

There are three strands in the philosophic and religious thought of the Hindus. They may be designated as (1) *Brahmaism* (2) *Vedanta* and (3) *Brahmanism*. Although they are correlated they stand for three different and distinct ideologies.

The essence of Brahmaism is summed up in a dogma which is stated in three different forms. They are—

(i) *Sarvam Khalvidam Brahma*[8]—All this is Brahma

(ii) *Aham Brahmasmi*[9]— Atmana (Self) is the same as Brahma. Therefore I am Brahma

(iii) *Tattvamasi*[10]—Atmana (Self) is the same as Brahma.

---

8 This is a much quoted verse from 3.14.1 of *Chandogya Upanishad* (c. 600 BCE, considered one of the earliest Upanishads), which is regarded as one of the 'Mahavakyas' or 'Great Pronouncements' of the Upanishads. See Ganganath Jha's 1923 Sanskrit–English edition of the Upanishad along with a translation of Sankara's Bhashya, *Chandogya Upanishad and Sri Sankara's Commentary—I*. The entire verse translates as: "All this is Brahma; beginning, ending and continuing in It. One ought to meditate upon It calmly. Now, because man consists in his will. According as his will is in this world, so will the man be after he has departed hence. He ought to have (this) will" (Jha 1923, 179–80). Max Müller in *The Upanishads: Part 1* (in the SBE series) renders this as: "All this is Brahman (n.) Let a man meditate on that (visible world) as beginning, ending, and breathing in it the Brahman). Now man is a creature of will. According to what his will is in this world, so will he be when he has departed this life. Let him therefore have this will and belief" (Müller 1879, 48).

9 This statement, meaning "I am Brahman" or "I am that", is regarded as another of the Mahavakyas, this one from *Brihadaranyaka Upanishad*, 1.4.10: "Verily in the beginning this was Brahman, that Brahman knew (its) Self only, saying, 'I am Brahman.' From it all this sprang. Thus, whatever Deva was awakened (so as to know Brahman), he indeed became that (Brahman); and the same with Rishis and men. The Rishi Vamadeva saw and understood it, singing, 'I was Manu (moon), I was the sun.' Therefore now also he who thus knows that he is Brahman, becomes all this, and even the Devas cannot prevent it, for he himself is their Self" (Müller 1879, 48).

10 Broken down as *tat tvam asi*. Literally "That thou art", meaning "Thou art that". It states the relationship between the individual and the Absolute and is frequently

Therefore thou art also Brahma.

They are called Mahavakyas, which means Great Sayings, and they sum up the essence of Brahmaism.

The following are the dogmas which sum up the teachings of Vedanta[11]—

I. Brahma is the only reality

II. The world is maya or unreal

III. Jiva and Brahma are—

(i) according to one school identical,

(ii) according to another not identical but are elements of him and not separate from him,

(iii) according to the third school they are distinct and separate.

The creed of Bramhanism may be summed up in the following dogmas—

(i) belief in the *chaturvarna*

(ii) sanctity and infallibility of the Vedas

(iii) sacrifices to gods the only way to salvation.

Most people know the distinction between the Vedanta and Brahmanism and the points of controversy between them. But very few people know the distinction between Brahmanism

---

repeated in the sixth chapter of the *Chandogya Upanishad*, culminating in 6.8.7. See Jha 1923, 132. "Now, that which is the subtle essence,—in That, has all this its Self; That is the Self; That is the True; That thou art, O Svetaketu." This is part of the father–son dialogue between Uddalaka Aruni and Shvetaketu. For the entire conversation that leads up to this definitive statement, see Müller 1879, 98–101.

11 Ambedkar is writing after both academic (such as the scholarly, Orientalist SBE series of books) as well as pop versions of Vedanta (those peddled by right-leaning supremacist voices such as Vivekananda's after the much-vaunted speech at the Parliament of World's Religions in Chicago in 1893, and sustained by the well-networked Ramakrishna Math) had established themselves as the front of some kind of political Brahmanism. See Meera Nanda's exposition of this in the context of the colonial period and its implications in post-independence history and for contemporary Hindutva (Nanda 2010). See also Freystad 2010 and Nanda 2004.

and Brahmaism.[12] Even Hindus are not aware of the doctrine of Brahmaism and the distinction between it and Vedanta. But the distinction is obvious. While Brahmaism[13] and Vedanta agree that Atman is the same as Brahma,[14] the two differ in that Brahmaism does not treat the world as unreal, while Vedanta does. This is the fundamental difference between the two.

The essence of Brahmaism is that the world is real and the reality behind the world is Brahma. Everything therefore is of the essence of Brahma.

There are two criticisms which have been levelled against Brahmaism. It is said that Brahmaism is a piece of impudence. For a man to say "I am Brahma" is a kind of arrogance. The other criticism levelled against Brahmaism is the inability of man to know Brahma. "I am Brahma" may appear to be impudence. But it can also be an assertion of one's own worth.[15] In a world where

---

12 The sentence here in the BAWS edition oddly reads: "But very few people know the distinction between Brahmanism and Vedanta." Since it almost repeats the previous sentence, and since Ambedkar means to distinguish here between Brahmanism and Brahmaism, this is likely an error either on the part of the BAWS editors or Ambedkar, and has been corrected as "Brahmanism and Brahmaism".

13 Brahmaism came to be discussed also because of the reformist Brahmo Samaj founded by Raja Rammohun Roy in 1828 in Bengal, which sought to propagate 'true Vedanta'. The Brahmos believed in what they called 'Adi Dharma' and 'casteless' Vedic Aryanism. While rejecting Brahmanism and caste, the Brahmos upheld the principle of the Brahman—the supreme being or spirit. There were debates within the Samaj over repudiating the Vedas. For an account of Brahmo Samaj and its history, see Kopf 1979. See also Hatcher 2007, who looks at the work of Tattvabodhini Sabha, an offshoot of the Brahmo Samaj. The Arya Samaj, founded in 1875 in Lahore by Dayananda Saraswati, believed in the supremacy of Vedas and Aryans. For an account of how Vivekananda and Ramakrishna Mission came to represent Vedanta for the times—and for the West—see Jackson 1994. See further 178n18 to this riddle.

14 Again, Ambedkar is improvising on Hopkins.

15 Related concepts in Buddhist thought are *attadipa* and *dhammadipa*. The scholar of religions Peter Schalk dwells upon this. "The reference to *dhammadipa* in the *Mahaparinibbana Sutta* (D.I.100), has to be translated as '(whoever) has the *dhamma* as (guiding) light'" (Schalk 2006, 86). Schalk's delineation of concepts related to this idea of each person being individually enlightened is worth citing at length: "In the *Mahaparinibbana Sutta*, the dying Buddha is reported to have said that the disciples

humanity suffers so much from an inferiority complex, such an assertion on the part of man is to be welcomed. Democracy demands that each individual shall have every opportunity for realizing his worth. It also requires that each individual shall know that he is as good as everybody else. Those who sneer at *Aham Brahmasmi* (I am Brahma) as an impudent utterance forget the other part of the Mahavakya, namely *Tattvamasi* (thou art also Brahma). If *Aham Brahmasmi* had stood alone without the conjunct of *Tattvamasi* it may have been possible to sneer at it. But with the conjunct of *Tattvanmsi* the charge of selfish arrogance cannot stand against Brahmaism.

It may well be that Brahma is unknowable. But all the same this theory of Brahma has certain social implications which have a tremendous value as a foundation for democracy.[16] If all

---

should not have any other *sarana* (refuge) other than the *dhamma* (D.II.100–01). He also uses the term *atta* (self), in connection with *dipa*: *attadipa* (having oneself as *dipa*). It is implied by the context that the monks should have themselves as *dipa* and not the dying or dead Buddha or anybody else. Furthermore, the Buddha introduces the concept of *dhammadipa*, which here is not *tatpurusa* 'the *dipa* of the *dhamma*', but which is *bahuvrihi* 'having the *dhamma* as *dipa*'. Therefore, we have four terms that are connected with each other in a semantic chain: *dhamma*, *dipa*, *atta* and *sarana*. Connecting these, the Buddha is reported to have said to Ananda: '...therefore, Ananda, dwell you (all), having yourselves as *dipa*, having yourselves as refuge, having no other refuge, having the *dhamma* as *dipa*, having the *dhamma* as refuge, having no other refuge' (D.II.100). *Atta* is of course here not 'the soul', but the logical counterpart of reference to somebody else than myself, to 'the other', who is made explicit in the text. The *atta* and the *dhamma* have common attributes, to be a *sarana* and to be a *dipa*. It is implied that *dipa* is a simile for *sarana*" (87). "D" here refers to *Digha Nikaya*, the Collection of Long Discourses of the Buddha. *Mahaparinibbana Sutta* is the sixteenth and longest of the thirty-four discourses (*suttas*) that make up the *Digha Nikaya*.

16 The word 'sramana', although used sparsely in Brahmanical literature, makes its first appearance in the *Brihadaranyaka Upanishad* IV.3.22: "There (in that state) a father is not a father, a mother is not a mother, the worlds are not the worlds, the gods are not the gods, the Vedas are not the Vedas. There a thief is not a thief, the murderer is not a murderer, a candala is not a candala, a paulkasa is not a paulkasa, a sramana is not a sramana, an ascetic is not an ascetic" (in Radhakrishnan 1998, 263). Sankara—the non-dualist Vedantic who literally used the second portion of *Jabala Upanishad* verse 4 (the portion sanctioning renunciation at any time of one's life) as his personal slogan—in his gloss on *Brihadaranyaka Upanishad* IV.3.22

persons are parts of Brahma then all are equal and all must enjoy the same liberty, which is what democracy means. Looked at from this point of view, Brahma may be unknowable. But there cannot be the slightest doubt that no doctrine could furnish a stronger foundation for democracy than the doctrine of Brahma.

To support democracy because we are all children of God is a very weak foundation for democracy to rest on. That is why democracy is so shaky wherever it made to rest on such a foundation. But to recognize and realize that you and I are parts of the same cosmic principle leaves room for no other theory of associated life[17] except democracy. It does not merely preach democracy. It makes democracy an obligation of one and all.

Western students of democracy have spread the belief that democracy has stemmed either from Christianity or from Plato

---

defined the 'state' that was beyond empirical distinctions as *avidya-kama-karma-vinirmuktah* (nescience-desire-ritual action–free). He argues that the 'Self in Deep Sleep' was essentially indivisible. (For Sankara's commentary on *Brihadaranyaka Upanishad* IV.3.22, see tr. Som Raj Gupta 2008, 925.) Sankara's gloss can be adduced to support Ambedkar's thesis that even if Brahma were unknowable the theory of Brahma has a "tremendous value as a foundation for democracy". Unfortunately, despite his tirades against the *samuchhaivadi* system of ashrama (see Notes 10, 16 and 17 to Riddle No. 17, p.132, 134–5) and his constant exhortation of Brahma, when it came to the question of varna, Sankara was steadfast in following the Manu line. However, the reason why Sankara failed to take the democratic impulse inherent to the (unaccountable) concept of Brahman to its logical conclusion at the social level may not be due to his theory of maya, which does not quite mean 'unreal'. (The annotators owe this note to Sibaji Bandyopadhyay.)

17 Ambedkar is drawing here on the Deweyan concept of 'associated life', which he picks up and develops further into a political tool at length in AoC. AoC 11.3 says: "The associated mode of life practised by the Sikhs and the Mahomedans produces fellow-feeling. The associated mode of life of the Hindus does not. Among Sikhs and Muslims there is a social cement which makes them *bhais* [brothers]. Among Hindus there is no such cement, and one Hindu does not regard another Hindu as his *bhai*" (2014, 256). In 14.2 of AoC: "Democracy is not merely a form of government. It is primarily a mode of associated living, of conjoint communicated experience" (260). Ambedkar uses Dewey's exact words from *Democracy and Education* (1916, 101). Both Dewey and Ambedkar believed that democracy should not be restricted to the political realm, but should also manifest itself in other areas, such as education, industry and the public sphere. On Dewey's influence on Ambedkar, see Mukherjee 2009, 356.

and that there is no other source of inspiration for democracy. If they had known that India too had developed the doctrine of Brahmaism which furnishes a better foundation for democracy they would not have been so dogmatic. India too must be admitted to have a contribution towards a theoretical foundation for democracy.

The question is what happened to this doctrine of Brahmaism?[18] It is quite obvious that Brahmaism had no social effects. It was not made the basis of dharma. When asked why this happened the answer is that Brahmaism is only philosophy, as though philosophy arises not out of social life but out of nothing and for nothing. Philosophy is no[t a] purely theoretic matter. It has practical potentialities. Philosophy has its roots in the problems of life and whatever theories philosophy propounds must return to society as instruments of re-constructing society. It is not enough to know. Those who know must endeavour to fulfil.

Why then did Brahmaism fail to produce a new society? This is a great riddle. It is not that the Brahmans did not recognize the doctrine of Brahmaism. They did. But they did not ask how they could support inequality between the Brahman and the Shudra, between man and woman, between casteman and outcaste.[19] The result is that we have on the one hand the most democratic principle of Brahmaism and on the other hand a society infested with castes, subcastes, outcastes, primitive tribes and criminal

---

18 It appears that Ambedkar, without naming the Brahmo Samaj and its various offshoots, is critiquing their reformist efforts, for despite speaking of everyone being accessible to Brahman and the Brahman residing in everyone (which means a spiritual democracy), in actual fact the ideologues of Brahmaism did little to ensure real democracy in the social realm. Many, including the populist Gandhi, finally did believe in the racist Aryan supremacy theory. On Gandhi's espousal of Aryanism, see Desai and Vahed 2015 and Roy 2014. On how European thinkers fell for the Aryan theory, see Figueira 2002.

19 In the BAWS edition, this sentence ends with a redundant question mark followed by a redundant sentence, "But they did not." Both have been deleted for sense.

tribes. Can there be a greater dilemma than this? What is more ridiculous is the teaching of the Great Shankaracharya.[20] For it was this Shankarcharya who taught that there is Brahma and this Brahma is real and that it pervades all and at the same time upheld all the inequities of the Brahmanic society. Only a lunatic could be happy with being the propounder of two such contradictions. Truly as the Brahman is like a cow, he can eat anything and everything as the cow does and remain a Brahman.[21]

---

20 'Adi' Sankara was an exponent of Advaita Vedanta, which advocated the nonduality of the self (atman) and the absolute (Brahman). He wrote extensive commentaries (*bhashyas*) on the Vedic canon (the *Brahma Sutras*, Upanishads and the *Bhagavad Gita*). To Ambedkar, Sankara is among the founder-propagators of Brahmaism.

21 Ambedkar makes a similar statement in his blistering critique of Gandhi and the Congress, *What Congress and Gandhi Have Done to the Untouchables* (1945). "I am quite aware that there are some protagonists of Hinduism who say that Hinduism is a very adaptable religion, that it can adjust itself to everything and absorb anything. I do not think many people would regard such a capacity in a religion as a virtue to be proud of just as no one would think highly of a child because it has developed the capacity to eat dung, and digest it. But that is another matter. It is quite true that Hinduism can adjust itself. The best example of its adjustability is the literary production called *Allahupanishad* which the Brahmans of the time of Akbar produced to give a place to his *Din-e-Ilahi* within Hinduism and to recognise it as the Seventh system of Hindu philosophy" (BAWS Vol 9, 1991, 195).

Riddle No. 23

Kali Yuga: Why have the Brahmans made it Unending?[1]

If there is any notion widespread among the Hindus and understood by every man and woman, adult or old, mature or immature, it is that of the Kali Yuga.[2] They are all aware of the fact that the present yuga is Kali Yuga and that they are living in the Kali Yuga. The theory of Kali Yuga has a psychological effect

---

1 The BAWS editors write: "This chapter contains 45 typed pages. Only 9 pages of this chapter at the beginning are numbered. While no other pages are numbered. Howsoever the text of this chapter has been found to be complete and without any loss of material."

2 Time for Hindus is both linear and cyclical (Doniger 2009, 57). Brahmanic Hinduism believes in cosmic time that has neither a beginning nor an end, and alternates between cycles of creation and cessation. Each Mahayuga consists of four yugas—Krita or Satya Yuga (the golden age), followed by Treta, Dwapara and Kali. Each era, shorter than the previous, is said to also be more degenerate and depraved than the preceding one. In Kali Yuga, there is disregard for varnashrama dharma—the Shudras and Untouchables wrest power—and chaos reigns, leading to complete destruction. In Kali Yuga, the *Bhagavad Gita* says (IX.32): "Even those who are of evil birth, women, Vaishyas and Shudras, having sought refuge in me will attain supreme liberation" (Debroy 2005, 137). Further, "the Kali Age is the dice throw of snake eyes, the present Age, the Iron Age, the Losing Age, the time when people are no damn good and die young, and barbarians invade India, the time when all bets are off. This fourth Age was always, from the start, entirely different from the first three in one essential respect: Unlike the other Ages, it is now, it is real. The four Ages are also often analogized to the four legs of dharma visualized as a cow who stands on four legs in the Winning Age, then becomes three-legged, two-legged, and totters on one leg in the Losing Age" (Doniger 2009, 57–8). According to P.V. Kane (1958, 687), the four names of the yugas came to be fixed around the fourth century BCE.

upon the minds of the people. It means that it is an unpropitious age. It is an immoral age.[3] It is therefore an age in which human effort will not bear any fruit. It is therefore necessary to inquire as to how such a notion arose. There are really four points which require elucidation. They are (1) What is Kali Yuga? (2) When did Kali Yuga begin? (3) When is the Kali Yuga to end? and (4) Why such a notion was spread among the people.[4]

---

3 Romila Thapar has argued that for the post-industrial West, linear time has been "associated with dialectical change" and cyclic time is seen as "primitive and archaic", especially when "change was progress as defined in nineteenth-century terms" (1996a, 5). Thapar rebuts critiques of the Hindu Brahmanic view of time as an Orientalist and missionary discourse, where cyclic time is seen as leading to "a negative eschatology" that is repetitive, unchanging and therefore "amounts to a refusal of history, for no event can be particular or unique and all events are liable to be repeated in the next cycle" (5–6). Arguing that cyclic time was used in cosmological contexts and linear time in historical contexts, Thapar offers a positive reading of the yugas: "But the four ages need not be perceived as enclosed units for it is said that the king's conduct characterizes the identity of the age and this ties ethics and social behaviour to time. Ultimately the possibility of the return of the cycle provides the necessary optimism for continuing human action and also gives a meaning to human action in the past: it makes history necessary" (24). Jaina and Buddhist notions of time—which Ambedkar does not discuss here—were not too different. Sharada Sugirtharajah points out (2003, 103) that "Orientalist constructions of Hindu time were largely based on selective texts such as Manu's Dharmashastra, the Puranas and the *Mahabharata*, while mathematical and astronomical views of time were ignored". On his part, Ambedkar factors in mathematical and astronomical views as well. Thapar says the *Manusmriti* came to be used "as their exploratory text into concepts of time and history" (1996a, 4). She speaks of there being more than one single category of time (both in the East and the West), and therefore characterising "societies as using either cyclic or linear time is an inadequate explanation for the centrality or other-wise of history" and that "cyclic time is not a characteristic of cultures which are historically stunted but an indication of historical complexity" (44). Ambedkar's concerns here appear to be, however, both moral and political and arise from an existential need to understand why what seems to be the best of times—the present—is ultimately looked at as Kali Yuga, the worst.

4 In Brahmanic Hinduism, the largest unit of cosmic time is a *kalpa*. "According to one concept, the *kalpa* is broken up into one thousand *maha*yugas, each lasting 4.32 million years. The *kalpa*, or 'Day of Brahma', is the longest conceived measure of time and is used to determine the duration of the universe. After the *kalpa* is complete, it is followed by an equally long 'Night of Brahma', a period of universal dissolution (*pralaya*)" (Lochtefeld 2002, 338).

I

To begin with the first point. For the purposes of this inquiry it is better to split the words Kali Yuga and consider them separately. What is meant by yuga? The word yuga occurs in the Rig Veda[5] in the sense of age, generation or tribe as in the expressions *Yuge Yuge* (in every age), *Uttara Yugani* (future ages), *Uttare Yuge* (later ages) and *Purvani Yugani* (former ages) etc. It occurs in connection with Manushy, Manusha, Manushah in which case it denotes generations of men. It just meant ages. Various attempts are made to ascertain the period the Vaidikas intended to be covered by the term 'yuga'. Yuga is derived from the Sanskrit root *'yuj'*, which means to join and may have had the same meaning as the astronomical term 'conjunction'.

Prof. Weber[6] suggests that the period of time known as yuga was connected with four lunar phases. Following this suggestion Mr Rangacharya has advanced the theory that "in all probability the earliest conception of a yuga meant the period of a month from new-moon when the Sun and the Moon see each other i.e., they are in conjunction."[7] This view is not accepted by others.

---

5 Ambedkar is likely drawing this from Bal Gangadhar Tilak's 1903 work, *The Arctic Home in the Vedas: Being Also a New Key to the Interpretation of Many Vedic Texts and Legends*, 159, where Tilak cites Muir (*Original Sanskrit Texts*) to say that the phrase *'yuge yuge'* is used at least in half a dozen places in the *Rig Veda*. While the Brahmanical Tilak and Buddhist-leaning Ambedkar come to depend on the same Orientalist scholars, the conclusions they arrive at are often irreconcilable. We must remember that Tilak (1865–1920) saw even the education of women and non-Brahmans as "a loss of nationality" (Jaffrelot 2005, 44).

6 Albrecht Weber (1825–1901) was a German Indologist and historian. He wrote a *History of Indian Literature* in 1878, dividing it into two periods—the Vedic and the Sanskrit (the second German edition of 1875 was first translated into English in 1878). Ambedkar is referring to p. 70 of the 1904 edition, which was part of Trübner's Oriental Series, where Weber says "the four yugas ... are connected with the four lunar phases, to which they evidently owe their origin, although all recollection of the fact had in later times died out." Weber was a friend of Max Müller, with a shared interest in Sanskrit literature.

7 [*The Yugas: A Question of Hindu Chronology and History*, p. 19.] This was authored by M. Rangacharya and published in the *Madras Christian College Magazine* in

For instance, according to Mr Shamasastry[8] the term yuga is in the sense of a single human year as in the Setu Mahatmya which is said to form part of the *Skanda Purana*.[9] According to the same authority it is used in the sense of a Parva or half a lunation, known as a white or dark half of a lunar month.

All these attempts do not help us to know what was the period which the Vaidikas intended to be covered by a yuga.

While in the literature of the Vaidikas or theologians there is no exactitude regarding the use of the term yuga, in the literature of the astronomers (writers on Vedanga Jyotish)[10] as distinguished from the Vaidikas the word yuga connotes a definite period. According to them, a yuga means a cycle of five years which are called (1) Samvatsara, (2) Parivatsara, (3)

1891 in issues 8 and 9. Again, Tilak who extensively discusses the idea of yuga, cites the same passage Ambedkar does. Rangacharya also prepared descriptive catalogues of Sanskrit manuscripts for Government Oriental Manuscripts Library, Madras, and among many works published *The Vedantasutras with the Sribhasya of Ramanujacarya*.

8 [Drapsa: The Vedic System of Eclipses (1938), p. 88.] The author is R. Shamasastry and the actual title is *Drapsa: The Vedic Cycle of Eclipses: A Key to Unlock the Treasures of the Vedas*. Shamasastry was a Sanskrit scholar and librarian at the Oriental Research Institute, Mysore, who discovered a copy of the *Arthashastra* in 1905 and published a Sanskrit edition in 1909 and an English translation in 1915.

9 Doniger (1993, 60) calls the *Skanda Purana* the most volatile of Sanskrit texts, "surely the shiftiest, or sandiest, of all" Puranas, continuously expanding and incorporating new traditions.

10 Vedanga literally means "limbs of the Veda" and refers to texts dated between the ninth and fifth centuries BCE dealing with phonetics and ritual injunctions, linguistics, grammar, etymology, lexicography, prosody, astronomy and astrology. *Vedanga Jyotishya*, dealing with the fraught subject of Vedic astronomy, is considered an addendum to the four Vedas. B.N. Narahari Achar (1998, 101) says: "*Vedanga Jyotisa* (VJ) is the general name by which one refers collectively to the earliest codified texts of astronomy of ancient India, the *Rg Jyotisa* (RJ), the *Yajusa Jyotisa* (YJ), and the *Atharva Jyotisa* (AJ). The RJ consists of 36 verses and the YJ of 44 verses and the authorship of these two is ascribed to Lagadha, whose disciple Suci composed and preserved the knowledge codified by his celebrated teacher. The AJ consists of 162 verses divided into fourteen chapters, but the author is unknown." According to Vahia and Yadav (2011, 71), "The concept of the yuga was introduced as a more sophisticated attempt to synchronise the solar and lunar calendars ... Two intercalary months, Amhaspati and Samsarpa, were added to complete a yuga."

Idvatsara, (4) Anuvatsara and (5) Vatsara.

Coming to Kali, it is one of the cycles made up of four yuga: Krita, Treta, Dwapara and Kali. What is the origin of the term Kali? The terms Krita, Treta, Dwapara and Kali are known to have been used in the three different connections. The earliest use of the term Kali as well as of other terms is connected with the game of dice.

From the *Rig Veda* it appears that the dice piece[11] that was used in the game was made of the brown fruit of the Vibhitaka tree being about the size of a nutmeg, nearly round with five slightly flattened sides. Later on the dice was made of four sides instead of five. Each side was marked with the different numerals 4, 3, 2 and 1. The side marked with 4 was called Krita, with 3 Treta, with 2 Dwapara and with 1 Kali. Shamasastry gives an account of how a game of dice formed part of sacrifice and how it was played. The following is his account:

> Taking a cow belonging to the sacrificer, a number of players used to go along the streets of a town or village, and making the cow the stake, they used to play at dice in different batches with those who deposited grain as their stake. Each player used to throw on the ground a hundred or more *Cowries* (shells), and when the number of the Cowries thus cast and fallen with their face upwards or downwards, as agreed upon, was exactly divisible by four then the sacrificer was declared to have won: but if otherwise he was defeated. With the grain thus won, four Brahmans used to be fed on the day of sacrifice.[12]

---

11 Earlier, in Riddle No. 13, Ambedkar says of the names of the yugas: "As a matter of fact, originally these are the names of the dices used by the Aryans at gambling." The Hymn of Dice in *Rig Veda* X.34.1–14 speaks of the perils of man addicted to gambling. Verse 10 from Griffith 1889 reads: "The gambler's wife is left forlorn and wretched: the mother mourns the son who wanders homeless./In constant fear, in debt, and seeking riches, he goes by night unto the home of others." On the names of the yugas and their connection to the dice game, see Gonzalez-Reimann 1989.

12 The reference is from Shamasastry 1908, 70. Ambedkar mentions and draws on Shamasastry's *Gavam Ayana* further on in the chapter but no citation is given.

Professor Eggeling's references[13] to Vedic literature leave no doubt about the prevalence of the game of dice almost from the earliest time. It is also clear from his references that the game was played with five dice, four of which were called Krita while the fifth was called Kali. He also points out[14] that there were various modes in which the game was played and says that according to the earliest mode of playing the game, if all the dice fell uniformly with the marked sides either upwards or downwards then the player won the game. The game of dice formed part of the Rajasuya and also of the sacrificial ceremony connected with the establishment of the sacred fire.[15]

These terms—Krita, Treta, Dwapara and Kali—were also used in mathematics. This is clear from the following passage from Abhayadevasuri's commentary on *Bhagavati Sutra,*[16] a

---

13 [See his note on the subject in his edition of *Satapatha Brahmana*, Vol, IV, p. 107.] Julius Eggeling's translations with extensive notes on the *Satapatha Brahmana*, comprising fourteen books in five parts, were published as part of the SBE series between 1882 to 1900.

14 Eggeling says in a footnote to the dice hymn: "The allusions to the game of dice in the early literature are not sufficiently definite to enable us to form a clear idea as to the manner in which the game was played. Sayana, on our passage (as on Taitt. S. I, 8, 16), remarks that the dice here used consisted either of gold cowries (shells) or of gold (dice shaped like) Vibhitaka nuts. That the (brown) fruit of the Vibhitaka tree (*Terminalia bellerica*)—being of about the size of a nutmeg, nearly round, with five slightly flattened sides—was commonly used for this purpose in early times, we know from the *Rig Veda*; but we do not know in what manner the dice were marked in those days" (Eggeling 1894, 106).

15 The correspondinp verse in *Satapatha Brahmana* reads: "...assuredly in the house of him who offers the Rajasuya, or who so knows this, the striking of that cow is approved of. On those dice he says, 'Play for the cow!' The two draught oxen of the original (hall-door) fire are the sacrificial fee." Discussing the *Mahabharata*, Alf Hiltebeitel has this to say: "...a canonically performed Rajasuya is not complete without a concluding dice match in which the sacrificing king is supposed to be victorious. Thus even though the Pandavas' Rajasuya is said to be complete, insofar as there is no mention that it includes a dice match, the poets imply that this component of the rite is left for the Kauravas, the other half of the divided family" (Hiltebeitel 1988, 224).

16 *Vyakhyaprajnapti* ('Exposition of Explanations'), commonly known as the *Bhagavati Sutra*, and attributed to Sudharmaswami (sixth century BCE), is the fifth of the

voluminous work on Jaina religion.

> In mathematical terminology an even number is called 'Yugma', and an odd number 'Ojah'. Here there are, however, two numbers deserving of the name 'Yugma' and two numbers deserving of the name 'Ojah'. Still, by the word 'Yugma' four Yugmas i.e., four numbers are meant. Of them Krita-yugma: Krita means accomplished, i.e., complete, for the reason that there is no other number after four, which bears a separate name (i.e., a name different from the four names Krita and others). That number which is not incomplete like Tryoja and other numbers, and which is a special even number is Kritayugma. As to Tryoja: that particular odd number which is uneven from above a Krityugma is Tryoja. As the Dwaparayugma:—That number which is another even number like Krityugma, but different from it and which is measured by two from the beginning or from above a Krityugma is Dwaparayugma— Dwapara is a special grammatical word. As to Kalyoja:—That special uneven number which is odd by Kali, i.e., to a Kritayugma is called Kalyoja. That number etc. which even divided by four, ends in complete division, Krityugma. In the series of numbers, the number four, though it need not be divided by four because it is itself four, is also called Krityugma.[17]

Shamasastry[18] mentions another sense in which these terms are used. According to him, they are used to mean the *parvas* of those names, such as Krita Parva, Treta Parva, Dwapara Parva and Kali Parva. A *parva* is a period of fifteen *tithis* or days, otherwise called *paksha*. For reasons connected with religious ceremonies, the exact time when a *parva* closed was regarded

---

twelve Jain agamas.

17 Ambedkar is once again drawing upon Shamasastry's citation (1908, 73) from Abhayadevasuri's work. Shamasastry discusses the *Bhagavati Sutra* on pp. 71, 74 and 128. For an edition with Abhayadevasuri's commentary, see Diparatnasagara 2000.

18 [Shamasastry, Drapsa, p.92–3.] The reference is to Shamasastry 1938.

as important. It was held that the *parvas* fell into four classes according to the time of their closing. They were held to close either (1) at sunrise, (2) at one quarter or *pada* of the day, (3) after two quarters or *padas* of the day or (4) at or after three quarters or *padas* of the day.[19] The first was called Krita Parva, the second Treta Parva, the third Dwapara Parva and the fourth Kali Parva.

Whatever the meaning in which the words Kali and yuga were used at one time, the term Kali Yuga has long since been used to designate a unit in the Hindu system of reckoning time. According to the Hindus there is a cycle of time which consists of four yugas, of which the Kali Yuga forms one. The other yugas are called Krita, Treta and Dwapara.

II

When did the present Kali Yuga begin? There are two different answers to the question. According to the *Aitareya Brahmana*[20] it began with Nabhanedishta, the son of Vaivasvata Manu. According to the Puranas, it began on the death of Krishna, after the battle of Mahabharata.

The first has been reduced to time terms by Dr Shamasastry,[21] who says that Kali Yuga began in 3101 B.C. The second has been worked out by Mr Gopal Aiyer[22] with meticulous care. His view is that the Mahabharata War commenced on the 14th of October and ended on the night of 31st October 1194 B.C.[23] He places the death of Krishna sixteen years after the close of

19 For an elaborate explanation of terms like *parva, tithi, paksha* etc. see Sewell et al 1896.

20 See Keith 1998 [1920].

21 [Gavam Ayana.] Shamasastry 1908, 101.

22 See Aiyer 1901.

23 Aiyer 1901, 104.

the war, basing his conclusion on the ground that Parikshit[24] was sixteen when he was installed on the throne, and reading it with the connected facts, namely that the Pandavas went on Mahaprasthan immediately after installing Parikshit on the throne and this they did on the very day Krishna died. This gives 1177 B.C. as the date of the commencement of the Kali Yuga.[25]

We have thus two different dates for the commencement of the Kali Yuga: 3101 B.C. and 1177 B.C. This is the first riddle about the Kali Yuga. Two explanations are forthcoming for these two widely separated dates for the commencement of one and the same yuga. One explanation is that 3101 B.C. is the date of the commencement of the *kalpa* and not of Kali and it was a mistake on the part of the copyist who misread *kalpa* for Kali and brought about this confusion. The other explanation is that given by Dr Shamasastry. According to him there were two Kali Yuga eras which must be distinguished, one beginning in 3101 B.C. and another beginning in 1260 or 1240 B.C.[26] The first lasted about 1,840 or 1,860 years, and was lost.

III

When is the Kali Yuga going to end? On this question the great Indian astronomer Gargacharya in his *Siddhanta,* when speaking of Salisuka Maurya, the fourth in succession from Asoka,[27] makes the following important observation:

Then the viciously valiant Greeks, after reducing Saketa,

---

24 Aiyer 1910, 54–5. The first Parikshit is believed to be a Kuru king of the Vedic era. The Parikshit referred to here is the son of Abhimanyu and Uttara, the grandson of Arjuna and Subhadra.

25 Aiyer, 54.

26 Shamasastry 1908, 139.

27 Ambedkar is deriving this from Aiyer 1901, 26. Max Müller in his *India: What it Can Teach Us* dates Garga's work to about 200 CE (Müller 1883, 297–8).

> Panchala country to Mathura, will reach Kusumadhwaja (Patna): Pushpapura being taken all provinces will undoubtedly be in disorder. The unconquerable Yavanas will not remain in the middle country. There will be cruel and dreadful war among themselves. Then after the destruction of the Greeks at the end of the Yuga, seven powerful Kings reign in Oudha.[28]

The important words are "after the destruction of the Greeks at the end of the yuga". These words give rise to two questions (1) which yuga did Garga have in mind? and (2) when did the defeat and destruction of the Greeks in India take place? Now the answers to these questions are not in doubt. By yuga, he means Kali Yuga and the destruction and defeat of the Greeks took place about 165 B.C. It is not merely a matter of inference from facts. There are direct statements in chapters 188 and 190 of the Vana Parva of the *Mahabharata* that the barbarian Sakas, Yavanas, Balhikas and many others will devastate Bharatvarsha "*at the end of the Kali Yuga*".[29]

The result which follows when the two statements are put together is that the Kali Yuga ended in 165 B.C. There is also another argument which supports this conclusion. According to the *Mahabharata*, Kali Yuga was to comprise a period of one thousand years.[30] If we accept the statement that the Kali Yuga began in 1171 B.C. and deduct one thousand years since then we cannot escape the conclusion that Kali Yuga should have ended by about 171 B.C. which is not very far from the historical fact referred to by Garga as happening at the close of the Kali Yuga.

---

28 [Quoted in R.C. Dutt in his 'Civilization in Ancient India'.] Ambedkar is citing Garga's work from Romesh Chunder's Dutt's *A History of Civilization in Ancient India Based on Sanscrit Literature*, Vol 3, 206.

29 Italicised in the BAWS edition, possibly indicated for emphasis in Ambedkar's typescript.

30 [Chronology of Ancient India, p. 117.]

There can therefore be no doubt that in the opinion of the chief astronomer,[31] Kali Yuga came to end by about 165 B.C. What is however the position? The position is that according to the Vaidika Brahmans, Kali Yuga has not ended. It still continues. This is clear from the terms of Sankalpa which is a declaration every Hindu makes even today before undertaking any religious ceremony. The Sankalpa is in the following terms:

> On the auspicious day and hour, in the second Parardha of First Brahma, which is called the Kalpa of the White Boar, in the period of Vaivasvata Manu, in the Kali Yuga, in the country of Jambudvipa in Bharatavarsha in the country of Bharat, in the luni-solar cycle of the sixty years which begins with Pradhava and ends with Kshaya or Akshaya and which is current, as ordained by Lord Vishnu, in the year (name), of the cycle, in the Southern or the Northern Ayana, as the case may be, in the white or dark half, on the Tithi. I (name) begin to perform the rite (name) the object of pleasing the Almighty.[32]

The question we have to consider is why and how the Vedic Brahmans manage to keep the Kali Yuga going on when the astronomer had said it was closed. The first thing to do is to ascertain what is the original period of the Kali Yuga. According to the *Vishnu Purana*: "The Kritayuga comprises 4,000 years, the Treta 3,000, the Dwapara 2,000 and the Kali 1,000. Thus those that know the past have declared."[33]

Thus Kali Yuga originally covered a period of 1,000 years only. It is obvious that even on this reckoning the Kali Yuga should have ended long ago, even according to the reckoning

---

31 [Garga's statement seems to be corroborated by the statement in the *Mahabharata* that the period of Kali Yuga is 1,000 years. For we add 171 to 1,000 we get 1171 which is said to be the beginning of Kali.] Ambedkar is referring to Garga as the chief astronomer.

32 [Shamasastry, Drapsa p. 84.]

33 Ambedkar is citing this from Aiyer 1901, 117–8.

of the Vedic Brahmans. But it has not. What is the reason? Obviously, because the period originally covered by the Kali Yuga came to be lengthened. This was done in two ways.

Firstly, it was done by adding two periods called Sandhya and Sandhyamsa before and after the commencement and the end of a yuga.[34] Authority for this can be found in the same passage of the *Vishnu Purana* already referred to and which reads as follows:

> The period that precedes a Yuga is called *Sandhya* ... and the period which comes after a Yuga is called *Sandhyamsa,* which lasts for a like period. The intervals between these Sandhyas and Sandhyamsas are known as the Yugas called Krita, Treta and the like.[35]

What was the period of Sandhya and Sandhyamsa? Was it uniform for all the yugas or did it differ with the yuga? Sandhya and Sandhyamsa periods were not uniform. They differed with each yuga. The following table [*next page*] gives some idea of the four yugas and their Sandhya and Sandhyamsa.

The Kali Yuga, instead of remaining as before a period of 1,000 years, was lengthened to a period of 1,200 years by the addition of Sandhya and Sandhyamsa.

Secondly, a new innovation was made. It was declared that the period fixed for the yugas was really a period of divine years and not human years. According to the Vedic Brahmans one divine day was equal to one human year so that the period of Kali Yuga which was 1,000 years plus 200 years of Sandhya and Sandhamsa i.e. 1,200 years in all became (1,200 x 360) equal to 4,32,000 years.[36] In these two ways the Vedic Brahmans, instead of declaring the end of Kali Yuga in 165 B.C. as the astronomer had said, extended its life to 4,32,000 years. No wonder Kali

34 This refers to the twilight of yugas and the part of twilight between yugas. Aiyer discussed this on 118, 122.

35 Aiyer 1901, 118.

36 Discussed and analysed in Aiyer 1901, 117, 122, 137.

Yuga continues even today and will continue for lakhs of years. There is no end to the Kali Yuga.[37]

Unit of a Mahayuga	Period	Dawn	Twilight	Total
Krita	4,000	400	400	4,800
Treta	3,000	300	300	3,600
Dwapara	2,000	200	200	2,400
Kali	1,000	100	100	1,200
Maha Yuga				12,000

IV

What does the Kali Yuga stand for? The Kali Yuga means an age of *adharma*, an age which is demoralized [immoral?] and an age in which the laws made by the king ought not to be obeyed. One question at once arises. Why was the Kali Yuga more demoralized than the preceding yugas? What was the moral condition of the Aryans in the yuga or yugas preceding the present Kali Yuga? Anyone who compares the habits and social practices of the later Aryans with those of the ancient Aryans[38]

37 Every scholar, including Thapar (1996, 14), uses the same tabular explanation.

38 While Ambedkar does believe there was an Aryan incursion, he differs strongly from Brahmanic appropriations (such as by B.G. Tilak or M.K. Gandhi) of the racial theory of Aryans and Dravidians propounded by European Indologists. AoC 5.2–3: "...the caste system came into being long after the different races of India had commingled in blood and culture. To hold that distinctions of castes are really distinctions of race, and to treat different castes as though they were so many different races, is a gross perversion of facts.... The caste system does not demarcate racial division. The caste system is a social division of people of the same race" (2014, 237–8). For how European thinkers shaped subcontinental thinking on these matters, see Figueira 2002. Ambedkar differs on this front from his predecessor, the radical thinker Jotiba Phule (1827–90) and his contemporary 'Periyar' E.V. Ramasamy Naicker (1879–1973) who turned the racial theory inside

will find a tremendous improvement almost amounting to a social revolution in their manners and morals.

The religion of the Vedic Aryans was full of barbaric and obscene observances. Human sacrifice formed a part of their religion and was called Naramedha yagna.[39] [40] Most elaborate descriptions of the rite are found in the *Yajur Veda Samhita*, *Yajur Veda Brahmanas*, the *Sankhyana* and *Vaitana Sutras*.[41] The

---

out, postulated a pre-Aryan golden age, and regarded the Brahmans as Aryans, and hence foreigners, who imposed the caste system upon the non-Brahmans, who were seen as an indigenous race. For Phule's writings, especially *Gulamgiri* (Slavery, 1873), see G.P. Deshpande (2002, 23–101). Periyar, on the eve of independence, quite radically called upon the Dravidian people of South India to "guard against the transfer of power from the British to the Aryans" (*The Hindu*, 11 February 1946). As sociologist T.K. Oommen (2005, 99) argues, "According to Periyar, Brahmans had tried to foist their language and social system on Dravidians to erase their race consciousness and, therefore, he constantly reminded the Dravidians to uphold their 'race consciousness'. However, Periyar did not advocate the superiority of one race over the other but insisted on [the] equality of all races. Thus the fundamental difference between Aryan Hinduism and Dravidian Hinduism is crucial: the former [is] hegemonic, but the latter is emancipatory."

39 Naramedha literally means human sacrifice. The prototype sacrifice comes of course from the sacrifice of Prajapati (who is both the subject and object of the sacrifice) described in the Purusha Sukta hymn of the *Rig Veda* (10.90). As Jamison and Brereton say in the introduction to their opus translation of *Rig Veda*: "this hymn is generally considered to have been a quite late addition to the text, perhaps to provide a charter myth for the varna system after it had taken more definite shape" (2014, 58). The Prajapati sacrifice of the Purusha, the primordial being, spawns all creation including the four varnas. In the *Mahabharata*, the word Naramedha occurs four times. On regarding this as a self-sacrifice, see Heesterman 1987.

40 On the prevalence of human sacrifice and 'tribal' populations, Iyengar says: "Other traces of the more elaborate rites of the Nishada Age are to be found in the human sacrifices, called Meriah, associated sometimes with the use of stone tools, which were prevalent among the modern Nishadas (loosely called Khonds in the Vizagapatam and Ganjam agency tracts), till the British Government put a stop to it in the middle of the last century" (1926/1988, 21). For a full-length study, see Padel 1995/2011.

41 For a survey of scholarly literature on this subject since the colonial period, see Parpola 2007. Parpola offers a summary of all the references to human sacrifice in Vedic and post-Vedic texts up to contemporary Tantra practices, and concludes that "human sacrifice and skull cults have survived to the present day especially in eastern India ... this Sakta tradition appears to be a direct continuation of the cultic practices involving human sacrifice" (177). In his latest work (2015, 172) Parpola proposes that the human victim in Vedic sacrifices was a harp-playing bard named

worship of genitals or what is called phallus worship was quite prevalent among the ancient Aryans. The cult of the phallus came to be known as Skambha and was recognized as part of Aryan religion, as may be seen in the hymn in *Atharva Veda* X.7.[42] Another instance of obscenity which disfigured the religion of the ancient Aryans is connected with the Ashvamedha Yajna or the horse sacrifice. A necessary part of the Ashvamedha was the introduction of the *sepas* (penis) of the *medha* (dead horse) into the *yoni* (vagina) of the chief wife of the *yajamana* (the sacrificer) accompanied by the recital of long series of mantras by the Brahman priests.[43] A mantra in the *Vajasaneya Samhita* (xxiii. 18)

---

after his musical instrument. "The sacrifice included a 'revival' ritual that involved swapping the severed heads of the human victim and the animal (horse) victim, resulting in two 'mythical' creatures of the kind described above by Magha. Thus *kimpurusa,* an old problem relating to human sacrifice in the early layer of Vedic rituals, turns out to be a folk-etymological translation loan from Dravidian *kinnara,* which may be the earliest recorded word from any South Asian language." See also Oldenberg 1988, especially 200–04, who has a narrow definition of the term, where he accepts killing but not as sacrifice, where through ritual and chanting "magic power clinging to a human corpse" is invoked. He suggests that the human sacrifice during the Vedic period might have been more symbolic and suggestive than established in actual practice.

42 The *skambha* (also *stambha*) is a sacrificial post (*yupa skambha*) understood to be the cosmic column as described in *Atharva Veda* Book 10, Hymn 7 comprising 44 verses. Verse 8, for instance, reads: "That universe which Prajapati created, wearing all forms, the highest, midmost, lowest,/How far did Skambha penetrate within it? What portion did he leave unpenetrated?" (Griffith 1917, 21–6). Many nativist and Indological scholars to this day argue that the latter-day Shiva and the linga/phallus worship has its roots in the *skambha* verses of the *Atharva Veda*. However, scholars like Francesco Pellizzi (2007) warn us against becoming quickly procrustean. For a view that links *skambha* to linga, see Srinivasan 1997.

43 The *Brihadaranyaka Upanishad* opens with a re-description of the Vedic Ashvamedha sacrifice. See Swami Madhavananda 1934. The Naramedha and Ashvamedha passages in Ambedkar here are derived from P.T. Srinivasa Iyengar's work *The Stone Age in India* first published in 1926. From the facsimile reprint of 1998: "The texts related to the Purushamedha contemplate in some places an actual human sacrifice and in others a symbolic one. Apparently the human sacrifice was so ancient that it had become too holy to be given up, and, later, on account of the growing moral sense of the more refined classes, was converted into a symbolic sacrifice" (Iyengar 1988, 21).

shows that there used to be a competition among the queens as to who was to receive this high honour of being served by the horse. Those who want to know more about it will find it in the commentary of Mahidhara on the *Yajur Veda* where he gives full description of the details of this obscene rite which had formed a part of the Aryan religion.[44]

The morals of the ancient Aryans were no better than their religion.[45]

We may next proceed to consider the marital relations of men and women. What does history say? In the beginning there was no law of marriage among the Aryans. It was a state of complete promiscuity both in the higher and lower classes of the society. There was no such thing as a question of prohibited degrees as the following instances will show.

Brahma married his own daughter Satarupa. Their son was Manu, the founder of the Pruthu dynasty, which preceded the

---

44 Mahidhara was a sixteenth-century commentator on the Vedas. His *Vedadipa* is commentary on the *Vajasaneya Samhita* of the White *Yajur Veda*. Prabhakar (1972, 347): "Yajurveda is known for its multiplicity of recensions or schools unlike the other Vedas. Sukla Yajurveda (SYV) is known by its fifteen/sixteen recensions while the Krsna Yajurveda by its eighty-six recensions." Ambedkar likely used Ralph Griffith's 1899 translation of the White *Yajur Veda*. Griffith says "Books XXII to XXV contain formulas of the Asvamedha or Horse-sacrifice, a very ancient and most important ceremony which only a King can perform. Its object is the acquisition of power and glory, acknowledged preeminence over neighbouring princes, and the general prosperity of the kingdom by the fulfilment of the wishes expressed in verse 22 of this Book" (204). Griffith adds an illuminating note on p. 212: "The Chief Queen calls on her fellow-wives for pity, as, to obtain a son, she has to pass the night in disgusting contiguity to the slaughtered horse: 'No one takes me (by force to the horse); (but if I go not of myself), the (spiteful) horse will lie with (another, as,) the (wicked) Subhadra who dwells in Kampila.'—[Albrecht] Weber, *History of Indian Literature*, p. 114. Subhadra: probably the wife of the King of Kampila in the country of the Panchalas in the North of India. The Chief Queen must submit to the revolting ceremony, or its benefits will go to another woman. See Ramayana, Book I. Canto XIII. Schlegel's edition."

45 At this point, Ambedkar repeats verbatim his own words that form the first portion of Riddle No. 13, "The Riddle of the Ahimsa", on gambling and drinking. See pages 85–7 on gambling and 88–90 on drinking.

rise of the Aiksvakas and the Ailas.[46]

Hiranyakashpu married his daughter Rohini.[47] Other cases of fathers marrying daughters are Vasishtha and Satarupa, Janhu and Janhavi,[48] and Surya and Usha.[49] That such marriages between father and daughters were common is indicated by the usage of recognizing *kanina* sons. *Kanina* sons mean sons born to unmarried daughters.[50] They were, in law, the sons of the father of the girl. Obviously they must be sons begotten by the father on his own daughter.

There are cases of father and son cohabiting with the same woman. Brahma is the father of Manu, and Satarupa is his mother.[51] This Satarupa is also the wife of Manu. Another case

---

46 In the *Rig Veda*, Brahma also commits incest with Saraswati (also called *Vac* or speech), who is said to be his mind-born daughter. This is reiterated in the *Matsya Purana* and *Shiva Purana*. Since the examples Ambedkar offers here are listed in the same sequence by the historian S.C. Sarkar, Ambedkar is likely drawing on Sarkar, who says father–daughter and brother–sister incest continued from the Vedic to Puranic periods and was practised among "Prthuite dynasties that flourished in N.E. India during the two centuries (or more) before the rise of the Aiksvakas and Ailas. According to these accounts, the first famous chiefs in that earlier period, Priyavrta and Uttanapaada, were sons of a 'Manu' who was begotten by 'Brahma' (='Prajapati' etc.) on his own daughter Satarupa whom he loved" (Sarkar 1928, 136).

47 After discussing the prevalence of incest among the kings, Sarkar speaks of the priestly classes: "Tradition also supplies similar particulars about the priestly groups: in an Angirasa genealogy (partly tinged with myths), 'the maiden Rohini, daughter of Hiranyakasipu' is stated to have become 'his *bharya*' as a result of karma" (1928, 137).

48 Janhavi is another name for the river Ganga, said to be born of the rishi Janhu, whom she woos. *Brahma Purana* (8.37–54): "Greedily seeking a husband, Ganga wooed him (Jahnu). Since he dissented, Ganga flooded his sacrificial hall." See King 2005, 161.

49 The reference here is to the *Rig Veda* (6.12.4) where the allegory of creation is told as a story of incestuous rape, and where the Sun god (also Prajapati/ Brahma/ Surya) penetrates Usha (dawn). Many scholars (see Leeming 2005) argue that creation myths across the world often feature incest. Ambedkar is perhaps drawing on Rajendralal Mitra (1881, 297), who calls this myth "offensively indelicate" as he narrates the story of "the rape of Usha by her father Brahma".

50 For instance, in *Mahabharata*, Karna is the *kanina* son of Kunti.

51 Manu was Brahma's mind-born son, and he marries Brahma's consort. Satarupa/

is that of Shraddha. She is the wife of Vivasvat. Their son is Manu. But Shraddha is also the wife of Manu, thus indicating the practice of father and son sharing a woman. It was open for a person to marry his brother's daughter. Dharma married ten daughters of Daksha though Daksha and Dharma were brothers.[52] One could also marry his uncle's daughter, as did Kasyapa who married thirteen women, all of whom were the daughters of Daksha, and Daksha was the brother of Kasyapa's father Marichi.

The case of Yama and Yami[53] mentioned in the *Rig Veda* is a notorious case, which throws a great deal of light on the question of marriages between brothers and sisters. Because Yama refused to cohabit with Yami it must not be supposed that such marriages did not exist.

The Adi Parva of the *Mahabharata* gives a genealogy which begins from Brahmadeva. According to this genealogy Brahma had three sons, Marichi, Daksha and Dharma, and one daughter whose name the genealogy unfortunately does not give. In this very genealogy it is stated that Daksha married the daughter of Brahma who was his sister and had a vast number of daughters, variously estimated as being between fifty and sixty. Other instances of marriages between brothers and sisters could be cited. They are Pushan and his sister Acchoda and Amavasu. Purukutsa and Narmada, Viprachiti and Simhika, Nahusa and Viraja, Sukra-Usanas and Go, Amsumat and Yasoda, Dasaratha and Kausalya, Rama and Sita;[54] Suka and Pivari; Draupadi and

---

Saraswati/ Gayatri are names that share an equivalence and are used synonymously in the Vedic texts.

52 Shraddha is a goddess who figures in *Rig Veda* and the Brahmanas, and is said to be the daughter of Vivasvat, the sun god (also known as Surya and Prajapati). In *Mahabharata*, she is known as the daughter of Daksha and wife of Dharma and also as the daughter of Vivasvat.

53 Discussed at length in Riddle No. 6, 75–7.

54 See The "Riddle of Rama and Krishna", 220.

Prasti are all cases of brothers marrying sisters.

The following cases show that there was no prohibition against a son cohabiting with his mother. There is the case of Pushan and his mother,[55] Manu and Satrupa and Manu and Shraddha. Attention may also be drawn to two other cases, Arjuna and Urvashi and Arjuna and Uttara. Uttara was married to Abhimanyu, son of Arjuna, when he [Abhimanyu] was barely sixteen. Uttara was associated with Arjuna. He taught her music and dancing. Uttara is described as being in love with Arjuna and the *Mahabharata* speaks of their getting married as a natural sequel to their love affair. The *Mahabharata* does not say that they were actually married but if they were, then Abhimanyu can be said to have married his mother. The Arjuna–Urvasi episode is more positive in its indication.[56]

Indra was the real father of Arjuna. Urvashi was the mistress of Indra and therefore in the position of a mother to Arjuna. She was a tutor to Arjuna and taught him music and dancing. Urvasi became enamoured by Arjuna and with the consent of his father, Indra, approached Arjuna for sexual intercourse. Arjuna refused to agree on the ground that she was like mother to him. Urvashi's conduct has historically more significant than Arjuna's denial and for two reasons. The very request by Urvashi to Arjuna and the consent by Indra show that Urvashi was following a well established practice.[57] Secondly, Urvashi in her reply to Arjuna

55 In *Rig Veda* 6.55: "Pusan, who driveth goats for steeds, the strong and mighty, who is called His Sister's lover, will we laud." Pushan woos his mother as well as his sister Surya. See also *Rig Veda* 10.85.

56 During the Pandavas' exile, Arjuna works as a dance teacher in the court of King Virata. His daughter Uttara falls in love with Arjuna, and seeks to marry him. Arjuna refuses, saying she is like his daughter and suggests that she marry his son Abhimanyu. In the Urvashi episode, Arjuna spurns the advances of the celestial nymph who is a consort of Indra, Arjuna's father.

57 Urvashi was the wife of Pururava and Arjuna was one of Pururava's descendants. Arjuna rejects Urvashi on the ground that he looked upon her as his mother.

tells him in a pointed manner that this was a well recognized custom and that all Arjuna's forefathers had accepted precisely similar invitations without any guilt being attached to them.

Nothing illustrates better the complete disregard of consanguinity in cohabitation in ancient India than the following story which is related in the second Adhyaya of the *Harivamsa*. According to it, Soma was the son of ten fathers—suggesting the existence of polyandry—each one of whom was called Pralheta.[58] Soma had a daughter Marisha. The ten fathers of Soma and Soma himself cohabited with Marisha. This is a case of ten grandfathers and a father married to a woman who was a grand-daughter and daughter to her husbands. In the same Adhyaya, the story of Daksha Prajapati is told. This Daksha Prajapati, who is the son of Soma, is said to have given his twenty-seven daughters to his father, Soma, for procreation. In the third Adhyaya of *Harivamsa* the author says that Daksha gave his daughter in marriage to his own father Brahma on whom Brahma begot a son who became famous as Narada. All these are cases of cohabitation of *sapinda* men with *sapinda* women.[59]

The ancient Aryan women were sold. The sale of daughters is evidenced by the Arsha form of marriage. According to the technical terms used, the father of the boy gave Go-Mithuna and

---

58 This is likely a misspelling of Prachetasas, a mystery figure in Vedic mythology. Wilson 1865 throws some light on this. Book 1, Ch 25 begins with the story Ambedkar adduces here. Prajapati Daksha, a contemporary of Lord Shiva, gives his twenty-seven daughters in marriage to Soma, and Soma is born from Marichi. But it is said that Daksha was also the son of a woman called Marichi, who in turn is referred to as the mother of Daksha. Thus it appears that Prachetasas were Daksha's fathers as well as Daksha's great grandsons. This confusion arises in Hindu families essentially because children are often named after their grandfather or great grandfather.

59 *Sapinda* means a relationship of "sharing a common body", a set of kindred seven generations on the father's side and five on the mother's. In his 1916 essay, "Castes in India", while discussing endogamy and exogamy, Ambedkar says "it is not that *sapindas* (blood-kin) cannot marry, but a marriage even between *sagotras* (of the same class) is regarded as a sacrilege" (BAWS Vol 1, 1979, 9).

took the girl. This is another way of saying that the girl was sold for a Go-Mithuna. Go-Mithuna means one cow and one bull, which was regarded as a reasonable price of a girl.[60] Not only daughters were sold by their fathers but wives also were sold by their husbands. The *Harivamsa* in its 79th Adhyaya describes how a religious rite called Punyaka-Vrata should be the fee that should be offered to the officiating priest.[61] It says that the wives of Brahmans should be purchased from their husbands and given to the officiating priest as his fee. It is quite obvious from this that Brahmans freely sold their wives for a consideration.

That the ancient Aryans let their women on rent for cohabitation to others is also a fact. In the *Mahabharata* there is an account of the life of Madhavi in Adhyayas 103 to 123. According to this account, Madhavi was the daughter of King Yayati.[62] Yayati made a gift of her to Galava, who was a rishi as a fee to a priest. Galava rented her out to three kings in succession but to each for a period necessary to beget a son on her. After the tenancy of the third king terminated, Madhavi was surrendered by Galava to his guru Vishwamitra who made her his wife. Vishwamitra kept her till he begot a son on her and gave her back to Galava. Galava returned her to her father Yayati.[63]

---

60 See the discussion on *Arsha* marriage in Riddle No. 19, p.156 and 159. In an *Arsha* marriage, a bride "is given in exchange for a pair of cattle for sacrifice" (Lochtefeld 2002, 523). Information on the *Arsha* form of marriage is given even in textbooks meant for today's civil service aspirants in India. See Singh 2008, A70.

61 The ritual fast of Punyaka Vrata is described from Chapters 77– 79 of the *Harivamsa*. A translation of Chapter 79 is available online. http://mahabharata-resources.org/harivamsa/vishnuparva/hv_2_079.html. Accessed 14 February 2016. The text used in this online project is based on Pandit Ramachandra Shastri Kinjawadekar's 1936 edition of *Harivamsa* published as part of the *Mahabharata*.

62 Writes Meyer 1953, 41: "The tale of the princess Madhavi reminds us of one of Boccaccio's novels."

63 When Galava insists on offering his guru Vishwamitra a *dakshina* (fee), Vishwamitra says, "Give me eight hundred horses that are as white as the rays of the moon and possess a single black ear each. O Galava! Go now and do not delay" (Debroy 2012, Vol 5, 435). Galava, a poor Brahman, finally ends up at King Yayati's palace

Polygamy and polyandry were raging in the ancient Aryan society.[64] The fact is so well known that it is unnecessary to record cases which show its existence. But what is probably not well known is the fact of promiscuity. Promiscuity in matters of sex becomes quite apparent if one were only to examine the rules of *niyoga* which the Aryan name for a system under which a woman who is wedded can beget on herself a progeny from another who is not her husband.[65] This system resulted in a

---

trying to find such horses, and Yayati says he does not have those kind of riches. He then offers his daughter Madhavi instead, saying: "Accept Madhavi, this daughter of mine. O lord! The only boon that I ask for is that I should have grandsons through my daughter" (Debroy 2012, Vol 5, 449). Madhavi, like some celestial nymphs, has the ability to turn herself into a virgin after sleeping with someone. Subsequently when Galava manages to return to his guru with the gifts including Madhavi, "Vishvamitra saw Galava and the bird and the maiden with the beautiful thighs and said, 'O Galava! Why did you not give her to me earlier? Then all the four sons would have been mine and would have extended the lineage. I will accept this maiden to have one son through her. Let all the horses remain in my hermitage'" (454).

64 A study closer to Ambedkar's times is N.K. Sidhanta's *The Heroic Age of India: A Comparative Study* first published in 1929. Sidhanta distinguishes between *niyoga* as a Vedic practice and polyandry that was prevalent among non-Aryans tribals. He speculates if the Pandavas were indeed non-Aryan, given that among certain northern hill tribes polyandry is practised even today (120–1; also see 154, 167). For a comprehensive survey of the subject with extensive citations from primary sources, see S.D. Singh 1978. Several ethnographic studies have proved that polyandry is practiced among certain tribes in the northern and southern hills. Gerald Berreman (1962) provides a good overview of literature on this. See also Vidyarthi and Rai 1976, especially the chapter "Polyandry in Tribal India", 395–410, where they say tribes like Todas (south) and Khasa (in Tibet) trace their ancestry to the Pandavas. See also 157n6.

65 *Niyoga*—when a husband is incapable of producing a child or dies intestate, the wife sleeps with or marries the husband's brother or a close relative to produce an heir. *Niyoga* is regarded as a variation of what is known as a levirate marriage in Judaism, where only a brother-in-law cohabits with a childless sister-in-law. Nineteenth-century Hindu ideologues like Dayananda Saraswati (who founded the Arya Samaj in 1875) sought to dress this up as proof of how there was widow remarriage in Vedic times and women were empowered. Citing this, Saraswati and Arya Samajists actively encouraged *niyoga* remarriage as way of preserving caste and of keeping the woman and thus property within a family, and crucially as a method to boost the Hindu population, given anxieties over demography, perceiving a threat from 'burgeoning' Muslims (see Jones 2006, 139–45). Many viewed this as 'licensed adultery' and a form of legitimising the rape of widowed women. See

complete state of promiscuity, for it was uncontrolled. In the first place, there was no limit to the number of *niyogas* open to a woman. Madhuti had one *niyoga* allowed to her.[66] Ambika had one actual *niyoga* and another proposed. Saradandayani had three. Pandu allowed his wife Kunti four *niyogas*. Vyusistasva was permitted to have seven and Vali is known to have allowed as many as seventeen *niyogas*, eleven on one and six on his second wife.[67] Just as there was no limit to the number of *niyogas* so also there was no definition of cases in which *niyoga* was permissible. *Niyoga* took place in the lifetime of the husband and even in cases where the husband was not overcome by any congenital incapacity to procreate. The initiative was probably taken by the wife. The choice of a man was left to her. She was free to find out with whom she would unite a *niyoga* and how many times, if she chose the same man. The *niyogas* were another name for illicit intercourse between men and women which might last for one night or twelve years or more with the husband a willing and a sleeping partner in this trade of fornication.

Ruchi Ram Sahni's 'scientific' critique (1897) and Llewellyn and Llewellyn (1993). A work contemporaneous with Ambedkar's writing that discusses polyandry, *niyoga*, deputed fathership and related issues at length is Meyer 1953.

66 Since there is no reference to a Madhuti or Madhuri in the *Mahabharata*, this could be a typographical error in the BAWS edition. Ambedkar must be referring to King Yayati's daughter Madhavi, also from *Mahabharata*, discussed earlier in Note 63.

67 All these are well-known references that form the genesis of the disputes over kingship in *Mahabharata*. The mother of Vichitravirya, Queen Satyavati (formerly a fisherwoman), gets her son and sage Vyasa (to whom authorship of *Mahabharata* is attributed) to perform *niyoga* with the widows of her son, Ambika and Ambalika. Says Wendy Doniger: "The *niyoga* of Vyasa (who appears in the epic as a kind of walking semen bank) is highly problematic. The widows of Vicitravirya reject him. Moreover, since Vyasa's relationship to Vicitravirya is clouded, being primarily maternal rather than paternal (he and Vicitravirya have the same mother but different fathers), he is far from the perfect *niyoga* surrogate. The tension for and against the *niyoga* persists in the myths, both in the form of two different sets of myths and in the form of unresolved paradoxes within each myth. Thus the wives of Vicitravirya both do and do not want to sleep with Vyasa, and their ambivalence is the direct source of the tragedy of the Mahabharata" (Doniger 1995, 175).

These were the manners and morals of common men in the ancient Aryan society.[68] What were the morals of the Brahmans? To tell the truth, they were no better than the common men. The looseness of the morals among the Brahmans is evidenced by many instances. But a few will suffice. The cases showing that the Brahmans used to sell their wives have already been referred to. I will give other cases showing looseness. Utanka is a pupil of Veda[69] (the *purohita* of Janamejaya III). The wife of Veda most calmly requests Utanka to take the place of her husband and 'approach' her for the sake of virtue. Another case that may be referred to in this connection is that of Uddalaka's wife. She is free to go to other Brahmans either of her own free will, or in response to invitations. Shvetaketu is her son by one of her husband's pupils.[70] These are not mere instances of laxity or adultery. These are cases of recognized latitudes allowed to Brahman women. Jatila Gautami was a Brahman woman and had seven husbands who were rishis. The *Mahabharata* says that the wives of the citizens admire Draupadi[71] in the company of

---

68 Ambedkar's ire here may appear moralistic, but it must be remembered that this was a time when both western Orientalists and nativists were holding up the 'Aryan' and Vedic period as ideal, and the Arya Samaj was not merely justifying practices like *niyoga* but also sought their revival.

69 Veda is a guru with a *nomen omen*. When Veda is away, his disciple Utanka (also spelt Uttanka) earns his guru's blessings by refusing to sleep with the guru's wife even as he is encouraged by other disciples to do so. This incident happens in the Adi Parva. In earlier stories, just like *niyoga* was accepted, a disciple sleeping with a guru's wife was also condoned, but by the time the Dharmasutras were composed it came to be condemned.

70 Vyasa tells Yudhishtira in the *Mahabharata*: "A man incurs no sin if intercourse with the preceptor's wife is for the sake of the preceptor. Through a disciple, Uddalaka had Shvetaketu as a son" (Debroy Vol 8, 2013, 229). The translator says in a note, "Shvetaketu was Uddalaka's son and their stories figure in the Upanishads, particularly *Chandogya Upanishad*. However, this bit about Shvetaketu being born to Uddalaka through a disciple is not mentioned elsewhere." For the Uddalaka–Shvetaketu dialogue in *Chandogya Upanishad* see 173n10 to Riddle No. 22.

71 See in this regard Khanna 1997, 103–20, who examines Mahasweta Devi's short story "Draupadi" and Gayatri Spivak's "ambiguous translator's foreword to the

her five husbands and compare her to Jatila Gautami with her seven husbands. Mamata is the wife of Utathya. But Brahaspati, the brother of Utathya, had free access to Mamata during the lifetime of Utathya. The only objection Mamata once raises to him is to ask him to wait on account of her pregnancy but does not say that approaches to her were either improper or unlawful.[72]

Such immoralities were so common among the Brahmans that Draupadi, when she was called a cow by Duryodhana for her polyandry, is said to have said she was sorry that her husbands were not born as Brahmans.

Let us examine the morality of the rishis. What do we find? The first thing we find is the prevalence of bestiality among the rishis. Take the case of the rishi called Vibhandaka. In Adhyaya 100 of the Vana Parva of the *Mahabharata* it is stated that he cohabited with a female deer and that the female deer bore a son to him who subsequently became known as Rishi Shranga. In Adhyaya 1 as well as in 118 of the Adi Parva of the *Mahabharata* there is a narration of how Pandu, the father of the Pandavas, received his curse from the Rishi by name Dama. Vyasa says that the Rishi Dama[73] was once engaged in the act of coitus with a

---

story" and offers a reading of the myth of Draupadi to ask "whether there is a space within it that might be epistemologically emancipatory for woman as subaltern."

72 Meyer discusses this (1953, 113–4): "Now there was once a famous wise Rishi, called Utathya. Mamata was the name of his much-prized wife. But Utathya's younger brother, the sacrificial priest of the heaven-dwellers, Brihaspati the majestic, forced himself on Mamata. But Mamata said to her brother-in-law, best among speakers, 'But I am with child by thine elder brother. Desist. And this offspring of Utathya within my body has already studied the Veda with its six auxiliary sciences. But thou art a man of irresistibly powerful seed. Two cannot find room here. But as things are so, do thou therefore now withdraw.' Though thus addressed by her aright, yet the noble-minded Brihaspati could not hold back his soul filled with love's urge. Then, with love's longing full, he united himself with her, who had none of love's longing." See also Debroy Vol 9, 2014, 425. See further Note 91 to this Riddle on 213–4.

73 Dama is likely a typographical error. The reference must be to Rishi Kindama (also spelt Kimdama). In Debroy (Vol 1, 2010, 298), Kimdama tells Pandu: "I am a sage

female deer in a jungle. While so engaged Pandu shot him with an arrow before the rishi was spent; as a result of it, Dama died. But before he died, Dama uttered a curse saying that if Pandu ever thought of approaching his wife, he would die instantly. Vyas tries to gloss this bestiality of the rishi by saying that the rishi and his wife had both taken the form of deer in fun and frolic. Other instances of such bestiality by the rishis will not be difficult to find if a diligent search was made in the ancient religious literature in India.

Another heinous practice which is associated with the rishis is cohabitation with women in the open and within the sight of the public. In Adhyaya 63 of the Adi Parva of the *Mahabharata* a description is given of how the Rishi Parashara had sexual intercourse with Satyavati, alias Matsya Gandha, a fisherman's girl. Vyasa says that he cohabited with her in the open and in public.[74] Another similar instance is to be found in Adhyaya 104 of the Adi Parva. It is stated therein that the Rishi Dirgha Tama cohabited with a woman in the sight of the public. There are many such instances mentioned in the *Mahabharata*. There is, however, no need to encumber the record with them. For the word *ayonija* is enough to prove the general existence of the practice. Most Hindus know that Sita, Draupadi and other renowned ladies are spoken of as *ayonija*. What they mean by *ayonija* is a child born by immaculate conception.[75] There is

---

named Kimdama, unparalleled in austerities. Ashamed of men, I was engaged in intercourse with this deer. Assuming the form of a deer, I roamed with other deer in this dense forest." Kimdama then curses Pandu, saying he would die if he ever had intercourse with any woman. See also 87n8 to Riddle No. 13.

74 In the *Mahabharata* (Adi Parva, 57.59–60 [Critical Edition]), before going to bed with Parashara, Satyavati says, "Sir, look, there are holy men standing on both the river banks. How can we lie with each other when they are looking at us?" (tr. J.A.B. Buitenen 1983, 133). Thereupon, Parasara created a fog that covered the entire region with darkness. Hence, at least technically, the mating was not done in public.

75 According to Doniger (1980, 50), "In the medical texts, it is clear that women can

however no warrant from etymological point of view to give such a meaning to the *ayoni*. The root meaning of the word *yoni* is "house".[76] *Yonija* means a child born or conceived in the house. *Ayonija* means a child born or conceived outside the house. If this is the correct etymology of *ayonija*, it testifies to the practice of indulging in sexual intercourse in the open within the sight of the public.

Another practice which evidences the revolting immorality of the rishis is in the *Chandyogya Upanishad*. According to this Upanishad it appears that the rishis had made a rule that while they were engaged in performing a *yajna*, if a woman expressed desire for sexual intercourse, the rishi who was approached should immediately, without waiting for the completion of the *yajna* and without caring to retire in a secluded spot, proceeded to commit sexual intercourse with her in the *yajna mandap* and in the sight of the public. This immoral performance of the rishi was elevated to the position of a religious observance and given the technical name of Vamadev Vrata,[77] which was later on

---

procreate unilaterally but men cannot; in the myths, the situation is reversed, and men, but not women, are capable of unilateral procreation (albeit men do it into a 'female' receptacle of some sort—any container at all)." Looking at the "remarkable pattern of mono-gender conception" in the *Mahabharata*, Mary Carroll Smith has this to say: "Male parthenogenic births in the *Mahabharata* occur without mothers as bearers or holders of the seed. Such births are called *ayonija* or 'non-womb birth'. *Ayonija* should perhaps be translated as 'born without the need of a female source', but even that translation fails to signify the full deprivation entailed in the parthenogenic births of the epic heroes" (1985, 79).

76 In the Monier-Williams Sanskrit dictionary *yoni* has many meanings and 'home' or 'a place of rest' is one of them. It also refers to a particular part of the sacrificial fire-pit or altar, as well as to the vagina or womb depending on the text and context.

77 This is from *Chandogya Upanishad*, Adhyaya 2, Khanda 13, and is also known as the Vamadevya hymn. For Max Müller's translation, see SBE Vol 1, 1897, 29–30. Alain Daniélou, the French Indologist and exponent of Shaivite Hinduism, quotes the verse: "The summons is the invocation of the deity; the request is the first hymn of praise. The act of lying next to the woman is the hymn of glory; meeting her face to face is the chorus; the height of passion is the consecration; and the separation is the final hymn. He who knows that the hymn to Vamadeva (the god of the left

revived as Vama Marga.[78]

This does not exhaust all that one finds in the ancient sacerdotal literature of the Aryans about the morality of the rishis. One phase of their moral life remains to be mentioned.

The ancient Aryans also seem to be possessed with the desire to have better progeny, which they accomplished by sending their wives to others, and it was mostly to the rishis, who were regarded by the Aryas as pedigree cattle. The rishis who figure in such cases form quite a formidable number. Indeed the rishis seemed to have made a regular trade in this kind of immorality and they were so lucky that even kings asked them to impregnate the queens. Let us now take the Devas.[79]

---

hand who represents the Tantric aspect of Shiva) is woven upon the act of love, re-creates himself in each act of union. His life will be long; his descendants and his livestock will be numerous; his fame widespread" (1987, 161). Daniélou also cites from Adhyaya 5, Khanda 5: "Woman is the hearth, the male organ is the fire; the caresses are the smoke, the vulva is the flame, penetration is the brand, and pleasure is the spark. In this fire, the gods receive the offering of semen, and a child is born" (161). A website dedicated to Hinduism offers more explicit version of these verses. See http://hinduwebsite.com/upanishads/essays/sex-in-Upanishads.asp, accessed 14 February 2016.

78 Vama Marga (also known as Left Hand Tantra) is how it features in Tantra, where the act of sex itself becomes a ritual. Ambedkar here avoids discussion of Buddhist Tantra where sex, too, is a means to enlightenment. Discussing Sakta Tantrism, Parpola (2015, 251) posits that they used a woman of any caste or even their mothers and daughters in these rituals. For a discussion on the cult of Vama Marga see Rinehart and Stewart (2000, 281), who argue that "any man takes any woman he happens to find; the followers worship a naked woman and consider that they attain greater merit by getting a female of the Bhangina caste or one in her monthly course. They worship her, eat the remainders of her food, and come into contact with her; they do not observe any distinction between what should be eaten and what should not be eaten."

79 [One does not know what to say of the scholar who first translated the Sanskrit word Deva as the English word god. It was the greatest blunder which has resulted in confusion and has prevented a proper understanding of the social life of the Aryans as revealed in the Vedic literature. That Deva was the name of a community is beyond question. That Rakshas, Daityas and Danavas are also names of different communities in the same manner as the words Arya and Dasyu are must also be accepted without question.] Most scholars and translators continue to render Devas as divine beings. It is not clear how and from where Ambedkar is making this

The Devas were a powerful and most licentious community. They even molested the wives of the rishis. The story of how Indra raped Ahalya, the wife of Rishi Gautama, is well known.[80] But the immoralities they committed on the Aryan women were unspeakable. The Devas as a community appears to have established an overlordship over the Aryan community in very early times. This overlordship had become so degenerated that the Aryan women had to prostitute themselves to satisfy the lust of the Devas. The Aryan took pride if his wife was in the keeping of a Deva and was impregnated by him. The mentions in the *Mahabharata* and in the *Harivamsa* of sons born to Arya women from Indra, Yama, Nasatya, Agni, Vayu and other Devas are so frequent that one is astounded to note the scale on which such illicit intercourse between the Devas and the Arya women was going on.

In course of time the relations between the Devas and the Aryans became stabilized and appear to have taken the form of feudalism. The Devas exacted two boons[81] from the Aryans.

The first boon was the *yajna*, which were periodic feasts given by the Aryans to the Devas in return for the protection of the Devas in their fight against the Rakshasas, Daityas and Danavas. The *yajnas* were nothing but feudal exactions of the Devas. If

---

argument. The Devas are akin to Greek gods in the sense that they are immortal, nothing more. See Parpola 2015, 106–13 for a discussion on how the terms *deva* and god are related across Saka, Parthian and Avestan kingdoms.

80 Ahalya literally means "not to be plowed". This tale of rape, which some commentators term seduction, is recounted first in the *Ramayana*. Wendy Doniger relates several versions of this story in *Splitting the Difference: Gender and Myth in Ancient Greece and India* (1999, 88–111).

81 [Whether the relations between the Devas and the Aryans were of the nature of the feudal relations between the Lord and the Villein has not yet been investigated largely because the Devas are not considered as a community of men. The boons claimed by the Devas from the Aryans are the same as those claimed by the Lord from his Vellein: (1) First fruits and (2) Primae Noctis.] This is explained in the next note.

they have not been so understood it is largely because the word Deva instead of thought to be the name of a community is regarded as a term for expressing the idea of god, which is quite wrong at any rate in the early stages of Aryan society.

The second boon claimed by the Devas against the Aryans was the prior right to enjoy an Aryan woman.[82] This was systematized at a very early date.

There is a mention of it in the *Rig Veda* in X.85.40.[83] According to it the first right over an Arya[84] female was that of Soma, second of Gandharva, third of Agni and lastly of the Aryan. Every Aryan woman was hypothecated to some Deva

---

82 Ambedkar is referring to what in medieval Europe the French called *Droit du seigneur*—the right of the feudal lord to sleep the first night with the bride of any one of his vassals. In *The Origin of the Family, Private Property and the State*, Friedrich Engels argues that the "right of first night" had an anthropological origin. In the Mesopotamian *Epic of Gilgamesh* the king-man-god of Uruk, Gilgamesh, is a tyrannical oppressor who leaves no virgin to her lover. This notorious practice continues to be reported in many parts of rural India where Dalit women, before getting married, are forced to sleep with the landlord. The Human Rights Watch 1999 report (30–1) says: "Rape is a common phenomenon in rural areas. Women are raped as part of caste custom or village tradition. According to Dalit activists, Dalit girls have been forced to have sex with the village landlord. In rural areas, 'women are induced into prostitution (Devadasi system) … which [is] forced on them in the name of religion.' The prevalence of rape in villages contributes to the greater incidence of child marriage in those areas. Early marriage between the ages of ten years and sixteen years persists in large part because of Dalit girls' vulnerability to sexual assault by upper-caste men; once a girl is raped, she becomes unmarriageable. An early marriage also gives parents greater control over the caste into which their children are married."

83 The verses 36–40 of *Rig Veda* 10.85 from Griffith's translation (1896) are worth citing to corroborate Ambedkar's point: "36. I take thy hand in mine for happy fortune that thou mayst reach old age with me thy husband. Gods, Aryaman, Bhaga, Savitar, Purandhi, have given thee to be my household's mistress. 37. O Pusan, send her on as most auspicious, her who shall be the sharer of my pleasures; Her who shall twine her loving arms about me, and welcome all my love and mine embraces. 38. For thee, with bridal train, they, first, escorted Surya to her home. Give to the husband in return, Agni, the wife with progeny. 39. Agni hath given the bride again with splendour and with ample life. Long lived be he who is her lord; a hundred autumns let him live. 40. Soma obtained her first of all; next the Gandharva was her lord. Agni was thy third husband: now one born of woman is thy fourth."

84 Ambedkar uses Arya and Aryan here almost interchangeably.

who had a right to enjoy her first on becoming puber [attaining puberty]. Before she could be married to an Aryan, she had to be redeemed by getting the right of the Deva extinguished by making him a proper payment. The description of the marriage ceremony given in the seventh Khandika of the first Adhyaya of the *Ashvalayan Grihyasutra* furnish the most cogent proof of the existence of the system. A careful and critical examination of the Sutra reveals that at the marriage three Devas were present—Aryaman, Varuna and Pushan—obviously because they had a right of prelibation over the bride.[85] The first thing that the bridegroom does is to bring her near a stone slab and make her stand on it, telling her, "Tread on this stone, like a stone be firm. Overcome the enemies; tread the foes down."[86] This means that the bridegroom does it to liberate the bride from the physical control of the three Devas whom he regards as his enemies. The Devas get angry and march on the bridegroom. The brother of the bride intervenes and tries to settle the dispute. He brings parched grain with a view to offer it the angry Devas, to buy off their rights over the bride. The brother then asks the bride to join her palms and make a hollow. He then fills the hollow of her palm with the parched grain and pours clarified butter on it and asks her to offer it to each Deva three times. This offering is called *avadana.* While the bride is making this *avadana* to the Deva, the brother of the bride utters a statement which is very significant. He says, "This girl is making this *avadana* to Aryaman Deva through Agni. Aryaman should therefore relinquish his

85 The verses being referred to say (Oldenberg 1886, 168–9): "To god Aryaman the girls have made sacrifice, to Agni; may he, god Aryaman, loosen her from this, and not from that place, Svaha! To god Varuna the girls have made sacrifice, to Agni; may he, god Varuna, &c. To god Pushan the girls have made sacrifice, to Agni; may he, god Pushan, &c."

86 This is verse 7 from the same text (Oldenberg 1886, 168). This rite, of treading on a millstone, is called *asmarohana.*

right over the girl and should not disturb the possession of the bridegroom." Separate *avadanas* are made by the bride to the other two Devas and in their case also the brother alters the same formula. After the *avadana* follows the *pradakshana* around the Agni, which is called *saptapadi,* after which the marriage of the bride and bridegroom becomes completely valid and good. All this of course is very illuminating and throws a flood of light on the utter subjection of the Aryans to the Devas and the moral degradation of the Devas as well as of the Aryans.

Lawyers know that *saptapadi* is the most essential ceremony in a Hindu marriage and that without it there is no marriage at law. But very few know why *saptapadi* has so great an importance. The reason is quite obvious. It is a test whether the Deva, who had his right of prelibation over the bride, was satisfied with the *avadana* and was prepared to release her. If the Deva allowed the bridegroom to take the bride away with him up to a distance covered by the *saptapadi*, it raised an irrefutable presumption that the Deva was satisfied with the compensation and that his right was extinguished and the girl was free to be the wife of another. The *saptapadi* cannot have any other meaning. The fact that *saptapadi* is necessary in every marriage shows how universally prevalent this kind of immorality had been among the Devas and the Aryans.

This survey cannot be complete without separate reference to the morals of Krishna. Since the beginning of Kali Yuga—which is associated with the death of Krishna—his morals became of considerable importance.[87] How do the morals of Krishna compare with those of the others? Full details are given

87 This sentence as found in the BAWS edition is error-prone: "Since the beginning of Kali Yuga, which is the same thing is associated with his death his morals became of considerable importance." It has been amended for coherence.

in another place about the sort of life Krishna led.[88] To that I will add here a few. Krishna belonged to the Vrasni (Yadava family). The Yadavas were polygamous. The Yadava kings are reported to have innumerable wives and innumerable sons—a stain from which Krishna himself was not free. But this Yadava family and Krishna's own house was not free from the stain of parental incest. The case of a father marrying his daughter is reported by the *Matsya Purana* to have occurred in the Yadava family. According to the *Matsya Purana*, King Taittiri, an ancestor of Krishna, married his own daughter and begot on her a son by the name Nala. The case of a son cohabiting with his mother is found in the conduct of Samba, the son of Krishna. The *Matsya Purana* tells how Samba lived an illicit life with the wives of Krishna, his father, and how Krishna got angry and cursed Samba and the guilty wives on that account.[89] There is a reference to this in the *Mahabharata* also. Satyabhama asked Draupadi the secret of her power over her five husbands. According to the *Mahabharata*, Draupadi warned her against talking or staying in private with her step-sons. This corroborates what the *Matsya Purana* has to say about Samba. Samba's is not the only case. His brother Pradyumna married his foster mother Mayavati, the wife of Sambara.

Such is the state of morals in the Aryan society before the death of Krishna. It is not possible to divide this history into definite yugas and to say what state of morals existed in the

88 See Appendix 1: The Riddle of Rama and Krishna on 232–46.

89 From the *Puranic Encyclopaedia* (Mani 1975, 677): "Samba was extremely handsome, and even the wives of Sri Krishna fell in love with him. Under the circumstances Samba tended to become wicked. Sri Krishna came to know of the unnatural attachment between his wives and Samba, from Narada, and cursed Samba that he would become a leper, and cursed his own wives, that they would be carried away by thieves and plunderers. Accordingly Samba became a leper and the wives of Sri Krishna were carried away by the Abhiras, after the submerging of Dvaraka."

Krita, what in Treta and what in Dwapara Yuga, which closed at the death of Krishna. If, however, we allow the ancient Aryans a spirit of progressive reform it is possible to say that the worst cases of immorality occurred in earliest age i.e. the Krita age, the less revolting in the Treta and the least revolting in the Dwapara and the best in the Kali age.

This line of thinking does not rest upon the mere general development of human society as we see all over the world. That instead of undergoing a moral decay, the ancient Aryan society was engaged in removing social evils by undertaking bold reforms is borne out by its story.

Devas and the rishis occupied a very high place in the eyes of the common Aryan, and as is usual the inferior always imitate their superior. What the superior class does forms a standard for the inferior. The immoralities which were prevalent in the Aryan society were largely the result of the imitation by the common man of the immoral acts and deeds of the Devas and the rishis. To stop the spread of immoralities in society, the leaders of the Aryan society introduced a reform of the greatest significance. They declared that acts and deeds of the Devas and the rishis are not to be cited[90] or treated as precedents. In this way one cause and source of immorality was removed by a bold and courageous stroke.

Other reforms were equally drastic. The *Mahabharata* refers to two reformers, Dirghatama[91] and Shvetaketu. It was laid

90 [The rules that Rishis' conduct is not to be cited or treated as precedent is laid down in *Gautama Dharmasutra*: Na Deva Charitam Chareta has reference to the bar enacted against treating the acts and deeds of the Devas as precedent. It is a floating verse whose source it has not been possible to locate.] In AoC 22.15 (2014, 303), Ambedkar says: "This may sound to be most extraordinary, most perverse, but the fact remains that Na Deva Charitam Chareta is an injunction issued to the Hindus by their shastras." It literally means "One should not follow the conduct of the gods."

91 Recall the story of Utathya and Mamata and how Brihaspati rapes Mamata in

down by Shvetaketu that marriage is indissoluble and there was to be no divorce. Two reforms are attributed to Dirghatama. He stopped polyandry and declared that a woman can have only one husband at a time. The second reform he is said to have carried out was to lay down conditions for regulating *niyoga*. The following were the most important of these conditions.

(i) The father or brother of the widow (or of the widow's husband) shall assemble the gurus who taught or sacrificed for the deceased husband and his relatives and shall appoint her to raise issue for the deceased husband.

(ii) (1) The husband, whether living or dead, must have no sons; (2) The gurus in a family council should decide to appoint the widow to raise issue for her husband; (3) The person appointed must be either the husband's brother or a *sapinda*, or *sagotra* of the husband or (according to Gautama) a *sapravara* or a person of the same caste; (4) The person appointed and the widow must be actuated by no lust but only by a sense of duty; (5) The person appointed must be anointed with ghee or oil (Narada Stripumsa, 82), must not speak with or kiss her or engage in the sportive dalliance with the women; (6) This relationship was to last till one son was born (or two according to some); (7) The widow must be comparatively young, she should not be old or sterile, or past child-bearing or sickly or unwilling or pregnant (Baud. Dh.S. II. 2.70, Narada Stripumsa 83–84); (8) After the birth of a son they were to regard themselves as father-in-law and daughter-in-law (Manu IX, 62). It is further made clear by the texts that if a brother-in-law has intercourse with his

---

205n75 to this riddle. The child born to Utathya and Mamata is Dirghatamas, who perhaps befittingly turns a reformer. The *Puranic Encyclopaedia* relates this story from *Mahabharata*: "At the time of the intercourse, when the semen of Brhaspati entered the womb, the child within it cried out 'Father! this passion is improper. Two persons have no place here. So withdraw your semen.' Brhaspati did not heed the request. The child in the womb repelled the semen that entered the womb with his foot and it dropped on the floor. Brhaspati who became angry, cursed the child. As a result, the boy was born blind. He got the name 'Dirghatamas' because he was born blind" (Mani 1975, 243).

> sister-in-law without appointment by elders or if he does so even when appointed by elders but the other circumstances do not exist (e.g., if the husband has a son), he would be guilty of the sin of incest.[92]

There were other reforms carried out by the ancient Aryan society necessary to improve its morals. One was to establish the rule of prohibited degrees for purposes of marriage to prevent recurrence of father–daughter, brother–sister, mother–son and grandfather–granddaughter marriages. The other was to declare sexual intercourse between the wife of the guru and the pupil a heinous sin. Equally clear is the evidence in support of an attempt to control gambling. Every treatise in the series called Dharmasutras contain references to laws made throwing on the king the duty and urgency of controlling gambling by state authorities under stringent laws.

All these reforms had taken effect long before the Kali Yuga started and it is natural to hold that from the point of view of morality the Kali Yuga was a better age. To call it an age in which morals were declining is not only without foundation but is an utter perversion.

This discussion about the Kali Yuga raised many riddles in the first place. How and when did the idea of Mahayuga arise? It is true that all over the world the idea of a golden age lying in the past has been prevalent.[93] Elsewhere the golden past is not deemed to return. But in the idea of the Mahayuga the golden past is not gone forever. It is to return after the cycle is complete.

---

92 [Kane Vol. II part I p. 601.] Ambedkar is quoting from Kane on the rules of *niyoga* obtained from various sources such as Narada, Manu and Vasishtha. Like Ambedkar, Kane too makes the point that while *niyoga* was rampant in earlier times, it came to be frowned upon and new rules were sought to be put in place, which indicates that societal life was getting better and not worse.

93 An erroneous sentence here in the BAWS edition has been removed. It reads: "But the idea of a Mahayuga is quite satisfied with the idea of a golden past prevalent elsewhere in India."

The second riddle is why was Kali Yuga not closed in 165 B.C.? When according to the astronomer it was due to end, why was it continued? The third riddle is the addition of Sandhya and Sandhyamsa periods to the Kali Yuga. It is quite obvious that these were later additions, for the *Vishnu Purana* states them separately. If they were original parts of Kali Yuga they would not have been stated separately why these additions were made. A fourth riddle is the change in the counting of the period. Originally the period of the Kali Yuga was said to be human years. Subsequently it was said to be a period of divine years with the result of the Kali Yuga—being confined to 1,200 years—became extended to 4,32,000 years. That this was an innovation is quite obvious. For the *Mahabharata* knows nothing about this calculation in terms of divine years. Why was this innovation made? What was the object of the Vedic Brahmans in thus indefinitely extending the period of the Kali Yuga? Was it to blackmail some Shudra king that the theory of Kali Yuga was invented and made unending so as to destroy his subjects from having any faith in his rule?

Appendix I

The Riddle of Rama and Krishna[1]

Rama is the hero of the *Ramayana*, whose author is Valmiki. The story of the *Ramayana* is a very short one. Besides it is simple and in itself there is nothing sensational about it.

... There is nothing in this story to make Rama the object of worship.[2] He is only a dutiful son. But Valmiki saw something

1 The BAWS editors write that they found this 49-page typed copy "in a well-bound file along with the MS of 'Symbols of Hinduism'", and included it as an Appendix to Part 3 of *Riddles in Hinduism*. This chapter caused much controversy upon its publication in BAWS Volume 4 in 1987, with a public burning in 1988 at a Maratha Mahamandal meeting in Amravati, and led to riots by the Shiv Sena. The first page of the Riddle in BAWS includes the note: "Government does not concur with the views expressed in this Chapter." In this edition, the riddle has been carefully edited from its original 9,400-word length to about 8,200 words. The cuts have been indicated with ellipses. For instance, at the outset Ambedkar recalls in bare outlines the well-known story of the *Ramanaya* in about 450 words which have been deleted so that we come to his argument per se.

2 The idea of Rama as a role model and the subject of devotion and bhakti, and the book of *Ramayana* itself becoming an object of veneration given its 'moral' message, was questioned by several writers from a Dalit and self-respect ('Shudra') standpoint in the twentieth century. Most famously, Periyar E.V. Ramasamy, in the year 1930, wrote a counter-narrative to the *Ramayana* in Tamil called *Iramayana Pathirangal* (The Characters of Ramayana), in which he attacked *Ramavataram*, the Tamil version of *Ramayana* written by the poet Kamban in the twelfth century. This was translated into Hindi as *Sacchi Ramayana* (The True Ramayana) by 'Periyar' Lalai Singh in 1968 and was banned within a year of its publication by the Uttar Pradesh government. For the troubled history of the Hindi edition, see Sarah Beth Hunt, *Hindi Dalit Literature and the Politics of Representation* (2014). Periyar saw the basic story of *Ramayana* as a tale of Aryan conquest of the Dravidian people. His critique sought "to radicalize the Tamils in southern India against Brahmanical supremacy and the domination of North Indian Sanskritic culture" (Udayakumar

extraordinary in Rama and that is why he undertook to compose the *Ramayana*.Valmiki asked Narada the following question:[3] "Tell me Oh! Narada, who is the most accomplished man on earth at the present time?" ...and then goes on to elaborate what he means by accomplished man. He defines his accomplished man as:

> Powerful, one who knows the secret of religion, one who knows gratitude, truthful, one who is ready to sacrifice his self-interest even when in distress to fulfil a religious vow, virtuous in his conduct, eager to safeguard the interests of all, strong, pleasing in appearance with power of self-control, able to subdue anger, illustrious, with no jealousy for the prosperity of others, and in war able to strike terror in the hearts of Gods.[4]

Narada then asks for time to consider and after mature deliberation tells him that the only person who can be said to possess these virtues is Rama, the son of Dasaratha. It is because of his virtues that Rama has come to be deified.[5]

2005, 55). In 1922, Periyar even advocated the burning of the *Ramayana* to counter the largely North Indian ritual of the burning of a Ravana effigy during Dussehra. His interpretation of *Ramayana* even came to be enacted in a play called *Keemayana*—literally a mincemeat of *Ramayana*—across the Tamil country during the Self-Respect Movement (on this, see Pandian 2006 and Geetha and Rajadurai 1998). For an account of anti-*Ramayana* literature by other Dravidian writers, see Udayakumar (2005, 55–6). In Bengal, Michael Madhusudan Dutt wrote *Meghnad-badh* in 1861, an epic poem on the foul murder of Ravana's son, Meghnad (Indrajit), at the hands of Lakshmana. The work is considered a modern classic. See Dutt 2010.

3 [Balakanda Sarga I. slokas 1–5.] Bala Kanda is the first of the seven books that comprise the *Ramayana*, and is considered, along with the last book, to be a later composition and an addendum to the core story in books II–VI.

4 Robert Goldman calls this one of the "most elaborate and well-known celebrations of the idealized South Asian male" (2004, 21).

5 In the core books of the *Ramayana*, books II–VI, Rama is portrayed as an ideal prince and warrior. Gradually, with the addition of books I and VII, and some interpolations in book VI, Rama is portrayed as an avatar of Vishnu and even a supreme being himself (Cush et al 2012, 659). This has been the subject of careful analysis right from the colonial period, when Wilson emphasized that "Rama, although an incarnation of Vishnu, commonly appears in his human character alone" (Pollock 1984, 505). John Muir also emphatically showed that the references

But is Rama a worthy personality of deification? Let those who accept him as an object worthy of worship, as a god, consider the following facts.

Rama's birth is miraculous and it may be that the suggestion that he was born from a *pinda* prepared by the sage Shrunga[6] is an allegorical gloss to cover the naked truth that he was begotten upon Kausalya by the sage Shrunga, although the two did not stand in the relationship of husband and wife. In any case, his birth, if not disreputable in its origin, is certainly unnatural.[7]

There are other incidents connected with the birth of Rama, the unsavoury character of which it will be difficult to deny.

Valmiki starts his *Ramayana* by emphasizing the fact that Rama is an avatar of Vishnu and it is Vishnu who agreed to take birth as Rama and be the son of Dasaratha. The god Brahma came to know of this and felt that, in order that this Rama avatar of Vishnu be a complete success, arrangements shall be made that Rama shall have powerful associates to help him and cooperate with him. There were none such existing then.

The gods agreed to carry out the command of Brahma and engaged themselves in wholesale acts of fornication not only against Apsaras, who were prostitutes, and not only against the unmarried daughters of Yakshas and Nagas, but also against the lawfully wedded wives of Ruksha, Vidhyadhar, Gandharvas, Kinnars and Vanaras and produced the Vanaras who became the associates of Rama.

---

to Rama's divine status are inconsistent enough with the rest of the story to have not formed part of the original poem. For more, see Pollock 2005.

6 This seems to be a reference to Rishi Shranga, the same priest born of cohabitation with a deer in the *Mahabharata* mentioned in Riddle No. 23 (see p.204). According to Sutherland (2004, 55–6), the story of Rishi Shranga (or Risyasranga) is not limited to the epics, but its use in the *Ramayana* is significant.

7 On the *putresti* and *ashvamedha* rituals conducted by Rishi Shranga on Dasaratha's behalf to beget sons, see Sutherland 2004, 58–9.

Rama's birth is thus accompanied by general debauchery, if not in his case certainly in the case of his associates. His marriage to Sita is not above comment. According to the *Buddha Ramayana*,[8] Sita was the sister of Rama; both were the children of Dasaratha. The *Ramayana* of Valmiki does not agree with the relationship mentioned in *Buddha Ramayana*. According to Valmiki, Sita was the daughter of the king Janaka of Videha and therefore not a sister of Rama. This is not convincing, for even according to Valmiki she is not the natural-born daughter of Janaka but a child found by a farmer in his field while ploughing it and presented by him to king Janaka and brought up by Janaka. It was therefore in a superficial sense that Sita could be said to be the daughter of Janaka. The story in the *Buddha Ramayana* is natural and not inconsistent with the Aryan rules[9] of marriage. If the story is true, then Rama's marriage to Sita is no ideal to be copied. In another sense Rama's marriage was not an ideal marriage. One of the virtues ascribed to Rama is that he was monogamous. It is difficult to understand how such a notion could have become common. For it has no foundation in fact. Even Valmiki refers[10] to the many wives of Rama. These were

---

8 Ambedkar is referring to the *Dasaratha Jataka*, part of the Buddhist Jataka tales. The short story, translated by V. Fausbøll in 1871, correlates to the Ayodhya Kanda, or Book II, of the *Ramayana*. In this version of the story, as Ambedkar highlights, Sita is Rama's sister. The end of every Jataka story identifies the characters in it with characters in the present, i.e. the Buddha and his circle. In the *Dasaratha Jataka*, the Buddha is identified with Rama and Sita with "Rahula's mother", his wife before his Enlightenment (Gombrich 1985, 434). See Gombrich 1985 for a summary and a comparison to another Jataka tale, and see Fausbøll 1871 for the full translation.

9 [Among the Aryans marriages between brothers and sisters were allowed.] For a detailed discussion of what happened around an Aryan marriage and how Devas had the "right of prelibation" over an Aryan bride, see Riddle No. 23, especially p.209–11.

10 [Ayodhyakanda Sarga VIII sloka 12.] The second book of the *Ramayana*, Ayodhya Kanda deals with the preparations for Rama's coronation and his exile to the forest. In Griffith 1895, 98, the relevant part is translated thus: "Her slave with us who serve thee, thou Wilt see thy son to Rama bow, And Sita's friends exult o'er all, While

of course in addition to his many concubines. In this he was the true son of his nominal father Dasaratha who had not only the three wives, referred to above, but many others.

Let us next consider his character as an individual and as a king.

In speaking of him as an individual I will refer to only two incidents, one relating to his treatment of Vali and other relating to his treatment of his own wife Sita. First let us consider the incident of Vali.

Vali and Sugriva were two brothers. They belonged to the Vanar race and came from a ruling family which had its own kingdom, the capital of which was Kishkindha. At the time when Sita was kidnapped by Ravana, Vali was reigning at Kishkindha. While Vali was on the throne he was engaged in a war with a Rakshasa named Mayavi. In the personal combat between the two, Mayavi ran for his life. Both Vali and Sugriva pursued him. Mayavi entered into a deep cavity in the earth. Vali asked Sugriva to wait at the mouth of the cavity and himself went inside. After some time, a flood of blood came from inside the cavity. Sugriva concluded that Vali must have been killed by Mayavi and came to Kishkindha and got himself declared king in place of Vali and made Hanuman his Prime Minister.

As a matter of fact, Vali was not killed. It was Mayavi who was killed by Vali. Vali came out of the cavity but did not find Sugriva there. He proceeded to Kishkindha and to his great surprise, he found that Sugriva had proclaimed himself king. Vali naturally became enraged at this act of treachery on the part of his brother Sugriva, and he had good ground to be. Sugriva should have ascertained, should not merely have assumed that

---

Bharat's wife shares Bharat's fall." Therefore, the 'wives' part is referred to as Sita's friends. In the Clay Sanskrit Library series, Pollock translates this as: "Delight is truly in store for Rama's exalted women, and all that is in store for your daughters-in-law is misery, at Bharata's downfall" (Pollock 2005, 77).

Vali was dead. Secondly, Vali had a son by the name Angad whom Sugriva should have made the king as the legitimate heir of Vali. He did neither of the two things. His was a clear case of usurpation. Vali drove out Sugriva and took back the throne. The two brothers became mortal enemies.

This occurred just after Ravana had kidnapped Sita. Rama and Laxmana were wandering in search of her. Sugriva and Hanuman were wandering in search of friends who could help them to regain the throne from Vali. The two parties met quite accidentally. After informing each other of their difficulties a compact was arrived at between the two. It was agreed that Rama should help Sugriva to kill Vali and to establish him on the throne of Kishkindha. On the part of Sugriva and Hanuman, it was agreed that they should help Rama to regain Sita. To enable Rama to fulfil his part of the compact, it was planned that Sugriva should wear a garland in his neck as to be easily distinguishable to Rama from Vali and that while the duel was going on, Rama should conceal himself behind a tree and then shoot an arrow at Vali and kill him. Accordingly a duel was arranged, Sugriva with a garland in his neck and while the duel was on, Rama standing behind a tree shot Vali with his arrow and opened the way for Sugriva to be the king of Kishkindha. This murder of Vali is the greatest blot on the character of Rama. It was a crime which was thoroughly unprovoked, for Vali had no quarrel with Rama. It was most cowardly act for Vali was unarmed. It was a planned and premeditated murder.[11]

11 In fact, Vali himself rebukes Rama in the text. From Goldman 2004, 35: "In this well-known passage, the stricken monkey king rebukes Rama for having shot him while he was engaged in battle with a third party. His reproach is a harsh one and includes a number of arguments. Vali argues that Rama has violated the rules of ethical behaviour in killing someone who has done him no harm, an offence compounded further by his having done so when his victim was off guard. The monkey further argues that even if Rama's action were to be regarded as falling under the rubric of hunting rather than of combat, it would still be wrongful since the skin, bones,

Consider his treatment of his own wife Sita. With the army collected for him by Sugriva and Hanuman, Rama invades Lanka. There too he plays the same mean part as he did as between the two brothers Vali and Sugriva. He takes the help of Bibhishana the brother of Ravana, promising him to kill Ravana and his son and place him on the vacant throne. Rama kills Ravana and also his son Indrajit. The first thing Rama does after the close of the fight is to give a decent burial to the dead body of Ravana. Thereafter he interests himself in the coronation of Bibhishana and it is after the coronation is over that he sends Hanuman to Sita and that too to inform her that he, Laxmana and Sugriva are hale and hearty and that they have killed Ravana.

The first thing he should have done after disposing of Ravana was to have gone to Sita. He does not do so. He finds more interest in the coronation than in Sita. Even when the coronation is over he does not go himself but sends Hanuman. And what is the message he sends? He does not ask Hanuman to bring her. He asks him to inform her that he is hale and hearty. It is Sita who expresses to Hanuman her desire to see Rama. Rama does not go to Sita, his own wife who was kidnapped and confined by Ravana for more than ten months. Sita is brought to him and what does Rama say to Sita when he sees her? It would be difficult to believe any man with ordinary human kindness could address his wife in such dire distress as Rama did to Sita when he met her in Lanka, if there was not the direct authority of Valmiki. This is how Rama addressed her[12]:

---

flesh, and so on of monkeys is forbidden to people of high caste. He also implies that Rama is cowardly, boasting that he himself would have proved victorious in a fair fight. Moreover, he claims that Rama is not merely unjust but foolish as well, since had he, Vali, been asked, he could have easily defeated Ravana and recovered Sita for him." Rama's response to Vali absolved his crime by claiming higher moral authority. See Goldman 2004, 35–6. Vali's acceptance of the argument indicates that the composers thought the argument valid.

12 [Yudhakanda Sarga II5 slokas 1–23.] Yuddha Kanda is Book VI of Valmiki's

> I have got you as a prize in a war after conquering my enemy your captor. I have recovered my honour and punished my enemy. People have witnessed my military prowess and I am glad my labours have been rewarded. I came here to kill Ravana and wash off the dishonour. I did not take this trouble for your sake.

Could there be anything more cruel than this conduct of Rama towards Sita? He does not stop there. He proceeded to tell her:

> I suspect your conduct. You must have been spoiled by Ravana. Your very sight is revolting to me. On you, daughter of Janaka, I allow you to go anywhere you like. I have nothing to do with you. I conquered you back and I am content for that was my object. I cannot think that Ravana would have failed to enjoy a woman as beautiful as you are.[13]

Quite naturally Sita calls Rama low and mean and tells him quite that she would have committed suicide and saved him all this if when Hanuman first came he had sent her a message that he abandoned her on the ground that she was kidnapped. To give him no excuse Sita undertakes to prove her purity. She enters the fire and comes out unscathed. The gods, satisfied with this evidence, proclaim that she is pure. It is then that Rama agrees to take her back to Ayodhya.

And what does he do with her when he brings her back to Ayodhya? Of course, he became king and she became queen. But while Rama remained king, Sita ceased to be a queen very soon. This incident reflects great infamy upon Rama. It is recorded by Valmiki in his *Ramayana* that some days after the coronation of

---

Ramayana. It is not clear which translated edition of Valmiki is being cited or paraphrased. Sarga 115 pertains to Rama disowning Sita and asking her to seek shelter elsewhere.

13 According to John Brockington (in Cush et al 2012, 797), this extant story of Rama's rejection of Sita may have been developed due to the growing importance of morality ascribed to the character of Rama as the text took shape and was interpolated. Sita too is portrayed as increasingly submissive.

Rama and Sita as king and queen, Sita conceived. Seeing that she was carrying, some residents of evil disposition began to calumniate Sita, suggesting that she must have conceived from Ravana while she was in Lanka and blaming Rama for taking such a woman back as his wife. This malicious gossip in the town was reported by Bhadra, the court joker, to Rama. Rama evidently was stung by this calumny. He was overwhelmed with a sense of disgrace. This is quite natural. What is quite unnatural is the means he adopts of getting rid of this disgrace. To get rid of this disgrace he takes the shortest cut and the swiftest means—namely to abandon her, a woman in a somewhat advanced state of pregnancy in a jungle, without friends, without provision, without even notice in a most treacherous manner. There is no doubt that the idea of abandoning Sita was not sudden and had not occurred to Rama on the spur of the moment. The genesis of the idea, the developing of it and the plan of executing are worth some detailed mention. When Bhadra reports to him the gossip about Sita which had spread in the town, Rama calls his brothers and tells them his feelings. He tells them Sita's purity and chastity was proved in Lanka, that the gods had vouched for it and that he absolutely believed in her innocence, purity and chastity.

> All the same the public are calumniating Sita and are blaming me and putting me to shame. No one can tolerate such disgrace. Honour is a great asset, Gods as well as great men strive to maintain it intact. I cannot bear this dishonour and disgrace. To save myself from such dishonour and disgrace I shall be ready even to abandon you. Don't think I shall hesitate to abandon Sita.

This shows that he had made up his mind to abandon Sita as the easiest way of saving himself from public calumny without waiting to consider whether the way was fair or foul. The life of Sita simply did not count. What counted was his own personal name and fame. He of course does not take the manly course of stopping this gossip, which as a king he could do and which as a husband who was convinced of his wife's innocence he was bound to do. He yielded to the public gossip and there are not wanting Hindus who use this as ground to prove that Rama was a democratic king when others could equally well say that he was a weak and cowardly monarch. Be that as it may, that diabolical plan of saving his name and his fame he discloses to his brothers but not to Sita, the only person who was affected by it and the only person who was entitled to have notice of it. But she is kept entirely in the dark. Rama keeps it away from Sita as a closely guarded secret and waits for an opportunity to put his plan into action. Eventually the cruel fate of Sita gives him the opportunity he was waiting for. Women who are carrying exhibit cravings for all sorts of things. Rama knew of this. So one day he asked Sita if there was anything for which she felt a craving. She said yes. Rama said what was it. She replied that she would like to live in the vicinity of the Ashrama of sage on the bank of the river Ganges and live on fruits and roots at least for one night. Rama simply jumped at the suggestion of Sita and said "Be easy my dear I shall see that you are sent there tomorrow". Sita treats this as an honest promise by a loving husband. But what does Rama do? He thinks it is a good opportunity for carrying through his plan of abandoning Sita.[14]

...Sita, abandoned by Rama and left to die in a jungle, went

---

14 This he does by convincing Lakshmana to take Sita to the countryside and abandon her. Goldman argues that unlike the Vali case and other instances in the text, here Rama affords no room for debate or a discussion on his decision, thereby making the choice all the more controversial. "In the case of the repudiation of Sita, it would appear that two of the central thrusts of Valmiki's *Ramayana*—the reinforcement of the system of male honour, here closely tied up with the construction of *ksatriyadharma*, and the emerging Vaishnava characterization of Rama as a new kind of god-king, a compassionate savior and redeemer who subsumes his 'caste-specific dharma under a larger, superordinate dharma'—have come into irreducible conflict" (Goldman 2004, 37–8).

for shelter in the Ashrama of Valmiki which was near about. Valmiki gave her protection and kept her in his Ashrama. There in course of time Sita gave birth to twin sons, called Kusa and Lava. The three lived with Valmiki. Valmiki brought up the boys and taught them to sing the Ramayana, which he had composed. For twelve years the boys lived in the forest in the Ashrama of Valmiki not far from Ayodhya where Rama continued to rule. Never once in those twelve years this model husband and loving father cared to inquire what had happened to Sita, whether she was living or whether she was dead. Twelve years after, Rama meets Sita in a strange manner. Rama decided to perform a Yadna[15] and issued invitation to all the rishis to attend and take part. For reasons best known to Rama himself no invitation was issued to Valmiki, although his Ashrama was near to Ayodhya. But Valmiki came to the Yadna of his own accord accompanied by the two sons of Sita, introducing them as his disciples. While the Yadna was going on the two boys performed recitations of Ramayana in the presence of the assembly. Rama was very pleased and made inquiries when he was informed that they were the sons of Sita. It was then he remembered Sita, and what does he do then? He does not send for Sita. He calls these innocent boys who knew nothing about their parents' sin, who were the only victims of a cruel destiny, to tell Valmiki that if Sita was pure and chaste she could present herself in the assembly to take a vow, thereby removing the calumny cast against herself and himself. This is a thing she had once done in Lanka. This is a thing she could have been asked to do again before she was sent away. There was no promise that after this vindication of her character Rama was prepared to take her back. Valmiki brings her to the assembly. When she was in front of Rama, Valmiki said, "O, son of Dasaratha, here is Sita whom you abandoned in

15 *Yadna* is the same as *yagna*, or sacrificial offering.

consequence of public disapprobation. She will now swear her purity if permitted by you. Here are your twin-born sons bred up by me in my hermitage." "I know," said Rama "that Sita is pure and that these are my sons. She performed an ordeal in Lanka in proof of her purity and therefore I took her back. But people here have doubts still, and let Sita perform an ordeal here that all these Rishis and people may witness it."

With eyes cast down on the ground and with hands folded Sita swore, "As I never thought of any man except Rama even in my mind, let mother Earth open and bury me. As I always loved Rama in words, in thoughts, and in deed, let mother Earth open and bury me!" As she uttered the oath, the earth verily opened and Sita was carried away inside seated on a golden *simhasana* (throne). Heavenly flowers fell on Sita's head while the audience looked on as in a trance.

That means that Sita preferred to die rather than return to Rama, who had behaved no better than a brute.[16]

Such is the tragedy of Sita and the crime of Rama the god.

Let me throw some searchlight on Rama the king.

Rama is held out as an ideal king. But can that conclusion be said to be founded in fact?

As a matter of fact Rama never functions as a king. He was a nominal king. The administration, as Valmiki states, was

16 Much has been written about Sita as an ultimately devotional wife, one that continues to be revered as a role model for Hindu women. But in fact the Sita of Valmiki's *Ramayana* is a more independent and well-rounded figure than in later versions (Cush et al 2012, 797). For different interpretations of Sita, see Doniger 1997 and Sutherland 1989. Writes Sutherland, "The character of Sita is a complex figure, like Draupadi's. Sita's actions belie much of her idealized description. Valmiki takes great pains to convince us of Sita's worth, devotion, and love, all of which are developed into a self-sacrificing, submissive, and pious creation. This carefully drawn figure is set against the more realistic Sita, one whose actions—such as her greed for the golden deer and her castigation of Lakshmana—are far from ideal. For Sita, these are the actions that lead to her abduction and confinement in the palace of Ravana" (1989, 76).

entrusted to Bharata, his brother. He had freed himself from the cares and worries about his kingdom and his subjects. Valmiki has very minutely described[17] the daily life of Rama after he became king. According to that account the day was divided into two parts. From morning to forenoon he was engaged in performing religious rites and ceremonies and offering devotion. The afternoon he spent alternately in the company of court jesters and in the *zenana*. When he got tired of the *zenana* he joined the company of jesters and when he got tired of jesters he went back to the *zenana*.[18] Valmiki also gives a detailed description of how Rama spent his life in the *zenana*. This *zenana* was housed in a park called Ashoka Vana. There Rama used to take his meal. The food according to Valmiki consisted of all kinds of delicious viands. They included flesh and fruits and liquor. Rama was not a teetotaller. He drank liquor copiously and Valmiki records that Rama saw to it that Sita joined with him in his drinking bouts.[19] From the description of the *zenana*, it was by no means a mean thing. There were Apsaras, Uraga and Kinnari accomplished in dancing and singing. There were other beautiful women brought from different parts. Rama sat in the midst of these women drinking and dancing. They pleased Rama and Rama garlanded them. Valmiki calls Rama as a "prince among women's men". This was not a day's affair. It was a regular course of his life.

As has already been said, Rama never attended to public business. He never observed the ancient rule of Indian kings of hearing the wrongs of his subjects and attempting to redress them. Only one occasion has been recorded by Valmiki when he

17 [Uttara Kanda Sarga 42 sloka 27.] Uttara Kanda, the last book of the *Ramayana*, concerns the final years of Rama and Sita, after their return to Ayodhya and Rama's coronation.

18 [Uttara Kanda Sarga 43 sloka 1.]

19 [Ibid., Sarga 42 sloka 8.]

personally heard the grievance of his subjects. But unfortunately the occasion turned out to be a tragic one. He took upon himself to redress the wrong but in doing so committed the worst crime that history has ever recorded. The incident is known as the murder of Sambuka the Shudra.[20] It is said by Valmiki that in Rama's reign there were no premature deaths in his kingdom. It happened, however, that a certain Brahman's son died a premature death. The bereaved father carried the body to the gate of the king's palace, and placing it there, cried aloud and bitterly reproached Rama for the death of his son, saying that it must be the consequence of some sin committed within his realm, and that the king himself was guilty if he did not punish it; and finally threatened to end his life there by sitting *dharna* (hunger strike)[21] against Rama unless his son was restored to life.

---

20 According to Paula Richman, "Among the deeds for which Rama has been most roundly condemned in south India, the beheading of Sambuka is preeminent" (2004, 125). The story has been used by the Dravidian movement and in anticaste literature to ridicule the idea of Rama as the embodiment of perfection. See for instance, *Sambuka Vadha* (The Slaying of Sambuka), written in Telugu by Tripuraneni Ramasvami Chaudari between 1914 and 1917; *Ramayana Natakam* (*Ramayana* drama), a Tamil play from 1954 by Thiruvarur K. Thangaraju, which was fiercer in its critique of Rama's treatment of Sambuka; and Kuvempu (Kuppalli Venkatappa Puttappa) (1904–94), a Jnanpith-winning Kannada author who wrote *Sudra Tapasvi* (1944), a novel based on Sambuka's life (see Richman 2004). Sikhamani, a contemporary Telugu Dalit poet, writes: "The sword that severed/ Shambuka's head could remain/ sharp and safe for centuries./ It has just changed hands/ and no longer recognises you./ No Manu to save you now!" See the poem "Steel Nibs are Sprouting…" in Satyanarayana and Tharu (2013, 554).

21 Ambedkar is referring to the ancient practice of a very Brahman form of protest. The scholar Catherine Weinberger-Thomas in her brilliant work on sati discusses *dharna* and its social origins at length (1999, 63–70). *Dharna* in Hindi literally means 'to place, hold' and "consists of sitting at the door (thereby blocking access) of the offender, in a sign of protest. Implicit in this act is the threat of not lifting the siege until one has received satisfaction, even if this means dying in the process. An exclusively Brahman prerogative in ancient India and religiously sanctioned since that time, *dharna* is a modern form of protest suicide. The murder of a Brahman—or responsibility for his death, which amounts to the same thing—is in fact the most abominable of all crimes, an inexpiable crime (in the absolute sense) that pursues its perpetrator, from rebirth to rebirth, with its disastrous effects. Indeed, its sole equivalent is the slaughter of a cow; but this is precisely because the cow incarnates

Rama thereupon consulted his council of eight learned rishis and Narada amongst them told Rama that some Shudra among his subjects must have been performing *tapasya* (ascetic exercises), and thereby going against *dharma* (sacred law); for according to it the practice of *tapasya* was proper to the twice-born alone, while the duty of the Shudras consisted only in the service of the twice-born. Rama was thus convinced that it was the sin committed by a Shudra in transgressing *dharma* in that manner, which was responsible for the death of the Brahman boy.

So Rama mounted his aerial car and scoured the countryside for the culprit. At last, in a wild region far away to the south he espied a man practising rigorous austerities of a certain kind. He approached the man, and with no more ado than to enquire of him and inform himself that he was a Shudra by the name Sambuka, who was practising *tapasya* with a view to going to heaven in his own earthly person and without so much as a warning, expostulation or the like addressed to him, cut off his head. And lo and behold! That very moment the dead Brahman boy in distant Ayodhya began to breathe again. Here in the wilds the gods rained flowers on the king from their joy at his having prevented a Shudra from gaining admission to their celestial abode through the power of the *tapasya*, which he had no right to perform. They also appeared before Rama and congratulated him on his deed. In answer to his prayer to them to revive the dead Brahman boy lying at the palace gate in Ayodhya, they informed him that he had already come to life. They then departed. Rama thence proceeded to the Ashrama which was

---

the very principle of Brahmanness. It is in this context that we can understand how a Brahman's threat of laying 'siege' would have been a tremendously effective means of coercion" (63–4). Weinberger-Thomas goes on to discuss how Mohandas Gandhi adapted to and excelled in this form of political blackmail parading as high moral ground, and links it to the anti-Mandal protests of 1990. This goes to show that *dharna*, which is a very popular form of and term for political protest in contemporary India, actually has rather Brahman roots.

nearby of the sage Agastya, who commended the step he had taken with Sambuka, and presented him with a divine bracelet. Rama then returned to his capital.

Such is Rama.

II

Now about Krishna.

...In the hands of Vyas, Krishna is a god among men. That is why he is made the hero of the *Mahabharata*. Does Krishna really deserve to be called a god among men? A short sketch of his life alone will help to give a correct answer. Krishna was born at Mathura at midnight on the eighth day of the month of Bhadra. His father was Vasudeva of the Yadu race, and his mother Devaki, daughter of Devaka, the brother of Ugrasen, king of Mathura. Ugrasen's wife had an illicit connection with Drumila, the Danava king of Saubha. From this illicit connection was born Kansa, who was in a sense the cousin of Devaki. Kansa imprisoned Ugrasen and usurped the throne of Mathura. Having heard from Narada or *daivavani,* a voice from heaven, that Devaki's eighth child would kill him, Kansa imprisoned both Devaki and her husband and killed six of their children as they were born one after another. The seventh child, Balarama, was miraculously transferred from Devaki's womb to that of Rohini, another wife of Vasudeva. When the eighth child, Krishna, was born, he was secretly borne by his father to the other side of the river Yamuna, where Nanda and his wife Yasoda, natives of Vraja, were then living. The Yamuna rolled back her waters to make way for the divine child; then Ananta, the chief of serpents, protected him with his ample hood from the heavy torrent of rain that was then falling. By a previous arrangement, Vasudeva exchanged his son for Nanda's newly born daughter, Yogindra or Mahamaya, and presented the latter to Kansa as his eighth child, but she flew away, telling him that the child which is being brought up by Nanda and Yasoda would kill him. This led Kansa to make a series of unsuccessful attempts to kill the child Krishna. With this object he sent to Vraja a number of Asuras in various forms. The killing of these Asuras and a number of other heroic deeds, impossible for an ordinary human child, are the chief staple of the Puranic account of Krishna's early life. Some of them are mentioned in the *Mahabharata* also. As might be expected, the authorities differ largely in their narration of these facts. I mention only some of them, following chiefly the later authorities.[22]

...Now these events filled Nanda with fear, and he seriously thought of leaving Vraja and moving to another settlement. While he was thus thinking, the place was infested with wolves which made great havoc among the cattle and made it quite unsafe.[23] This fixed the wavering intention of the nomads and they moved with all their belongings to the pleasant woodland named Vrindavan. Krishna was then only seven years old.

After his removal to this new settlement, Krishna killed quite a large number of Asuras. One of them was Aristha, who came in the form of a bull; another, Kesin, who was disguised as a horse. And five others, Vratrasura, Bakasura, Aghasura, Bhomasura and Sankhasura, the last a Yaksha. More important than these was Kaliya, a snake chief, who lived with his family in a whirlpool of the Yamuna and thus poisoned its water. Krishna one day threw himself on Kaliya's hood and danced so wildly as to make him vomit blood. He would thus have killed him, but on the

22 Here, Ambedkar recounts the stories of Krishna sucking the life-blood out of a malicious nurse while suckling on her breast as a baby, breaking a cart meant to crush his infant self and uprooting a tree he was tethered to. The emphasis remains on how ridiculous these stories seem when ascribed to a baby, even if it is the god Krishna.

23 This account is from chapter 52 from the *Harivamsa*. According to Lorenz (2007, 98), this is the only instance of the story in any of the texts dealing with Krishna's early life.

intervention of the snake's family, he spared him and allowed him to move away to another abode.

The subjugation of Kaliya was followed by *vastra-harana*, the carrying away of clothes, a hard nut to crack for worshippers and admirers of the Puranic Krishna. The whole narration is so obscene, that even the merest outlines will, I fear, be felt to be indelicate. But I must give them in as decent a form as is possible, to make my brief account of Krishna's doings as full as I can. Some *gopis*[24] had dived into the waters of the Yamuna for a bath, leaving their clothes on the banks, as is said to still be the custom in some parts of the country. Krishna seized the clothes and with them climbed upon a tree on the riverside. When asked to return them, he refused to do so unless the women approached the tree and each begged her own dress for herself. This they could do only by coming naked out of the water and presenting themselves naked before Krishna. When they did this, Krishna was pleased and he gave them their clothes. This story is found in the *Bhagavata*.[25]

The next of Krishna's feats was the uplifting of the Govardhan Hill. The Gopas were about to celebrate their annual sacrifices to Indra, the god of rain, and began to make grand preparations for it. Krishna pointed out to them that as they were a pastoral and not an agricultural tribe, their real gods were kine, hills

---

24 Meaning 'a female cowherder', the *gopis* in plural refer to the group of married or maiden women who are devoted to the worship of Krishna (Schweig 2007, 448). Within certain Vaishnava traditions, the *gopis* are honoured as the ultimate example of devotion.

25 The *Bhagavata Purana*, dated to the sixth to eighth centuries CE, is the principal textual source on Krishna's incarnation and activities. The text concerns itself with Vishnu and his incarnations, with Krishna featuring in the tenth book, which makes up one-quarter of the whole text of twelve books. While the other Puranas have almost no traditional commentary, *Bhagavata Purana* has eighty-one Sanskrit commentaries alone, attesting to its popularity (Bryant 2007, 111–2). For an exposition of the *Bhagavata Purana's* place in the Puranic canon, see Bryant 2007, chapter 3. For a contemporary translation of the tenth book, see Bryant 2004.

and woods, and then only they should worship, and not such gods as the rain-giving Indra. The Gopas were convinced, and giving up their intention of worshipping Indra, celebrated a grand sacrifice to the hill Govardhan, the nourisher of kine, accompanied with feasting and dancing. Indra was, as he could not but be, greatly enraged at this affront offered to him, and as punishment, he poured rain on the Gopa settlement for seven days and nights continually. Krishna, undaunted, uprooted the hill and held it up as an umbrella over the settlement and thus protected the Gopas and their cattle from the ruinous effects of Indra's wrath. As to the jealousy between Indra and the Krishna of the *Rig Veda*[26] and that between the former and the Vishnu of the *Satapatha Brahmana*, I have already spoken in my first lecture.[27]

Krishna's youthful career was full of illicit intimacy with the young women of Vrindavan, which is called his Rasa Lila. Rasa is a sort of circular dance in which the hands of the dancers, men and women, are joined together. It is said to be still prevalent among some of the wild tribes of this country. Krishna, it is stated, was in the habit of enjoying this dance with the young Gopis of Vrindavan, who loved him passionately. One of these dances is described in the *Vishnu Purana*, the *Harivamsa* and the *Bhagavata*.[28] All these authorities interpret the Gopis' love for

26 According to Bryant (2007, 16n6), hymns 8.96.13–15 speak of a battle of Indra against an army of ten thousand led by a Krishna Drapsa, who early commentators interpreted as a reference to a "pre-Aryan Krishna battling the Indra deity of the intruding Indo-Aryan tribes". Jamison and Brereton's translation makes no reference to Krishna (2014, 1199–1201) and Bryant deems these connections with Krishna unconvincing at best, since mostly the word *krishna* is used as an adjective, meaning 'black' (Bryant 2007, 4).

27 It is has not been possible to establish what lecture Ambedkar is referring to. We could infer that Ambedkar perhaps delivered some of the essays in this unpublished work as lectures.

28 Along with the *Mahabharata*, these are the three primary texts that refer to Krishna's life. Lorenz (2007, 99) shows the difference in the details of this part of Krishna's story in the *Harivamsa* as compared to the *Bhagavata Purana*. "The short account in

Krishna as piety—love to god, and see nothing wrong in their amorous dealings with him—dealings which, in the case of any other person, would be highly reprehensible according to their own admission. All agree as to the general character of the affair—the scene, the time and season, the drawing of the women with sweet music, the dance, the amorous feelings of the women for Krishna, and their expression in various ways. But while the *Vishnu Purana* tries—not always successfully—to keep within the limits of decency, the *Harivamsa* begins to be plainly indecent,[29] and the *Bhagavata* throws away all reserve and revels in indecency.[30]

---

the *Harivamsa* does not present any explicit theology or moral instructions, as in the *Bhagavata Purana*, where the whole affair takes up five chapters. Krishna does not attract the *gopis* by his nocturnal flute-playing. In fact, Krishna of the *Harivamsa* is not a flute-player at all. In the *Harivamsa*, it is the girls who take the initiative in the autumnal lovemaking. The *Harivamsa* does not explicitly mention that Krishna made love to married women, while the *Bhagavata Purana* is clear about this." For detailed comparisons between the *Harivamsa*, *Bhagavata Purana* and *Vishnu Purana*, see Sheth 1984 and Preciado-Solis 1984.

29 Says Sheth (1984, 14, quoted in Coleman 2010, 391), "The *[Harivamsa]* speaks frankly of Krishna's physical love with the women, which is quite earthy in comparison with the later erotico-mystical love portrayed in the *Visnu Purana* and the *Bhagavata Purana*. Understanding Krishna as a human hero, the bard of the *Harivamsa*, unlike the authors of the *Visnu Purana* and the *Bhagavata Purana*, is embarrassed by Krishna's making love to several women and does not attempt any justification of it."

30 The *Panchadhyaya* are the five chapters in the tenth book of *Bhagavata Purana* that deal with Krishna's amorous relations with the *gopis*. Schweig's summary of the *Bhagavata* version goes thus: "The Rasa Lila story commences on an enchanting autumn evening as the full moon is rising. Krishna himself is so inspired by the beauteous landscape that he is moved toward amorous love, and produces irresistible flute music, alluring the *gopis*. They suddenly abandon everything—their household duties, their families, their homes, even their physical bodies—to run off to the forest to be with him. Several chapters earlier (*Bhagavata Purana* 10.22), the *gopis* had performed a particular form of worship in order to gain the favour of the supreme goddess, with the intention of attaining Krishna as their husband. It is in the Rasa Lila that the *gopis* are said to have this desire fulfilled. The climactic scene occurs when the *gopis* form a great circle around Krishna, who miraculously duplicates himself so that he can dance with each and every *gopi* simultaneously, though each feels that Krishna is with her alone" (Schweig 2007, 449). For a translation of the Rasa Lila from *Bhagavata Purana*, see Schweig 2005.

Of all his indecencies the worst is his illicit life with one Gopi by the name Radha. Krishna's illicit relations with Radha are portrayed in the *Brahmavaivarta Purana*.[31] Krishna is married to Rukmini, the daughter of King Rukmangad. Radha was married to…[32] Krishna abandons his lawfully wedded wife Rukmini and seduces Radha, the wife of another man and lives with her in sin, without remorse.

Krishna was a warrior and a politician even at a very early age, we are told, when he was in his twelfth year. Every one of his acts whether as a warrior or as a politician was an immoral act.[33] His first act in this sphere was the assassination of his maternal uncle Kamsa. "Assassination" is not too strong a term for it, for though Kamsa had given him provocation, he was not killed in the course of a battle or even in a single combat. The story is that, having heard god Krishna's youthful feats at Vrindavan, Kamsa got frightened and determined to secure his death by confronting him with a great athlete in an open exhibition of arms. Accordingly he announced the celebration of a *dhanuryajna*, a bow sacrifice, and invited Krishna, Balarama

---

But many have argued (see Coleman 2010, 392) that, though the descriptions in *Bhagavata Purana* are more explicit and clear than *Harivamsa*, they are nonetheless ambiguous with respect to sex. So Ambedkar's accusations of indecency need to be read contextually.

31 The *Brahmavaivarta Purana* is one the eighteen Puranas; of its four parts, the last deals with the life of Krishna. The amorous relationship between the two is also prominent in *Bhagavata Purana*. See Schweig 2005, 147.

32 Ellipses as in the BAWS edition. It's not clear who Radha's husband was, but like the other *gopis*, she was a married woman who is drawn into the Rasa Lila with Krishna.

33 As an advisor to the Pandavas, Krishna often resorted to "unscrupulous means" to advance his cause, emphasizing that his actions and the battle in general ultimately upheld the cosmic order (Cush et al 2012, 426). In another brilliant work, "Essays on the Bhagwat Gita: Philosophic Defence of Counter-Revolution" in the section titled "Krishna and His Gita", Ambedkar says the *Bhagavad Gita* contains "an unheard of defence of murder" (BAWS Vol 3, 1987b, 364). He calls it a book that "offers a philosophic basis to the theory of Chaturvarna by linking it to the theory of innate, inborn qualities in men" (361).

and their Gopa friends to it. Akrura, an adherent of Krishna, but an officer of Kamsa, was deputed by the latter to bring the brothers to Mathura. They came, determined to kill Kamsa. He had provoked not only them, but other Yadavas also, whom his persecution had compelled to leave Mathura. The brothers were therefore supported by a conspiracy against him. Having arrived at Mathura, they desired to change their simple Gopa dress for a more decent one, and asked for clothes from Kamsa's washerman, whom they met in the street. As the man behaved insolently with them, they killed him and took from his stock whatever clothes they liked. They then met Kubja, a hunch-backed woman who served as Kamsa's perfumer. At their request she anointed them with sandal paste and in return was cured by Krishna of her bodily deformity. The *Bhagavata* makes him visit her on a subsequent occasion and describes his union with her with its characteristic indecency. However, on the present occasion, the brothers anointed by Kubja and garlanded by Sudama, a flower-seller, entered the place of sacrifice and broke the great bow to which the sacrifice was to be offered. The frightened Kamsa sent an elephant named Kuvalayapida to kill them. Krishna killed the elephant and entered the arena. There the brothers encountered Kamsa's chosen athletes, Chanura, Mustika, Toshalaka and Andhra. Krishna killed Chanura and Toshalaka and Balarama the other two. Frustrated in his plan of securing Krishna's death by stratagem, Kamsa ordered the brothers and their Gopa friends to be turned out and banished from his kingdom, their herds to be confiscated and Vasudeva, Nanda and his own father Ugrasen to be assassinated. At this Krishna got up on the platform on which Kamsa was seated and, seizing him by the hair, threw him down on the ground and killed him. Having consoled Kamsa's weeping wives he ordered a royal cremation for him, and refusing the kingdom offered him by Ugrasen, installed the latter on the throne and invited his banished relatives to return to Mathura.

The next episode is Krishna's fight with Jarasandha, emperor of Magadha, and Kalayavana. Jarasandha was the son-in-law of Kamsa. Enraged by Krishna's assassination of Kamsa, Jarasandha is said to have invaded Mathura seventeen times and to have been every time repulsed by Krishna. Fearing, however, that an eighteenth invasion would be disastrous to the city, Krishna removed the Yadavas to Dwarka at the west end of the Gujarat peninsula. After the removal of the Yadavas from Mathura, the city was besieged by Kalayavana at the instigation of Jarasandha. While pursuing the unarmed Krishna, however, out of the city, the invader was burnt to ashes, by fire issuing from the eyes of King Muchakunda, who had been sleeping in a mountain cave and whom he had awakened with a kick, mistaking him for Krishna. Krishna defeated the army of Kalayavana but while flying to Dwarka with the booty, he was overtaken by Jarasandha. He, however, evaded his enemy by climbing a hill and flying to Dwarka after jumping down from it.

Krishna was now, for the first time, married. He married Rukmini, the daughter of Bhishmaka, king of Vidarbha. Her father, at Jarasandha's advice, was making preparations to get her married to Sishupala, Krishna's cousin and king of Chedi. But Krishna carried her off on the day before the proposed marriage. The *Bhagavata* says she had fallen in love with Krishna and had addressed a love letter to him. This does not seem to be true. For Krishna did not remain a true and faithful husband of Rukmini.[34] Rukmini was gradually followed by an enormously vast army of co-wives, till the number of Krishna's consorts rose to sixteen thousand one hundred and eight.[35] His children numbered

34 It is not clear what the connection is between Rukmini addressing a love letter to Krishna and Krishna subsequently being unfaithful to her.

35 In *Bhagavata Purana*, it is said that every one of the wives had fervently wished for

one lakh and eighty-thousand. The chief of his wives were the well-known eight—Rukmini, Satyabhama, Jambavati, Kalindi, Mitrabinda, Satya, Bhadra and Lakshmana. The remaining sixteen thousand and one hundred were married to him on the same day. They belonged originally to the harem of King Naraka of Pragjyotish whom Krishna defeated and killed at the invitation of Indra, whose mother's earrings had been carried away by Naraka. While paying a visit after the battle to Indra's heaven in company with Satyabhama, this lady took fancy to Indra's famous *parijat* tree. To oblige his wife, Krishna had to fight with the god whom he had just favoured. Indra, though the chief of the Vedic gods, and though he was helped by the latter on this occasion, was indeed no match for the "Incarnation of the Supreme Being" and was forced to part with his favourite flower-tree, which was thus carried to Dwarka and planted there.

The story of how he obtained his chief eight wives is very interesting. The story of how he got Rukmini is already told. Satyabhama was the daughter of Satrajit, a Vadava chief who gave her away in marriage to Krishna because he was afraid of him and wished to buy his favour. Jambavati was the daughter of Jambavana, a bear chief, against whom Krishna waged a long war to recover a precious gem he had taken away from a Yadava. Jambavana was defeated and presented his daughter to Krishna as a peace-offering. Kalindi went through a series of austerities in order to get Krishna as her husband and her devotion was rewarded by the marriage she had sought. Mitrabinda was a cousin of Krishna and was carried off by him from the Svayamvara grounds. Satya was the daughter of Nagnajit, king

---

Krishna to be her husband, which was fulfilled, "yet due to Krishna's special power of duplication and his ability to act lovingly with each wife, each one considered Krishna to be her husband alone: 'Seeing that Achyuta stayed at home and never left the house, each princess regarded her beloved as exclusively her own. These women were not aware of his real nature'" (Schweig 2007, 444).

of Ayodhya, and was won by Krishna when he had achieved a brave feat of arms, namely, killing a number of naughty bulls belonging to Nagnajit. Bhadra was another cousin of Krishna and was married by him in the usual way. Lakshmana was the daughter of Brihatsena, king of Madra, and was carried off by him from the Swayamavara grounds.

Krishna's part in Arjuna's marriage with Subhadra, sister of Balarama and Krishna's half sister, is noteworthy. In the course of his travels, Arjuna arrived at the holy place of Prabhasa, and was received by Krishna on the hill of Raivataka. There he was enamoured of Subhadra and asked Krishna how he could get her. Krishna advised him to carry her off as a brave Kshatriya without depending upon the chances of a Svayamvara, the usual Kshatriya form of marriage. The Yadavas were at first enraged at this outrage, but when Krishna convinced them that Arjuna would be a very worthy husband for Subhadra, and that by carrying her off he had done nothing unworthy of a hero, they consented to the union. And how could they do otherwise? Krishna did not simply argue like us, poor talkers. He, as we have already seen, had backed his precepts by example.

It is interesting to note how Krishna disposed of Jarasandha and Sishupala, who created trouble at the Rajasuya performed by Yudhishtira. Jarasandha had imprisoned a large number of kings and intended to sacrifice them to Rudra. Unless he was killed and the imprisoned princes released and given an opportunity to pay homage to Yudhishtira, the latter's claim as emperor could not be established. Krishna therefore proceeded with Bhima and Arjuna to Rajagriha, Jarasandha's capital, and challenged him to a single combat with anyone of them he might choose. Such a challenge could not be refused by a Kshatriya, and Jarasandha, at the anticipation of death at his opponent's hand, declared his son Sahadev as his heir apparent and chose Bhima as his opponent. The combat lasted thirteen days, and Jarasandha at length met with a painful death at his rival's hand. Having put Sahadev on his father's throne, and invited the released princes to attend Yudhishtira's Rajasuya, Krishna and his friends returned to Indraprastha.

In due course the Rajasuya came off. Of the various functions and duties connected with the ceremony, Krishna is said to have taken charge of washing the feet of the Brahmans. This is a sure indication of the comparative modernness of the *Mahabharata*, at any rate, of this story. For in ancient times, even when the supremacy of the Brahmans had been established, the Kshatriyas never paid them any servile honour. However, when the sacrifice was over, the time came for Yudhishtira to make presents to the assembled princes, priests and other persons deserving honour. To whom must honour be paid first?

Yudhishtira asked Bhishma's opinion on the matter; the latter replied that Krishna was the person to be honoured first. Accordingly Sahadeva, at Yudhishtira's command, presented the Arghya, the mark of honour, to Krishna, and the latter accepted it. This upset Sishupala, who made a long speech challenging Krishna's right to the honour and abusing the Pandavas for paying any honour and Krishna for accepting it. Bhishma made another speech narrating Krishna's exploits and achievements at length, and declaring his divinity. Sishupala rose again, rebutted Bhishma's arguments one after another, and grossly abused him. It is pointed out by Krishna's recent biographers, that of the charges brought against Krishna by Sishupala, there is no mention of his dealings with the Vrindavan Gopis, a sure indication, according to them, that when the *Mahabharatha* was composed, the story of these dealings of Krishna, a story made so much of by the writers of the Puranas and the later poets, was not conceived. However, at the end of Sishupala's speech Bhishma, who saw that Yudhishtira was afraid lest Sishupala and his followers might obstruct the completion of the ceremony, said, addressing them, that if they were resolved to die they might challenge the divine Krishna himself to fight. At this Sishupala challenged Krishna, who rose in response and narrated his opponent's numerous misdeeds. Then with the words, "At the request of his mother, my aunt, I have pardoned a hundred of Sishupala's offences. But I cannot pardon the insulting words he has spoken of me before the assembled princes; I kill him before you all." He threw his *chakra* at him and cut off his head.

Krishna's actions during the Mahabharata War may now be reviewed. The following are some of them:

1. When Satyaki, Krishna's friend, was hard pressed by Bhurisrava, son of Somadatta, Krishna induced Arjuna to cut off his arms, and thereby made it easy for Satyaki to kill him.

2. When Abhimanyu was unfairly surrounded and killed by seven Kaurava warriors, Arjuna vowed the death of the ring leader, Jayadratha, the next day before sunset, or, failing that, his own death by entering into fire. When the sun was about to set, and Jayadratha remained unslain, Krishna miraculously hid the sun, on which Jayadratha came out; Krishna then uncovered the sun, and Arjuna killed Jayadratha when he was unaware.

3. Despairing of Drona being ever killed by fair means, Krishna advised the Pandavas to kill him unfairly. If he could be made to cast down his arms, he could, Krishna said, be killed easily. This could be done if he was told that his son, Asvathama, was dead. Bhima tried the suggested device. He killed an elephant named after Drona's son and told him that Asvathama was killed. The warrior was somewhat depressed by the news, but did not quite believe it. At this juncture he was hard pressed by a number of sages to cease fighting and prepare himself for heaven with meditations worthy of a Brahman. This checked the hero still more and he applied to the truthful Yudhishtira for correct information about his son. Finding Yudhishtira unwilling to tell a lie, Krishna overcame his reluctance by a long

exhortation, in the course of which he announced his ethics of untruth in the following edifying text from Vasishtha's Smriti.

"In marriage, in amorous dealings, when one's life is in danger, when the whole of one's possession is going to be lost, and when a Brahman's interest is at stake, untruth should be told. The wise have said that speaking untruth on these five occasions is not a sin." Yudhishtira's scruples were stifled, and he said to his preceptor, "Yes, Asvathama is killed," adding in a low voice, "that is, an elephant"; the last words, however, were not heard by Drona. His depression was complete, and on hearing some bitterly reproachful words from Bhima, he gave up his arms, and while sitting in a meditative posture, was killed by Dhristhadyumna.

4. When Bhima was unsuccessfully fighting with Duryodhana by the side of the Dvaipayana lake, Krishna reminded him through Arjuna that he had vowed the breaking of his opponent's thighs. Now striking a rival below the navel was unfair, but as Duryodhana could not be killed except by such an unfair means, Krishna advised Bhima to adopt the same and Bhima did.

The death of Krishna throws a flood of light on his morals. Krishna died as the ruler of Dwarka. What was this Dwarka like, and what sort of death awaited him?

In founding his city of Dwarka, he had taken care to settle thousands of "unfortunates" there. As the *Harivamsa* said: "O, hero having conquered the abodes of the Daityas (giants) with the help of brave Yadus, the Lord settled thousands of public women in Dwarka." Dancing, singing and drinking by men and women, married and prostitutes, filled the city of Dwarka. We get a description of a sea trip in which these women formed a principal source of enjoyment. Excited by their singing and dancing, the brothers Krishna and Balarama joined in the dancing with their wives. They were followed by the other Yadava chiefs and by Arjuna and Narada. Then a fresh excitement was sought. Men and women all fell into the sea and at Krishna's suggestion, the gentlemen began *jalakrida*, a water sport with the ladies, Krishna leading one party, and Balarama another, while the courtesans added to the amusement with their music. This was followed by eating and drinking and this again by a special musical performance, in which the leaders themselves exhibited their respective skill in handling various musical instruments.

It will thus be seen what a jolly people these Yadavas were, and with what contempt they would have treated the objections urged nowadays by the Brahmans and such other purists against *nautch* parties and the native theatres. It was in one of these revels—a drunken revel—that the Yadavas were destroyed. They, it is said, had incurred the displeasure of a number of sages by a childish trick played on the latter by some of their boys. These boys disguised Samba, one of Krishna's sons, as a woman with child, tying an iron pestle below his navel, and asked the sages to say what child the "woman" would give birth to. The enraged sage said "she" would produce an iron pestle which would be the ruin of the Yadavas. Fearing the worst consequences from this curse, the boys took the pestle to the sea-side and rubbed it away. But its particles came out in the form of *erakas,* a kind of reed, and its last remaining bit, which had been thrown into the sea, was afterwards recovered and used by a hunter as the point of an arrow.

Now it was with these *erakas* that the Yadavas killed themselves. They had gone in large parties to the holy place of Prabhasa. They indulged in drinking there and this proved their ruin. The evils of drinking there had been found out at length by Krishna and some other Yadava leaders, and it was prohibited on pain of death by a public notification. But the prohibition had no effect. The drunken Yadavas at first quarrelled and then began to fight and kill one another. When some of Krishna's own sons were killed he himself joined in the fight and killed a large number of his own people. He then went in search of Balarama. He found him in a meditative posture and saw his spirit passing out of his body in the form of a large serpent i.e., Sesha Naga, the divine snake whom he had incarnated. Krishna now felt that it was time for him also to pass away. He then bade farewell to his father and his wives, telling them that he had sent for Arjuna, who would take charge of them. Then he seated himself under a tree, hidden by its leafy and outstretching branches, and composed his mind in meditation. While thus sitting, a hunter named Jara mistook him for a deer and hit him with an arrow, one pointed with the last remaining bit of the fatal pestle. Discovering his mistake, the man fell at Krishna's feet and was pardoned and Krishna flew away to heaven, illumining all sides by its dazzling light. Arjuna came and proceeded towards Hastinapur with the surviving Yadava men and women. But his good genius having left him, he had lost the power of his hitherto mighty arm and his unrivalled skill as an archer. A number of Ahiras, armed only with *lathis*, attacked his party and carried off many of the women, and he reached Hastinapur only with a small remnant. After Arjuna's departure, the sea engulfed Dwarka, and nothing was left to speak of the Yadavas, their glories, their domestic broils and their revels.

List of all the Riddles featured in the BAWS edition of **Riddles in Hinduism**

(Riddles in italics are featured in this annotated edition)

Appendix II

"The Towel, the Tar Brush and the Hammer"

Unnamati Syama Sundar

"The Press in India is an accomplice of the Congress," said Dr B.R. Ambedkar in 1945 in his blistering attack on Gandhi and the Congress party (BAWS Vol 9, 1991, 199). In the same breath, Ambedkar lamented the blackout in the news of the Muslim League, the Justice Party of Madras, and his own party at the time, the All-India Scheduled Castes Federation. Despite serious lack of resources, he founded and oversaw the running of four newspapers in his lifetime. The first one was the fortnightly *Mook Nayak* (Leader of the Voiceless), established in 1920 with help from Shahu Maharaj of Kolhapur (a pioneer who was the first to implement the policy of reservation in his state). Dhananjay Keer writes in his biography of Ambedkar, "How violent and unfavourable were the times can be seen from the fact that the *Kesari* refused even to announce its publication although solicited to do so as a paid advertisement! And this happened when Tilak was yet alive!" (1954/1990, 41). The exclamation marks seem a little out of place, but then Keer was a hack who wrote worshipful biographies of Tilak and Vinayak Damodar Savarkar as well.

Ambedkar explains why we need not be so surprised: "In 1918, when the non-Brahmins and the Backward Classes had started an agitation for separate representation in the legislature,

Shankar in *Hindustan Times,* 17 February 1933. Republished in the Telugu newspaper *Krishna Patrika* on 4 March 1933. Courtesy: NMML

Mr Tilak at a public meeting held in Sholapur said that he did not understand why the oil pressers, tobacco shopkeepers, washermen, etc.—that was his description of the Non-Brahmins and the Backward classes—should want to go in the legislature. In his opinion, their business was to obey the laws and not to aspire for power to make laws." In 1942, when Lord Linlithgow invited fifty-two important Indians from a cross-section of the population to enlist the cooperation of all Indians in the war effort, Ambedkar quoted the response of Congress stalwart Vallabhai Patel, who found it funny: "The Viceroy sent for the leaders of the Hindu Mahasabha, he sent for the leaders of the Muslim League and he sent for Ghanchis (oil pressers), Mochis (cobblers) and the rest" (BAWS Vol 9, 1991, 209). The current prime minister, Narendra Modi, said to be a Ghanchi, is

Shankar in *Shankar's Weekly*, 11 December 1949. Ambedkar's favourite little girl, the Hindu Code Bill, is depicted like Hitler's favourite little girl. Courtesy: NMML

installing a 182-metre high 'Statue of Unity' for the same Patel.

This is the background against which we must see Eeran in one his *Filmindia* cartoons on the Constitution showing an uncharacteristically bare-chested Ambedkar with a *janeu* dangling across him, and *padukas* for footwear as sweepers and women step out of a car to walk into parliament. The caption carries the sobriquet 'Modern Manu', the most incongruous title for someone who ended the Mahad Satyagraha movement on 25 December 1927 by making a bonfire of a copy of the *Manusmriti*, the book that brings Manu fame.

The controversy that broke out in 2012 around K. Shankar Pillai's cartoon of Ambedkar in NCERT's Class XI Political Science textbook, *Indian Constitution at Work*, on the slow pace of the drafting of the Constitution, led to many interpretations and debates among research scholars and in the media. This one cartoon posed several questions to a historian. As a self-taught cartoonist, working on Telugu newspaper cartoons in colonial India for my MPhil at the Jawaharlal Nehru University, I realised that research on colonial-era cartoons was scant. The so-called nationalist press, which as Ambedkar says was nothing but a Congress and Brahman press, served as a vehicle of propaganda for Gandhi (who ran a few well-funded newspapers himself).

Cartoons in most newspapers largely upheld these prejudices. Gandhi appeared in these cartoons as a demigod, a saint, a leader whom the drummer boys dared not lampoon. Besides Gandhi, the British Viceroy occupied center-stage. If these were the heroes, there were villains too: Ambedkar and Muhammad Ali Jinnah. Any leader who bitterly criticized the policies of the Congress was a victim of the cartoonist's nib. Ambedkar was mostly portrayed negatively as a villain and buffoon during the Round Table Conference (1930–31), the Poona Pact (1932), when he was Labour Member of the Viceroy's Executive Council (1942–46), during the drafting of the Constitution and

Earan in *Filmindia*, December 1950. Courtesy: National Film Archives of India, Pune

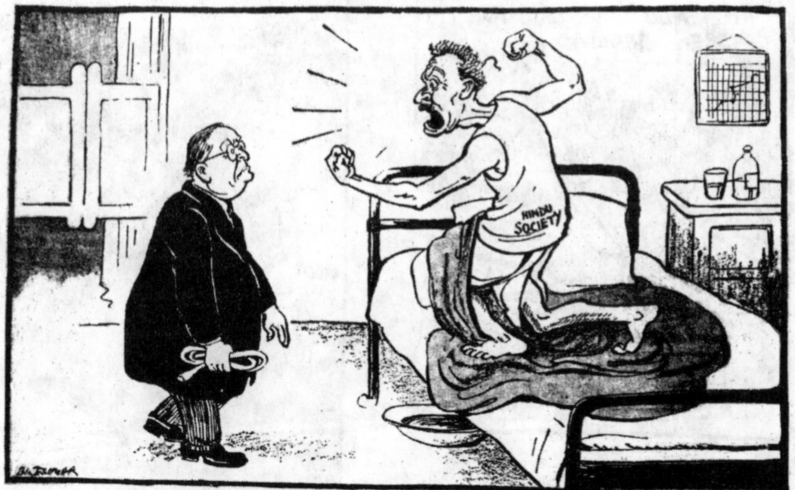

There is much opposition to Dr. Ambedkar's Hindu Code Bill.

Bireshwar in *National Herald*, 26 February 1949. Courtesy: National Library, Kolkata

the Hindu Code Bill controversy. He was shown as someone out to destroy the Sanatana Hindu Dharma.

The two Shankar cartoons featured here may at first glance appear sympathetic to Ambedkar, but there's a catch: the Hindu Code Bill is depicted as Ambedkar's favourite little girl, echoing what back then was an iconic image of Hitler taking a walk with his favourite little girl, Helga Goebbels (one of the daughters of Joseph Goebbels). Varnashrama is depicted by Shankar in 1933 as a goddess on a pedestal being tainted with tar by the little-known Sanatanist leader from Madras M.K. Acharya, and Gandhi is shown wiping it with a towel, while Ambedkar—who was actually at the centre of this debate after the Poona Pact—is shown striking at the very foundation with a hammer, but to Shankar it appears that not a chip or dent is made by him.

Oommen in *The Leader*, 30 September 1951. The caption implies that it was neither the ruling Congress nor the Opposition but Brahmanism that defeated the Hindu Code Bill in parliament. Courtesy: NMML

Shankar's cartoon, c.1949, as reproduced in the NCERT Class XI textbook.

After Ambedkar embraced Buddhism in 1956, Bal Thackeray in *Maratha*, the mouthpiece the Samyukta Maharashtra Movement in the 1950s. Courtesy: NMML

Unnamati Syama Sundar's response in May 2012 on his Facebook page to the controversy following Shankar's cartoon featured in the NCERT textbook.

Bibliography

Achar, B. N. Narahari. 1998. "Enigma of the Five-Year Yuga of Vedanga Jyotisa." *Indian Journal of History of Science* 33 (2): 101–11.

Agarwal, Bina. 1994. *A Field of One's Own: Gender and Land Rights in South Asia*. Cambridge: Cambridge University Press.

Aiyer, Velandai Gopala. 1901. *The Chronology of Ancient India*. Madras: G.A. Natesan.

Alsdorf, Ludwig. 2010. *The History of Vegetarianism and Cow-Veneration in India*. London: Routledge.

Ambedkar, B.R. 1979. "Castes in India: Their Mechanism, Genesis and Development." *Indian Antiquary* 41: 81–95. Repr. BAWS, Vol 1, 5–22. Bombay: Education Department, Government of Maharashtra. (Orig. pub. 1917.)

——. 1979. "Thoughts on Linguistic States". In BAWS, Vol 4, 137–71. Bombay: Education Department, Government of Maharashtra.

——. 1987a. *Riddles in Hinduism*. In BAWS, Vol 4. Bombay: Education Department, Government of Maharashtra.

——. 1987b. "Krishna and His Gita". In BAWS, Vol 3, 375–80. Bombay: Education Department, Government of Maharashtra.

——. 1990. *The Untouchables: Who Were They and Why They Became Untouchable*. In BAWS, Vol 7. Bombay: Education Department, Government of Maharashtra. (Orig. publ. 1948.)

——. 1990. *Who Were the Shudras?* In BAWS, Vol 7. Bombay: Education Department, Government of Maharashtra. (Orig. publ. 1946.)

——. 1991. *What Congress and Gandhi Have Done to the Untouchables*. In BAWS, Vol 9. Bombay: Education Department, Government of Maharashtra. (Orig. publ. 1945.)

——. 2003. "A letter to Jawaharlal Nehru regarding the Book 'Buddha and His Dhamma'." In BAWS, Vol 17, Part 1, 444–5. Bombay: Education Department, Government of Maharashtra.

——. 2014. *Annihilation of Caste: The Annotated Critical Edition*. New Delhi: Navayana. (Orig. publ. 1936.)

Banerji, Sures Chandra. 1989. *A Companion to Sanskrit Literature*. New

Delhi: Motilal Banarsidass.

Bandyopadhyay, Sibaji. 2014. "Of Gambling: A Few Lessons from the *Mahabharata*", in Ed. Bandyopadhyay and Arindam Chakrabarti. *Mahabharata Now: Narration, Aesthetics, Ethics*. New Delhi: Routledge.

——. 2016. *Three Essays on the Mahabharata: Exercises in Literary Hermeneutics*. Hyderabad: Orient BlackSwan.

Benson, James. Ed. 2010. *Mahadeva Vedantin: Mimamsanyayasamgraha: A Compendium of the Principles of Mimamsa*. Wiesbaden: Harrassowitz Verlag.

Berreman, Gerald. 1962. "Pahari Polyandry: A Comparison." *American Anthropologist*, New Series, 64 (1) Part 1 (Feb 1962): 60–75.

Bhattacharya, Ramkrishna. 2011a. "History of Indian Materialism." http://www.carvaka4india.com/2011/12/history-of-indian-materialism.html, accessed 19 March 2016.

——. 2011b. *Studies on the Carvaka/Lokayata*. New Delhi: Anthem Press.

Bloomfield, Maurice. 1890. "The Kaucika-sutra of the Atharva-veda." *Journal of the American Oriental Society* 14: i–424.

——. 1897. *Hymns of the Atharva Veda Together with Extracts from the Ritual Books and Commentaries*. Sacred Books of the East Vol 42. Oxford: Clarendon Press.

Blunt, E.A.H. 1931. *The Caste System of Northern India with Special Reference to the United Provinces of Agra and Oudh*. London: Oxford University Press.

Bosworth, A. B. 1996. "The Historical Setting of Megasthenes' Indica." *Classical Philology* 91 (2): 113–27.

Brockington, J. 1998. *The Sanskrit Epics*. Leiden: Brill.

Bryant, Edwin F. Ed. 2004. *Krishna: the Beautiful Legend of God (Srimad Bhagavata Purana Book 10)*. London: Penguin.

——. 2007. *Krishna: A Sourcebook*. Oxford: Oxford University Press.

Buckle, Henry Thomas. 1884/2011. *History of Civilization in England*. Cambridge: Cambridge University Press.

Bühler, George. 1879. *The Sacred Laws of the Aryas as taught in the schools of Apastamba, Gautama, Vasistha and Baudhayana, Part I: Apastamba and Gautama*. Sacred Books of the East Vol 2. Oxford: Clarendon Press.

——. 1882. *The Sacred Laws of the Aryas as taught in the schools of Apastamba, Gautama, Vashishta and Baudhayana, Part II: Vasistha and Baudhayana.* Sacred Books of the East Vol 14. Oxford: Clarendon Press.

——. 1886. *The Laws of Manu*. Sacred Books of the East Vol 25. Oxford: Clarendon Press.

Census of India, 1911. 1913. Delhi: Office of the Superintendent of Government Printing, India.

Chakravarti, Mahadev. 1979. "Beef-eating in Ancient India." *Social Scientist* 7 (11): 51–5.

Chakravarti, Uma. 1995. "Gender, Caste and Labour: Ideological and Material Structure of Widowhood." *Economic and Political Weekly* 30(36) (Sep 9, 1995): 2248–56.

——. 2003. *Gendering Caste: Through a Feminist Lens*. Calcutta: Stree.

Chattopadhyaya, Debiprasad. 1990. *Carvaka/Lokayata: An Anthology of Source Materials and Some Recent Studies*. New Delhi: Indian Council of Philosophical Research.

Clooney, Francis X, S.J. 1990. *Thinking Ritually: Rediscovering the Purva Mimamsa of Jaimini*. Vienna: De Nobili Research Library.

Coleman, Tracy. 2010. "Viraha-Bhakti and Stridharma: Re-Reading the Story of Krsna and the Gopis in the Harivamsa and the Bhagavata Purana", *Journal of the American Oriental Society* 130 (3): 385–412.

Cowell, E.B. and A.E. Gough. 1882. *The Sarva-Darsana-Samgraha by Madhavacharya*. London: Trubner and Co.

Cush, Denise, Catherine Robinson, and Michael York, eds. 2012. *Encyclopedia of Hinduism*. London: Routledge.

Daniélou, Alain. 1987. *While the Gods Play: Shaiva Oracles and Predictions on the Cycles of History*. Tr. Barbara Bailey and Michael Baker. Vermont: Inner Traditions International.

Debroy, Bibek. Tr. 2005 *The Bhagavad Gita*. New Delhi: Penguin

——. Tr. 2010–14. *The Mahabharata*. New Delhi: Penguin.

Desai, Ashwin, and Goolam Vahed. 2015. *The South African Gandhi: Stretcher-Bearer of Empire*. New Delhi: Navayana.

Deshpande, G.P. Ed. 2002. *Selected Writings of Jotirao Phule*. New Delhi: LeftWord.

Dewey, John. 1916. *Democracy and Education: An Introduction to the Philosophy of Education*. New York: The Macmillan Company.

Diparatnasagara, Muni. Ed. 2000. *Bhagavati Arigasutra (with Abhayadevasuri's commentary)*, Agama Suttani, Vol 6. Ahmedabad: Agama Sruta Prakasan.

Dirks, Nicholas B. 2001. *Castes of Mind: Colonialism and the Making of Modern India*. New Delhi: Permanent Black.

Doniger, Wendy. 1981. *The Rig Veda: An anthology: One hundred and eight hymns, selected, translated and annotated*. London: Penguin.

——. 1985. *Women, Androgynes, Mythical Beasts*. Chicago: University of Chicago Press.

——. Ed. 1991. With Brian K. Smith. *The Laws of Manu*. New Delhi: Penguin Books.

——. 1993. Ed. *Purana Perennis: Reciprocity and Transformation in Hindu and Jaina Texts*. New York: SUNY Press.

——. 1995. "Begetting on Margin: Adultery and Surrogate Pseudomarriage in Hinduism." In *From the Margins of Hindu Marriage: Essays on Gender, Religion, and Culture*. Eds. Lindsey Harlan and Paul B. Courtright, 160–83. New York: Oxford University Press.

——. 1997. "Sita and Helen, Ahalya and Alcmena: A Comparative Study." *History of Religions* 37 (1): 21–49.

——. 1999. *Splitting the Difference: Gender and Myth in Ancient Greece and India*. Chicago: University of Chicago Press.

——. 2009. *The Hindus: An Alternative History*. New York: Penguin.

——. 2014. *On Hinduism*. Oxford: Oxford University Press.

Dutt, Michael Madhusudan. 2010. *The Poem of the Killing of Meghnad*. Tr. William Radice. New Delhi: Penguin.

Dutt, Romesh Chunder. 1889. *A History of Civilization in Ancient India Based on Sanscrit Literature* (3 vols). Calcutta: Thacker, Spink and Co.

Embree, Ainslie T. Ed. 1991. *Sources of Indian Tradition*, Vol 1. New Delhi: Penguin.

Eggeling, Julius. Tr. 1882–1900. *The Satapatha Brahmana, according to the text of the Madhyandina School*. Sacred Books of the East Vols 12, 26, 41, 43, 44. Oxford: Clarendon Press.

Fausbøll, V. Tr. 1871. *The Dasaratha Jataka, Being the Buddhist Story of King*

Rama. Copenhagen: Hagerup.

Figueira, Dorothy. 2002/2015. *Aryans, Jews, Brahmins: Theorizing Authority through Myths of Identity*. New York: SUNY Press/New Delhi: Navayana.

Frede, Victoria. 2011. *Doubt, Atheism, and the Nineteenth-Century Russian Intelligentsia*. Madison: University of Wisconsin Press.

Freystad, Kathinka. 2010. "From Analogies to Narrative Entanglement: Invoking Scientific Authority in Indian New Age Spirituality." In *Handbook of Religion and the Authority of Science*. Eds. James R. Lewis and Olav Hammer, 41–66. Leiden: Brill.

Gandhi, M.K. [Mahatma]. 1965. *My Varnashrama Dharma*. Ed. Anand T. Hingorani. Bombay: Bharatiya Vidya Bhavan.

——. 2009. *The Bhagvad Gita According to Gandhi*. Ed. John Strohmeier. Berkeley: North Atlantic Books.

Ganguli, K.M. Tr. 1883–96. *The Mahabharata of Krishna-Dwaipayana Vyasa Translated into English Prose*. Calcutta: Bharata Press.

——. 2004. Tr. *The Mahabharata*. Vol 4. New Delhi: Munshiram Manoharlal.

Geetha, V. and S.V. Rajadurai. 1998. *Towards a Non-Brahmin Millennium: From Iyothee Thass to Periyar*. Calcutta: Samya.

Goldman, Robert P. 2004. "Resisting Rama: Dharmic Debates on Gender and Hierarchy and the Work of the Valmiki Ramayana." In *The Ramayana Revisited*. Ed. Mandakranta Bose, 19–46. Oxford: Oxford University Press.

Gombrich, Richard. 1985. "The Vessantara Jataka, the Ramayana and the Dasaratha Jataka." *Journal of the American Oriental Society* 105 (3): 427–37.

Gonzalez-Reimann, Luis. 1989. "The Ancient Vedic Dice Game and the Names of the Four World Ages in Hinduism." In *World Archaeoastronomy, Selected Papers from the 2nd Oxford International Conference on Archaeoastronomy Held at Mérida, Yucatán*, México, 13–17 January, 1986. Ed. A.F. Aveni, 195–202. Cambridge: Cambridge University Press.

Green, Nile. 2011. *Bombay Islam: The Religious Economy of the West Indian Ocean, 1840–1915*. New York: Cambridge University Press.

Griffith, Ralph T.H. 1895 [1870–74]. *The Ramayana of Valmiki Translated into English verse.* Benares: E. J. Lazarus and Co.

——. 1899. *The Texts of the White Yajurveda: Translated with a Popular Commentary*. Benares: E.J. Lazarus and Co.

——. 1916–17. *The Hymns of the Atharva Veda* (2 vols). Benares: E.J. Lazarus and Co.

Gupta, Som Raj. Tr. 2008. *The Word Speaks to the Man: Wisdom of Sankara* Volume V, Part Two. Delhi: Motilal Banarsidass.

Guru, Gopal. 1991. "Hinduisation of Ambedkar in Maharashtra." *Economic and Political Weekly* 26 (7) (Feb. 16, 1991): 339–41.

Hansen, Thomas Blom. 2001. *Violence in Urban India: Identity Politics, 'Mumbai', and the Postcolonial City.* Delhi: Permanent Black.

Hatcher, Brian A. 2007. "Bourgeois Vedanta: The Colonial Roots of Middle-class Hinduism." *Journal of American Academy of Religion* 75 (2): 298–323.

Heestermen, J.C. 1987. "Self-Sacrifice in Vedic Ritual", In *Gilgul: Essays on Transformation, Revolution, and Permanence in the History of Religions.* Eds. Guy G. Stroumsa, Shaul Shaked and David Shulman, 91–106. Leiden: Brill.

Hiltebeitel, Alf. 1988. *The Cult of Draupadi, Volume 1: Mythologies: From Gingee to Kuruksetra*. Chicago: University of Chicago Press.

Hopkins, Edward Washburn. 1902. *The Great Epic of India: Character and Origin of the Mahabharata*. London: C. Scribner's Sons.

Human Rights Watch. 1999. *Broken People: Caste Violence Against India's "Untouchables"*. New York: Human Rights Watch.

Hunt, Sarah Beth. 2014. *Hindi Dalit Literature and the Politics of Representation*. New Delhi: Routledge.

Iyengar, P.T. Srinavasa. 1988 (1926). *The Stone Age in India*. New Delhi: Asian Education Services.

Jackson, Carl T. 1994. *Vedanta for the West: The Ramakrishna Movement in the United States*. Bloomington: Indian University Press.

Jaffrelot, Christophe. 2005. *Dr Ambedkar and Untouchability: Analysing and Fighting Caste*. New Delhi: Permanent Black.

——. 2010. *Religion, Caste, and Politics in India*. Delhi: Primus Books.

Jaiswal, Suvira. 2001. "Female Images in the Arthasastra of Kautilya." *Social Scientist* 29 (3/4): 51–59.

Jamison, Stephanie. 1996. *Sacrificed Wife/Sacrificer's Wife: Women, Ritual and Hospitality in Ancient India*. Oxford: Oxford University Press.

——. and Joel P. Brereton. 2014. *The Rigveda: The Earliest Religious Poetry of India*. New York: Oxford University Press.

Jayaswal, Kashi Prasad. 1924. *Hindu Polity: A Constitutional History of India in Hindu Times*. Calcutta: Butterworth.

Jha, D.N. 2009. *The Myth of the Holy Cow.* New Delhi: Navayana.

Jha, Ganganath. 1923. *Chandogya Upanishad and Sri Sankara's Commentary–I*. Madras: V.C. Seshacharri.

——. 1942. *The Purva Mimamsa Sutras of Jaimini*. Allahabad: Panini Office.

——. 1999. *The Nyaya-Sutras of Gautama* (4 vols). New Delhi: Motilal Banarsidass.

Jolly, Julius. 1880. *The Institutes of Vishnu*. Sacred Books of the East Vol 7. Oxford: Clarendon Press.

Jones, Kenneth W. 2006. *Arya Dharm: Hindu Consciousness in 19th Century Punjab*. Delhi: Manohar. (Orig. publ. 1976.)

Kane, P.V. 1968–77 [1930–53]. *History of Dharmasastra* (5 vols, 2nd edition). Poona: Bhandarkar Oriental Research Institute.

Kannabiran, Kalpana. 1995. "Judiciary, Social Reform and Debate on 'Religious Prostitution' in Colonial India." *Economic and Political Weekly* 30 (43): WS59–WS69.

Keith, A.B. 1998 (1920). *Rigveda Brahmanas: The Aitareya and Kausitaki Brahmanas of the Rigveda*. Delhi: Motilal Banarsidass.

Ketkar, S.V. 1998 (1909). *History of Caste in India*. New Delhi: Low Price Publications.

Khanna, Ranjana. 1997. "In Search of a Voice for Dopdi/Draupadi: Writing the Other Woman's Story Out of the 'Dark Continent'." In *Women's Lives/Women's Times: New Essays on Auto/Biography*. Eds. Trev Lynn Broughton and Linda R. Anderson, 103–21. New York: SUNY Press.

King, Anna. 2005. "The Ganga: Waters of Devotion." In *The Intimate Other: Love Divine in Indic Religions*. Eds. Anna S. King and J. L.

Brockington, 153–93. Hyderabad: Orient BlackSwan.

Kinjawadekar, Pandit Ramachandra Shastri. 1936. *Harivamsa.* Pune: Chitrashala Press.

Klostermaier, Klaus A. 1972. "Hinduism in Bombay." *Religion* 2 (2): 83–91.

——. 2007. *A Survey of Hinduism.* New York: SUNY Press.

Kopf, David. 1979. *The Brahmo Samaj and the Shaping of the Modern Indian Mind.* Princeton: Princeton University Press.

Kosambi, D.D. 1956/2008. *An Introduction to the Study of Indian History.* Reprint. Bombay: Popular Prakashan.

Krishnarao, Bhavaraju Venkata. 1942. *A History of the Early Dynasties of Andhradesa, c. 200–625 A.D.* Madras: V. Ramaswamy Sastrulu and Sons.

Lane, Christopher. 2012. *The Age of Doubt: Tracing the Roots of Our Religious Uncertainty.* New Haven and London: Yale University Press.

Law, B.C. 1922/2005. *Kshatriya Clans in Buddhist India.* New Delhi: Ajay Book Service.

——. 1926/2007. *Ancient Indian Tribes.* New Delhi: Motilal Banarsidass. Reissued New Delhi: Law Press.

Leeming, David. 2005. *The Oxford Companion to World Mythology.* Oxford: Oxford University Press.

Lingat, Robert. 1973. *The Classical Law of India.* Tr. J. Duncan M. Derrett. Berkeley: University of California Press. http://www.ucpress.edu/op.php?isbn=9780520018983, accessed 21 March 2016.

Llewellyn, J.E. and J.S. Llewellyn. 1993. *The Arya Samaj as a Fundamentalist Movement: A Study in Comparative Fundamentalism.* New Delhi: Manohar.

Lochtefeld, James. 2002. *The Illustrated Encyclopedia of Hinduism.* Vol 1. New York: Rosen Publishing Group.

Lokhandwalla, T. 1955. "The Bohras: A Muslim community of Gujarat." *Studia Islamica* 3: 117–35.

Lorenz, Ekkehard. 2007. "The Harivamsa: The Dynasty of Krishna." In *Krishna: A Sourcebook.* Ed. Edwin F. Bryant, 95–110. Oxford: Oxford University Press.

Lorenzen, David N. 2002. "Early Evidence for Tantric Religion." In *The*

Roots of Tantra. Eds. Katherine Anne Harper and Robert L. Brown, 25–36. SUNY Press, New York.

——. 2006. "Who Invented Hinduism?" In *Who Invented Hinduism: Essays on Religion in History*, 1–36. New Delhi: Yoda Press.

Macauliffe, Max Arthur. 1875. "The Fair at Sakhi Sarwar." *Calcutta Review* 60.

Mani, Vettam. 1975. *Puranic Encyclopaedia: A Comprehensive Dictionary with Special Reference to the Epic and Puranic Literature*. New Delhi: Motilal Banarsidass.

Mayne, John Dawson. 1878/2008. *Treatise on Hindu Law and Usage*, Madras: Higginbothams. 16th edn. Revised by Justice Ranganath Misra. New Delhi: Bharat Law House.

Meyer, Johann Jakob. 1953. *Sexual Life in Ancient India: A Study in the Comparative History of Indian Culture*. New York: Barnes & Noble.

Mies, Maria. 1986. *Patriarchy and Accumulation on a World Scale: Women in the International Division of Labour.* London: Zed Books.

Miletski, Hani. 2005. "A History of Bestiality." In *Bestiality and Zoophilia: Sexual Relations with Animals*. Eds. Andrea M. Beetz and Anthony Louis Podberscek, 1–22. Purdue: Purdue University Press.

Mir, Farina. 2010. *The Social Space of Language: Vernacular Culture in British Colonial Punjab*. Berkeley and Los Angeles: University of California Press.

Mitra, Rajendralal. 1881. *Indo-Aryans: Contributions Towards the Elucidation of Their Ancient and Mediaeval History* (2 vols). Calcutta: W. Newman & Co.

Monier-Williams, Sir Monier. 1883. *Brahmanism and Hinduism*. London: J. Murray.

Mookerji, Radha Kumud. 1947 (1989). *Ancient Indian Education: Brahmanical and Buddhist*. Delhi: Motilal Banarsidass.

Müller, Max. 1859. *A History of Ancient Sanskrit Literature so far as it illustrates the Primitive Religion of the Brahmans*. London: Williams and Norgate.

——. 1879. *The Upanishads: Part 1*. Sacred Books of the East Vol 1. Oxford: Clarendon Press.

——. 1883. *India: What it Can Teach Us*. London: Longmans.

Muir, John. 1868–72 [1858–70]. *Original Sanskrit Texts on the Origin and History of the People of India, their Religion and Institutions* (5 vols, 2nd edition). London: Trübner and Co.

Mukherjee, Arun P. 2009. "B.R. Ambedkar, John Dewey, and the Meaning of Democracy." *New Literary History* 40 (2): 345–70.

Nair, Janaki. 1994. "The Devadasi, Dharma and the State." *Economic and Political Weekly* 29 (50) (Dec. 10, 1994): 3157–59 + 3161–67.

Nanda, Meera. 2004. "Postmodernism, Hindu nationalism and 'Vedic science'." *Frontline*, 2 and 16 January 2004.

——. 2010. "Madame Blavatsky's Children: Modern Hindu Encounters with Darwinism." In *Handbook of Religion and the Authority of Science*. Eds. James R. Lewis and Olav Hammer, 279–344. Leiden: Brill.

Narasu, P. Lakshmi. 2002. *Religion of the Modern Buddhist*. Ed. G. Aloysius. Delhi: Wordsmiths.

——. 1907. *The Essence of Buddhism*. Madras: Srinivasa Varadachari & Co.

O'Hanlon, Rosalind. 1985. *Caste, Conflict and Ideology: Mahatma Jotirao Phule and Low-Caste Protest in Nineteenth-Century Western India*. Cambridge: Cambridge University Press.

Oldenberg, Hermann. 1886. *The Grihya-sutras, rules of Vedic domestic ceremonies* (2 vols). Oxford: Clarendon Press.

——. 1988. *The Religion of the Veda*. Tr. Shridhar B. Shrotri. New Delhi: Motilal Banarsidass.

Olivelle, Patrick. 1993. *The Asrama System: The history and hermeneutics of a religious institution*. Oxford: Oxford University Press.

——. 1999. *The Dharmasutras: The Law Codes of Ancient India*. Oxford: Oxford University Press.

——. 2005. *Manu's Code of Law: A Critical Edition and Translation of the Manava-Dharmasastra*. New York: Oxford University Press.

——. 2008. *Collected Essays: I*. Firenze: Firenze University Press.

Oommen, T.K. 2005. *Crisis and Contention in Indian Society*. New Delhi: SAGE.

Padel, Felix. 1995. *The Sacrifice of Human Being: British Rule and the Konds of Orissa*. New Delhi: Oxford University Press.

——. 2011. *Sacrificing People: Invasions of a Tribal People*. Hyderabad:

Orient Blackswan.

Padoux, André. 2002. "What do we mean by Tantrism?" In *The Roots of Tantra*. Eds. Katherine Anne Harper and Robert L. Brown, 17–24. New York: SUNY Press.

Pandian, M.S.S. 2006. *Brahmin and Non-Brahmin: Genealogies of the Tamil Political Present*. Ranikhet: Permanent Black.

Pargiter, F. Eden. 1904. *The Markandeya Purana*. Calcutta: The Asiatic Society.

Parpola, Asko. 2007. "Human Sacrifice in India in Vedic Times and Before." In *The Strange World of Human Sacrifice*. Ed. Jan N. Bremmer, 157–78. Leuven: Peeters.

——. 2015. *The Roots of Hinduism: The Early Aryans and the Indus Civilization*. New York: Oxford University Press.

Pellizzi, Francesco. 2007. "Some Notes on Sacrifice, Shamanism and the Artifact." *Res 51* (Spring 2007): 239–46.

Pollock, Sheldon. 1984. "The Divine King in the Indian Epic." *Journal of the American Oriental Society* 104: 505–28.

——. 2005. Tr. *Ramayana II: Ayodhya*. New York: Clay Sanskrit Library and New York University Press.

Prabhakar, C.L. 1972. "The Recensions of the Sukla Yajurveda." *Archív Orientalni* 40 (Jan 1, 1972): 347–53.

Preciado-Solis, Benjamin. 1984. *The Krishna Cycle in the Puranas*. Delhi: Motilal Banarsidass.

Radhakrishnan, S.1960. *The Brahma Sutra: The Philosophy of Spiritual Life*. London: George Allen & Unwin Ltd.

——. 1998. Tr. *The Principal Upanisads*. New Delhi: HarperCollins.

Rangacharya, M. 1891. "The Yugas: A Question of Hindu Chronology and History." *Madras Christian College Magazine* 8 & 9.

Rangarajan. L.N. Ed. and tr. 1992. *Kautilya: The Arthashastra*. New Delhi: Penguin.

Rattu, Nanak Chand. 1997. *Last Few Years of Dr Ambedkar*. New Delhi: Amrit Publishing House.

Rege, Sharmila. 2013. *Against the Madness of Manu: B.R. Ambedkar's Writings on Brahmanical Patriarchy*. New Delhi: Navayana.

Rhys Davids, T.W and C.A.F. Tr. 2007. *The Digha-Nikaya: Dialogues of the*

Buddha Volume III. New Delhi: Motilal Banarsidass.

Rhys Davids, T. W. 2007. "Introduction: Kassapa-S han da Sutta" [The Naked Ascetic]. In *Dialogues of the Buddha* Volume I. Delhi: Motilal Banarsidass.

Richman, Paula. 2004. "Why Can't a Shudra Perform Asceticism? Sambuka in Three Modern South Indian Plays." In *The Ramayana Revisited*. Ed. Mandakranṭa Bose, 125–48. Oxford: Oxford University Press.

Rinehart, Robin and Tony K. Stewart. 2000. "The Anonymous Agama Prakasa: Preface to a Nineteenth-Century Gujarati Polemic." In *Tantra in Practice*. Ed. David Gordon White, 266–84. New Jersey: Princeton University Press.

Rocher, Ludo. 1986. *A History of Indian literature: The Puranas*. Wiesbaden: Harrassowitz.

——. 2002. Ed. and tr. *Jimutavahana's Dayabhaga: The Hindu Law of Inheritance in Bengal*. Oxford: Oxford University Press.

——. 2003. "The Dharmasastras." In *The Blackwell Companion to Hinduism*. Ed. Gavin Flood, 102–15. Oxford: Blackwell Publishing.

——. 2012. *Studies in Hindu Law and Dharmasastra*. London: Anthem Press.

Roy, Arundhati. 2014. "The Doctor and the Saint." In *Annihilation of Caste: The Annotated Critical Edition*. Ed. S. Anand. New Delhi: Navayana.

Roy, Kumkum. 1994. "Defining the Household: Some Aspects of Prescription and Practice in Early India." *Social Scientist* 22 (1/2) (Jan–Feb 1994): 3–18.

Sahni, Ruchi Ram. 1897. *Niyoga Doctrine of the Arya Samaj: Being a Literal Translation of that Portion of the Sattyarth Prakash which Treats of the Doctrine and Practice of Niyoga with Some Remarks*. Lahore: Punjab Economical Press.

Sarkar, S.C. 1928. *Some Aspects of the Earliest Social History of India (Pre-Buddhistic Ages)*. London: Oxford University Press.

Sarup, Lakshman. Tr. 1967. *The Nighantu and the Nirukta: The Oldest Indian Treatise on Etymology, Philology and Semantics*. Delhi: Motilal Banarsidass.

Satyanarayana, K. and Susie Tharu. Ed. 2013. *From Those Stubs, Steel Nibs Are Sprouting: New Dalit Writing from South India, Dossier II Kannada and Telugu*. New Delhi: HarperCollins.

Schalk, Peter. 2006. "Semantic Transformations of the Dhammadipa." In *Buddhism, Conflict and Violence in Modern Sri Lanka*. Ed. Mahinda Deegalle. New York: Routledge.

Schweig, Graham M. 2005. *Dance of Divine Love: India's Classic Sacred Love Story: The Rasa Lila of Krishna*. Princeton: Princeton University Press.

——. 2007. "The Divine Feminine in the Theology of Krishna." In *Krishna: A Sourcebook*. Ed. Edwin F. Bryant, 441–74. Oxford: Oxford University Press.

Sen, Benoychandra. 1942. *Some Historical Aspects of the Inscriptions of Bengal: Pre-Muhammadan Epochs.* Calcutta: University of Calcutta.

Sewell, Robert, Sankara Balakrshna Dikshit and Robert Gustav Schram. 1896. *The Indian calendar, with tables for the conversion of Hindu and Muhammadaninto A.D. dates, and vice versa*. London: Swan Sonnenschein and Co.

Shamasastry, R. 1908. *Gavam Ayana, the Vedic Era: An Exposition of a Forgotten Sacrificial Calendar of the Vedic Poets, Including an Account of the Origin of the Yugas, Chiefly on the Basis of the Vedas and Contemporary History of Foreign Nations.* Mysore: University of Mysore.

——. 1938. *Drapsa: The Vedic Cycle of Eclipses: A Key to Unlock the Treasures of the Vedas*. Mysore: Sree Panchacharya Electric Press.

Shastri, Gaurinath Bhattacharya. 2002. *Introduction to Tantra* (2 vols). New Delhi: Cosmo Publications (Reprint).

Sheth, Noel. 1984. *The Divinity of Krishna*. Delhi: Munshiram Manoharlal.

Siderits, Mark. 2007. *Buddhism as Philosophy: An Introduction.* London: Ashgate.

Sidhanta, N.K. 1929/1996. *The Heroic Age of India: A Comparatice Study*. London: Kegan, Paul, Trench, Trubner & Co. Reprinted New York: Routledge.

Singh, Vipul. 2008. *The Pearson Indian History Manual for the UPSC Civil Services Preliminary Examinations.* New Delhi: Pearson/Dorling Kindersley.

Singh, Sarva Daman. 1978. *Polyandry in Ancient India*. New Delhi: Motilal Banarsidass.

Singh, Upinder. 2009. *A History of Ancient and Early Medieval India: From the Stone Age to the 12th Century*. New Delhi: Pearson Longman.

Sivananda, Swami. 1949/2009. *Brahma Sutras: Text, Word-to-word Meaning, Translation, and Commentary.* Teri-Garhwal: Divine Life Society.

Smith, Mary Carroll. 1985. "Epic Parthenogenesis." *Journal of South Asian Literature* 20 (1) Part I: Essays on the *Mahabharata*: 79–92.

Srinivasan, Doris M. 1997. *Many Heads, Arms, and Eyes: Origin, Meaning, and Form of Multiplicity in Indian Art*. Leiden: Brill.

Stork, Hélène. 1992. "Mothering Rituals in Tamilnadu: Some magico-Religious beliefs." In *Roles and Rituals for Hindu Women*. Ed. Julia Leslie, 89–105. New Delhi: Motilal Banarsidass.

Swami Madhavananda. Tr. 1934. *The Brihadaranyaka Upanisad with the Commentary of Sankaracharya*. Almora: Advaita Ahsrama.

Sugirtharajah, Sharada. 2003. *Imagining Hinduism: A Postcolonial Perspective*. New York: Routledge.

Sutherland, Sally J. 1989. "Sita and Draupadi: Aggressive Behavior and Female Role-Models in the Sanskrit Epics." *Journal of the American Oriental Society* 109 (1): 63–79.

——. 2004. "Gendered Narratives: Gender, Space, and Narrative Structures in Valmiki's Balakanda." In *The Ramayana Revisited*. Ed. Mandakranta Bose, 47–85. Oxford: Oxford University Press.

Teltumbde, Anand. 2015. *Mahad: The Making of the First Dalit Revolt*. New Delhi: Aakar Books.

Tilak, Bal Gangadhar. 1903. *The Arctic Home in the Vedas: Being Also a New Key to the Interpretation of Many Vedic Texts and Legends.* Poona: Kesari.

Thapar, Romila. 1978. *Ancient Indian Social History: Some Interpretations*. Delhi: Orient Longman.

——. 1989. "Syndicated Hindusim." In *Hinduism Reconsidered*. Eds. Günther-Dietz Sontheimer and Hermann Kulke, 54–81. Delhi: Manohar.

——. 1996a. *Time as a Metaphor of History: Early India*. New Delhi: Oxford University Press.

——. 1996b/1990. *A History of India*. New Delhi: Penguin.

——. 2009. "Historical Consciousness in Early India." In *Different Types of History*. Ed. Bharati Ray. Delhi: Pearson Longman.

Thibaut, George. 1890. *The Vedanta Sutras with the Commentary of Sankaracarya*. Part I. Sacred Books of the East Vol 34. Oxford: Clarendon Press.

——. 1896. *The Vedanta Sutras with the Commentary of Sankaracarya*, Part II. Sacred Books of the East Vol 38. Oxford: Clarendon Press.

Uberoi, Patricia. Ed. 1993. *Family, Kinship and Marriage in India*. New Delhi: Oxford University Press.

Udayakumar, S.P. 2005. *Presenting the Past: Anxious History and Ancient Future in Hindutva India*. Westport: Praeger.

Urban, Hugh B. 1999. "The Extreme Orient: The Construction of 'Tantrism'as a Category in the Orientalist Imagination." *Religion* 29: 123–46.

——. 2003. *Tantra: Sex, Secrecy, Politics, and Power in the Study of Religion*. Berkeley: University of California Press.

Vahia, M.N and Nisha Yadav. 2011. "The Origin and Growth of Astronomy, as Viewed from an Indian Context." In *Highlighting the History of Astronomy in the Asia-Pacific Region*. Eds. Wayne Orchiston, Tsuko Nakamura and Richard G. Strom, 61–84. New York: Springer.

van Buitenen, J.A.B. 1983. *The Mahabharata*. Chicago: University of Chicago Press.

Vattanky, John. 2003. *A System of Indian Logic: The Nyaya Theory of Inference*. London: Routledge Curzon.

Vidyarthi, Lalita Prasad and Binay Kumar Rai. 1976. *The Tribal Culture of India*. New Delhi: Concept.

Visvanathan, Meera. 2011. "Cosmology and Critique: Charting a History of the Purusha Sukta". In *Insights and Interventions: Essays in Honour of Uma Chakravarti*. Ed. Kumkum Roy, 143–68. Delhi: Primus Books.

Weber, Albrecht. 1878/1904. *History of Indian Literature*: London: Kegan Paul, Trench and Trübner.

Wedemeyer, Christian K. 2014. *Making Sense of Tantric Buddhism History, Semiology, and Transgression in the Indian Traditions*. New York: Columbia University Press.

Weinberger-Thomas, Catherine. 1999. *Ashes of Immortality: Widow-Burning in India.* Chicago: University of Chicago Press.

White, Charles S. J. 1972. "The Sai Baba Movement: Approaches to the Study of Indian Saints." *The Journal of Asian Studies* 31 (4) (Aug 1972): 863–78.

White, David Gordon. 2003. *Kiss of the Yogini: "Tantric Sex" in its South Asian Contexts.* Chicago: The University of Chicago Press.

Wilson, H.H. 1850–88. *Rig-Veda Sanhita* (6 vols). London, Trubner & Co.

——. 1864–1870. *The Vishnu Purana: a system of Hindu mythology and tradition* (5 vols). London: Trubner & Co.

Winternitz, Maurice. 1927 (1977). *A History of Indian Literature* Vol 1. Delhi: Oriental Books.

Witzel, Michael. 2003. "Vedas and Upanisads." In *The Blackwell Companion to Hinduism*. Ed. Gavin Flood, 68–101. Oxford: Blackwell Publishing.

Woodroffe, Sir John. (As Arthur Avalon). Tr. 1913. *Mahanirvana Tantra: Tantra of the Great Liberation.* http://www.sacred-texts.com/tantra/maha/index.htm, accessed 20 March 2016.

Zavos, John. 2001. "Defending Hindu Tradition: Sanatana Dharma as a Symbol of Orthodoxy in Colonial India." *Religion* 31: 109–123.

Zimmer, Heinrich Robert. 1972. *Myths and symbols in Indian art and civilization*, Vol 6. Princeton: Princeton University Press.

Acknowledgements

The publisher wishes to thank Kancha Ilaiah for readily agreeing to write the introduction, and Unnamati Syama Sundar for sharing some of his archival work on cartoons from the nationalist and post-independence period that depict Ambedkar. The review feedback of Prof Sibaji Bandyopadhyay has enriched the annotations. He went through both Ambedkar's riddles and the notes with great care, and generously led us towards readings that shed further light on texts and ideas. Rakshit Sonawane's responses to Ilaiah's essay and the preface were most useful. Thanks are also due to Pratap Bhanu Mehta for making the time to read the manuscript and respond. Saumya Sethia for being around; Sanjiv Palliwal and Rajeev Kumar for their patience.

Index